MANAGING WITH
INFORMATION
TECHNOLOGY

Richard Ennals and Phil Molyneux (Eds)

MANAGING WITH INFORMATION TECHNOLOGY

Springer-Verlag
London Berlin Heidelberg New York
Paris Tokyo Hong Kong
Barcelona Budapest

Richard Ennals, MA, PGCE
Philip Molyneux, BSc, MSc

School of Operations Management and
    Quantitative Methods
Kingston Business School
Kingston University
Kingston upon Thames KT2 7LB
Surrey, UK

ISBN 978-3-540-19795-9   ISBN 978-1-4471-3299-8 (eBook)
DOI 10.1007/978-1-4471-3299-8

British Library Cataloguing in Publication Data
Managing with Information Technology
    I. Ennals, J. R.   II. Molyneux, Philip
    658.4038011

Library of Congress Cataloging-in-Publication Data
Managing with information technology / Richard Ennals and Philip
Molyneux, eds.
       p.   cm.
    Includes bibliographical references and indexes.

    1. Management information systems.   I. Ennals, J. R. (John Richard),
1951– . II. Molyneux, Phil, 1950– .
    HD30.213.M35   1993
    658.4′038—dc20   93–6018

Typeset by The Electronic Book Factory Ltd, Fife, Scotland
Printed by Anthenæum Press Ltd, Newcastle upon Tyne
34/3830-543210 Printed on acid-free paper

Preface

The language of business and management, and of information technology, is being employed across all sectors of economic and social activity. In recent years computers and information technology (IT) in general have moved from being a scarce resource to being a more generally available commodity, without a corresponding increase in understanding of how the new generation of tools can be used. IT is available on individual desktops, supporting decision making and communication, but often conventional organizations have failed to adapt, individuals lack competence and confidence, and senior managers lack both the strategic insight to develop appropriate strategies and the humility to accept that they need to learn.

As each sector, whether business, education, public sector management or the community and voluntary sector, realizes that the potential of IT is not being exploited to the full, calls are issued for the development of new "hybrid managers", a term coined to describe the gap in understanding and competence that is to be filled.

The two editors work in the hybrid field of business information technology, which is a melting pot of ideas and experience from numerous traditional disciplines. The pace of change is such that no one individual could ever be abreast of all technical and business developments, but the field is now sufficiently mature for us to identify certain underlying issues and principles, and areas of research for the coming years.

As each individual manager encounters unfamiliar problems, he or she is likely to feel exposed and uncertain. There is a wealth of insights and experience that can be made available, often already existing in published form, having been originally intended for a different audience. Springer-Verlag, for example, has published extensively in the area of information technology for a technical specialist audience, but advances in hardware and software development, and reductions in cost, mean that the technology is now available to a wider audience than sought access to the earlier literature. The new audience will often require old ideas to be re-expressed in new vocabulary. The same applies to management and business development, which has a new importance for information technology specialists taking on new roles in unfamiliar contexts and cultures.

Managing with Information Technology has been a collaborative effort, bringing together colleagues at Kingston University from Kingston Business School and the School of Information Systems, together with external partners from industry, education, and the community and voluntary sectors. We have welcomed the opportunity to share our ideas and experience.

The original seminar series from which the book derives benefited from the support of the Department of Trade and Industry Advanced Information Technology Awareness Programme.

We are grateful for the support of John Watson and Linda Schofield of Springer UK, who have taken a personal interest in the project from the start.

We would like to express particular thanks to David Miles, Clare Townsend, Eva Smith and Maureen Beard of Kingston Business School for their support during the writing of this book, as well as to our wives Bobbie and Beryl. They have had to manage with us as we have managed with information technology.

Kingston University   *Richard Ennals*
July 1992   *Phil Molyneux*

Contents

Section IV. Hybrid Managers

Section V. Knowledge Based Training Systems

Section VI. Human Centred Systems

Contributors

Richard Ennals (Co-editor)
Professor and Head, School of Operations Management
and Quantitative Methods, Kingston Business School,
Kingston University, Kingston Hill, Kingston upon
Thames, Surrey KT2 7LB, UK

Phil Molyneux (Co-editor)
Senior Lecturer in Business Computing, Kingston
Business School, Kingston University, Kingston Hill,
Kingston upon Thames, Surrey KT2 7LB, UK

Jonathan H. Briggs
Senior Lecturer, School of Information Systems, Faculty
of Technology, Kingston University, Penrhyn Road,
Kingston upon Thames, Surrey KT1 2EE, UK

David Browne
Senior Lecturer, Kingston Business School, Kingston
University, Kingston Hill, Kingston upon Thames,
Surrey KT2 7LB, UK

Mike Chesher
European Communications Manager, GE Information
Systems, and Lecturer, Kingston Business School,
Kingston University, Kingston Hill, Kingston upon
Thames, Surrey KT2 7LB, UK

Stuart Fitz-Gerald
Course Director, BSc Business Information Technology,
Kingston Business School, Kingston University,
Kingston Hill, Kingston upon Thames, Surrey KT2
7LB, UK

Karamjit Gill
Director, SEAKE Centre, Brighton University, Mithras
House, Lewes Road, Brighton BN2 4AT, UK, and
Professor, Human-Centred Systems, Universita Degli
Studi di Urbino, Via Saffi 15, I-61029 Urbino (PS), Italy

Kevin Harris
Head of Information, Community Development
Foundation, 60 Highbury Grove, London N5 2AG, UK

David Hopson
The Disktop Publishing Corporation Ltd, 47 Darville
Road, Stoke Newington, London N16

Chris Hutchison
Senior Lecturer, School of Information Systems, Faculty
of Technology, Kingston University, Penrhyn Road,
Kingston upon Thames, Surrey KT1 2EE, UK

Stewart Judd
Principal IT Adviser, Confederation of British Industry,
Centre Point, 103 New Oxford Street, London WC1A
1DV, UK

Ann Leeming
Course Director, MBA (Information Technology
Management), City University Business School,
Frobisher Cresent, Barbican Centre, London EC2Y
8HB, UK

Robin Matthews
Principal Lecturer, School of Business Strategy and
Development, and Director, Industrial Performance
Unit, Kingston Business School, Kingston University,
Kingston Hill, Kingston upon Thames, Surrey KT2
7LB, UK

Nicholas Oates
Lecturer in Pharmacology, Imperial College of Science,
Technology and Medicine, St Mary's Hospital Medical
School, London W2 1PG, UK

Juliet Sheppard
Professor and Head, School of Business Strategy and
Development, Kingston Business School, Kingston
University, Kingston Hill, Kingston upon Thames,
Surrey KT2 7LB, UK

Anthony Shoebridge
Managing Director, EIS Consultants Ltd, 4 Berghen Mews, Blythe Road, London W14 OHN, UK

Walter Skok
Principal Lecturer in Business Computing, Kingston Business School, Kingston University, Kingston Hill, Kingston upon Thames, Surrey KT2 7LB, UK

Gail Swaffield
Senior IT Consultant, Masons, Solicitors and Privy Council Agents, 30 Aylesbury Street, London EC1R 0ER, UK

Robert M. Taylor
Senior Consultant, Knowledge Based Systems Centre, Touche Ross Management Consultants, 1 Little New Street, London EC4A 3TR, UK

Chris Tompsett
Senior Lecturer, School of Information Systems, Faculty of Technology, Kingston University, Penrhyn Road, Kingston upon Thames, Surrey KT1 2EE, UK

Peijie Wang
Research Assistant, Kingston Business School, Kingston University, Kingston Hill, Kingston upon Thames, Surrey KT2 7LB, UK

Christine Warner
Course Director, MSc Information Systems Design and Management, School of Information Systems, Faculty of Technology, Kingston University, Penrhyn Road, Kingston upon Thames, Surrey KT1 2EE, UK

Sheenagh Wreyford
Lecturer, Kingston Business School, Kingston University, Kingston Hill, Kingston upon Thames, Surrey KT2 7LB, UK

Ara Yeghiazarian
Senior Lecturer, Kingston Business School, Kingston University, Kingston Hill, Kingston upon Thames, Surrey KT2 7LB, UK

I | FUNDAMENTALS OF BUSINESS INFORMATION TECHNOLOGY

Editorial Overview

The pressures of business and the technical complexities of information technology (IT) combine to produce new challenges for managers. It is fashionable to concentrate on the strategic uses of IT, and to disregard technical issues, but Phil Molyneux (Chapter 1) argues that advances in technology cannot remove the fundamental need for clarity in describing problems and approaches to their solutions.

Programming in some form will always be required, although it may be perceived as developing spreadsheet applications or working within an environment with a graphical user interface. Software consultancy expertise will remain expensive and rare, so the burden will continue to devolve, at least in part, to end users. This is reflected in the new generation of extensions to business spreadsheets and packages, and reports from the *Financial Times* concerning the future of software at work.

In a provocative and wide-ranging chapter, Molyneux criticizes orthodox solutions to the "software crisis" which besets industry, and presents the case for declarative programming. He concentrates on the innovative functional language Miranda, which offers the prospect of transforming our understanding of conventional business techniques such as critical path analysis, because the notation can be regarded as program scripts. Mathematical understanding is rewarded with problem-solving power. Management scientists and operations research specialists can use computers without sacrificing the power of their chosen formalisms.

Molyneux offers insights into the potential offered by fifth generation computing systems, based on logic programming and functional programming, and rejects suggestions that conventional software development methodologies offer a secure basis for future business systems. His arguments have radical implications for business and for IT professionals, and suggest the need for changes in both undergraduate education and management development. In particular, he challenges the divide that has developed between the two cultures of management and technology, and presents a new view of mathematics as providing a bridge, where the focus of attention is abstraction, rather than numbers.

Hybrid management involves ongoing debate: Phil Molyneux has cast the first stone, the ripples from which are spreading through academic business and computer science. The debate is important for the IT industry, which requires senior managers to understand and use the new generation of tools, and to engage in dialogue.

1 | Declarative Programming

Phil Molyneux

Introduction

The introduction to almost every text on software engineering or software development opens with a description of the Software Crisis. The complaints are that software projects are late, over budget, incorrect and do not do what the user intended (see for example, Ghezzi et al. 1991; Macro and Buxton 1987; Sommerville 1989 and Ince 1989). The same problems arise in the broader areas of exploiting information technology (IT) or designing and implementing information systems. One of the consequences of this state of affairs has been the conclusion that software developers have:

> not yet achieved the balance of practical skills and theoretical knowledge required of a true professional (R.L. Baber in McDermid 1991, p. 63).

Views such as this have led in turn to more soul searching among organizations concerned with the design of curricula for software developers, information system developers and other allied trades (see, for example, Denning et al. 1988; Tucker et al. 1991; British Computer Society 1989). Perhaps this is inevitable for such young disciplines, which are themselves hybrids of applied mathematics, science, engineering, cognitive psychology, sociology and other subjects. This chapter takes the view that the discussions about some of the difficulties can be understood only by having some knowledge of the language (or languages) that are used. As Denning et al. (1988) put it, in a section on the role of programming:

> It is also clear that access to the distinctions of any domain is given through language and that most of the distinctions of computing are embodied in programming notations. Hence programming languages are useful tools for gaining access to the distinctions of the discipline.

This is not to say that knowledge of programming languages or notations is a sufficient condition to understand the problems of constructing software or information systems – as mentioned above, many disciplines have their contribution to make. Much of the discussion on the education of students in this area has been as if there were two opposing camps: "theoretician" and "information system designers". As Robin Milner (winner of the 1992 Turing Award) puts it in the British Computer Society report on undergraduate curricula (British Computer Society 1989):

> [This] strength is lost if, five or ten years hence, computing is taught mainly in two kinds of course: design-oriented engineering courses (including software engineering) on the one hand, and theoretically oriented courses (perhaps within mathematics departments) on the other.

The strength that Milner is referring to is that of developing a combination of skills and understanding, covering both design-oriented engineering and theoretical aspects of computing.

In this chapter we recognize that many people will not have the time or inclination to invest their energies in learning programming, but present sufficient of the issues concerned with notations in computing to indicate the main problems and debates. In a later section we outline some of the reasons why programming has been viewed as a "hard" activity, and in the following section we describe the impact of this on software production and the software crisis. Next, we discuss some of the desirable features of notations for programming and how declarative programming languages provide these features. The final section discusses some myths and misconceptions about declarative programming – in essence, answering the question:

> If declarative languages are so good, why isn't everyone using them?

Why Is Programming Difficult?

For a long time it has been noticed that most students find their first (and even their second and third!) contact with computing and programming somewhat daunting: indeed, many teachers of programming have noticed that only a very small proportion of computing students really "resonate" with the subject (Knuth 1985). Even those who do go on to become information systems engineers or software engineers observe that producing quality software within budget is a difficult activity. We have already referred to the "software crisis" and the interrelationship between practical skills and theoretical knowledge. In this section we shall discuss one aspect, namely the mental model of computation and computers that programmers have learnt or acquired through their education and training. The main point we wish to illustrate is that conventional programming languages and many software packages for business have required the user to have a particular model of a computer – the von Neumann model – in mind when writing programs. It should be stressed that while this chapter deals with some of the more formal, notational aspects of software development, this should be regarded as part of an overall process involving more human and managerial aspects.

Conventional programming languages evolved as abstractions from a von Neumann model of sequential computers. The von Neumann model, which was developed by John von Neumann in the 1940s during the development of the first electronic computers, is illustrated in Fig. 1.1. The fact that most users are introduced to a computer via this model is a tribute that should not be undervalued. Even users who regard themselves as non-technical end-users will have been given this mental model. A look at any introductory book on MS DOS invariably has a similar diagram in the first chapter (though perhaps not giving von Neumann explicit credit!). Even texts that introduce Windows interfaces rather than a command line interface assume that the user will have the von Neumann model as their underlying mental model of computation.

In the model, the CPU has a program counter which contains the memory address of the next instruction to obey. The abstract machine

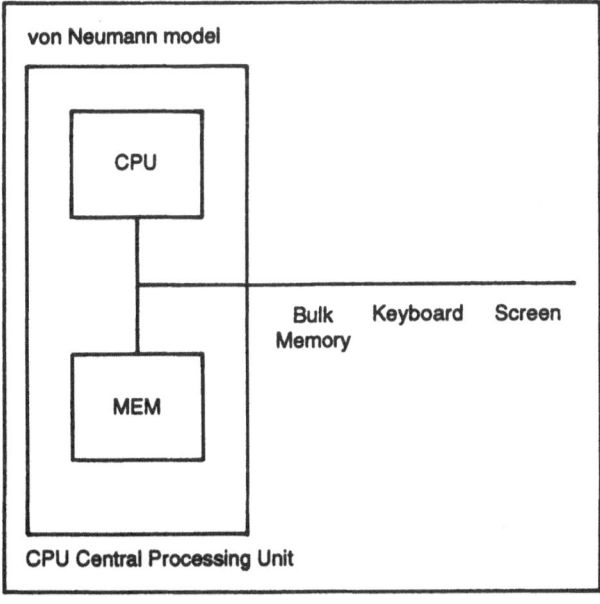

Fig. 1.1. The von Neumann model.

operates by getting the next instruction (by referring to the program counter) and executing it (which may involve getting some data from memory, updating the program counter, and so on). The meaning of the contents of any memory cell depends entirely on the context within which a program uses it.

Conventional languages – whether procedural or imperative – all contain some explicit abstraction of the memory and program counter. This applies to widely used conventional languages such as FORTRAN, COBOL, Pascal, Modula-2 and Ada. It also applies to many common business packages that ordinary users may not regard as programming languages. For example, popular spreadsheet packages such as Lotus 123 and Quattro provide the memory cells explicitly as a two-dimensional (or more) array of cells displayed on the screen. Spreadsheet users call their programs macros, perhaps in order to make beginners less nervous, but they are indeed programming. A recent *Financial Times* survey (1992) reported that:

> Uncontrolled use of spreadsheet packages risks the danger of amateur programmers producing incorrect business models on which important decisions might be based.

Macro and Buxton (1987, p. 8) emphasize the problem by explaining that the "smallness, cheapness and latent power of the micro" will lead to an order of magnitude increase in amateur programmers.

The following (in Pascal) is an example statement in a program:

$$x := x + 1 ;$$

The meaning of the statement is:

> Look up the value of the memory location with name "x"
> Evaluate the expression "value of" $(x) + 1$
> Overwrite the memory location with name "x"
> Obey the next statement

This means that within the statement there are three different "worlds":

$x :=$ refers to the world of computer memory
    $;$ refers to the world of computer control
    $x + 1$ refers to the world of ordinary maths

Notice that the problem to be solved (add 1 to a number) is only part of the task a programmer has to organize. The programmer has to describe what is to be computed in some formal language, organize the sequence of computation into small steps and also organize the management of memory. In this context, "formal" means a notation that is amenable to automatic computation by a machine. John Backus' 1978 Turing Award lecture strongly argued that the conventional style that this example embodies requires the programmer to think about the semantics of several worlds at the same time. This, he argued, is a major factor in making program writing difficult (Backus 1978). Ironically, Backus received his Turing Award primarily for the development of FORTRAN – one of the most widely used imperative programming languages.

Backus' Turing Award lecture also contains one of the most quoted arguments in favour of adopting a functional style of programming and developing languages that more directly support such a style, and was influential in the development and usage of languages that support the separation of concerns about the different worlds. This should enable the programmer to describe what is to be computed (though inevitably in some formal language), while the management of memory and sequencing of control is automated.

It should be stressed that this will make programming *easier*, but not necessarily *easy*. There is still room for many other errors of design and implementation. Programmers call their errors bugs to preserve their sanity; that number of mistakes would not be psychologically acceptable.

Other Solutions

Before describing the main declarative languages (and, indeed, defining what we mean by declarative) we mention briefly other suggested solutions to the software crisis.

Find a Proof System for Languages that Contain an Implicit Model of the von Neumann Machine

This has been expounded strongly by people such as Dijkstra (see for example many of the articles in Dijkstra 1982). However, it has been found that using these proof systems to help derive programs from their specifications gives rise to further difficulties (see, for example, Goguen 1992).

Structured Programming Promotes a Disciplined Use of Control Constructs

Dijkstra's famous 1968 letter to the *Communications of the ACM*, "Goto statement considered harmful", prompted a huge amount of correspondence on this topic. Much of the debate at the time concentrated on abstinence from the GOTO control statement rather than on the disciplined use of program control. In the next section we shall argue that it is not abstinence from control and memory assignment statements that is important, but rather an awareness of their disciplined usage.

*Many Structured Design Methodologies or Methods
have been Proposed*

While passing on best practice in the management of information systems projects, some authors fear that they have falsely claimed to remove the need to have some awareness of programming generally – to quote Dijkstra (1989) again:

> *If you carefully read its literature and analyze what its devotees actually do, you will discover that software engineering has accepted as its charter: How to program if you cannot.*

Supplying Powerful Programming Tools has been the Aim of Many of the So-called Fourth Generation Languages

When you look at the various products that claim fourth generation language (4GL) status, it becomes increasingly unclear whether such a classification is useful.

"It's Hard Anyway"

There will undoubtedly continue to be those that take pride in never using a manual but somehow getting by. We just hope that their software is only used by themselves.

Wadge and Ashcroft (1985) give an amusing classification of the various schools of solutions to the software crisis for interested readers.

A Declarative Style of Programming and Languages

This section presents a declarative style of programming and the main classes of languages that support such a style. We do not claim that declarative programming provides a panacea, but rather that the importance of such a style and languages lies in the natural evolution of expressiveness and elegance of notation that is provided. This progression should not be thought of as conventional languages with the assignment statement removed (just as structured programming was not just FORTRAN with the GOTO statement removed). Declarative programs can be viewed as descriptions of values, expressions and algorithms which do not make explicit reference to the sequencing of calculations or the organization of memory allocation. To consider why this is an advantage we should first consider the desirable features of any programming notation.

1. *Expressiveness:* there should be powerful means of combining small programs or expressions into large ones.

2. *Protection:* the language should provide automatic means for checking for common errors. This has led to powerful type-checking mechanisms (so that, for example, we only allow numbers to be used with arithmetic operations. While this may sound obvious, remember that at the machine level, the meaning of data depends on what is done with it. Some systems programming languages will quite happily allow you to multiply two characters by suitably interpreting the data representing the characters – many novice C programmers have come unstuck this way.)

3. *Abstraction mechanisms:* general means to construct user defined data types should be provided. This ensures that the usage to which some value is put can be checked by the language automatically. It should be possible to abstract common patterns of computation.

4. *Elegance:* this inevitably means a more mathematical notation since we wish programs to be amenable to formal reasoning and to transforming specifications into programs.

5. *Efficiency:* the languages should be amenable to reasoning about their space and time efficiency. They should be amenable to usage on parallel computers without special or extra notation. Finally, we require reasonably fast implementations – otherwise they will be regarded as academic toys.

Paul Hudak, in his tutorial on functional programming (1990), puts it more succinctly, as:

> *Abstraction, Abstraction, Abstraction.*
> *The answer to the question: "What are the three most important things in programming?"*

While the word "abstract" when used in common parlance is often meant in a pejorative sense, in IT (and in programming in particular) abstraction is the essential activity which models the real-world data and processes by the data structures and expressions provided by the programming language. The move to a declarative style in programming can be viewed as part of a general trend towards enabling the notations we use for specifying solutions to problems also to be notations that can be executed on a computer.

Languages Supporting a Declarative Style

There are two main classes of languages which support a declarative style of programming: functional languages and logic languages. A functional program is an expression to be evaluated in the context of some definitions of data values and functions. Expressions themselves are built from the application of functions to particular arguments. A logic program can be viewed as a logical assertion describing relationships between data, using ideas from first order logic.

The concepts of function, relation, and first order logic are regarded as part of elementary mathematics, much of which is (or could be) introduced at school level – they are concepts that should be part of almost anyone's intellectual toolbox. It should be emphasized that while more advanced topics would be required to understand the theoretical underpinnings of the languages and their implementations, the usage of these languages does not require anything beyond school maths. The next two sections give example usage in both types of language to illustrate their particular styles.

Functional Programming Example

Here is a possible sorting algorithm expressed in quasi- English:

To sort a list of objects:
IF the length of the list is zero
THEN return the list (since it must be ordered)
ELSE
Split the list into several parts
Sort the parts
Join the sorted parts together

The above specification leads to many of the usual sorting algorithms depending on the choice of split and join. The quicksort algorithm chooses one element of the list and splits the list by finding all elements less than the chosen element and all those greater than it.   √

Here is quicksort expressed in Miranda, a modern pure functional language (Miranda is a trade mark of Research Software Limited).

```
sort [] = []
sort (a:xs)
       = sort [b | b <- xs ; b <= a]
         ++
         [a]
         ++
         sort [b | b <- xs ; b > a]
```

This example illustrates the use of equations and pattern matching in defining functions in Miranda. The two equations define a function whose name is sort. The first equation states that when sort is applied to the empty list (the pattern []) the result is the empty list. The second equation states that when sort is applied to a non-empty list with first element a and xs as the rest of the list, then the result is given by the expression to the right of the equals sign. This expression can be read as:

The list resulting from sort applied to a list of all elements of xs *less than or equal to* a *concatenated with the list just containing* a *concatenated with sort applied to a list of all elements of* xs *greater than* a

The notation

$$[b \mid b <- xs \; ; \; b <= a]$$

is an example of list comprehension notation, which is based on the usual notation for sets and provides a concise notation for expressing many iterations over lists. This expression can be read as:

The list of all b *such that* b *comes from* xs *and* b *is less than or equal to* a.

In other words, this is the list of all the elements of xs that are less than or equal to a.

The advocates of functional programming claim that programs can be written as quickly as specifications, and in many ways functional languages can be used as specification languages. Some of the ideas and features found in modern functional languages like Miranda are:

1. *Purely functional:* there are no side effects or imperative features of any kind. This means that the same function applied to the same actual argument must produce the same result. This is not true of conventional languages like FORTRAN or Pascal, in the sense that functions or procedures in conventional languages may update some global variable, which therefore makes the state of computation implicitly dependent on the history of the computation.

2. *Higher order functions:* functions are first class citizens and can be treated just like any other data. This means that functions can take functions as arguments and/or return functions as results. The major strength that this gives is to improve modularity by enabling common patterns of function application to be abstracted.

3. *Lazy evaluation:* arguments to functions are evaluated only when needed. This evaluation strategy can be summarized as:

Don't do today what you can put off until tomorrow because you might never have to do it.

This provides programmers with a powerful means of gluing together small modules, since it frees them from concerns about evaluation order. Lazy evaluation promotes modularity by separating the definition of data structures from their usage. This is frequently illustrated by examples which define infinitely large data structures independently of their usage.

Hughes (1989) argues that higher order functions and lazy evaluation are the two main ideas that make functional languages more expressive and more elegant than conventional languages. The review article by Hudak (1989) gives the reader a very thorough overview of the ideas and development of functional programming, and should be essential reading for anyone interested in the area. Both these papers contain many examples to illustrate the ideas.

Of course, any language intended for practical use must contain some features beyond the basic elegant ideas. In Miranda (and other modern functional languages) these include

1. *Polymorphic strong typing:* every expression has a type that can be deduced at compile time. This has two main advantages over the type systems found in conventional languages such as Pascal:
   (a) The type of every expression can be inferred and type specifications can be used as a self check for the programmer.
   (b) Functions and data structures can have a flexible or polymorphic type. This means that the sort function defined above can take a list of any type.
2. *User defined datatypes:* general means for users to define their own concrete and abstract datatypes.
3. *Programming environment:* an interface to the operating system is provided, along with a library mechanism to enable programs to be developed from separate modules. The interested reader should consult the Miranda manual for further details (Research Software 1989).

Logic Programming Example

The style of logic programming arose from research in the areas of natural language processing and automatic theorem proving (Cohen 1988). Proofs are developed automatically using a technique known as resolution theorem proving (Robinson 1992). As a simple example, consider a logic program for appending two lists together. The following two statements in English express the logical relationships that must hold between two lists (called *Xs* and *Ys*) and the list formed by appending them together:

IF Xs *is the empty list*
THEN it is true that the answer is Ys

*IF Xs has head X and tail Ts and the result of appending Ts and
Ys is Tapp
THEN it is true that the answer is X followed by Tapp*

This can be directly implemented as a Prolog program (Prolog is the main language used for logic programming):

append ([], Ys, Ys).
append ([X | Ts], Ys, [X | Tapp]) :- append (Ts, Ys, Tapp).

In this notation, [X | Ts] can be read as "a list with head X and tail Ts", and :- can be read as "if".

Each of the lines is termed a clause, following the terminology of logic. The equivalent of executing a program in Prolog is termed posing a query in the context of a set of clauses.

A query is itself a form of clause, in which we wish to find if there are values for variables it may contain that would make the clause true. For example:

append([1, 2,], [3], Zs)

would return:

Zs is [1, 2, 3].

Because Prolog programs represent relations between data rather than functions, the distinction between inputs and outputs is blurred. We could choose to use the same program to find all the splits of a list:

append (Xs, Ys, [1, 2, 3])

will return:

[] [1, 2, 3]
[1] [2, 3]
[1, 2] [3]
[1, 2, 3] []

This is because all of the above lists satisfy the relation that when appended together they produce [1, 2, 3].

Logic programming enables the representation of knowledge in a machine-independent manner, which enables concise programs that are amenable to reasoning about. Many of the virtues we have claimed for functional languages would apply to logic programming. Indeed, since there are some relations that are not functions, logic programming could be regarded as an extension of functional programming (consider the relation "is–taller–than"). Combining the best ideas and features of both styles is, however, still a research issue, and the interested reader is referred to Cohen (1988, 1990), Darlington et al. (1986), Reddy (1986) and Shapiro (1989).

Conclusion

This final section concludes with some answers to the obvious question:

> *If declarative languages are so good, why isn't everyone using and teaching them?"*

The first three points draw on Hudak's (1989) discussion of myths and misconceptions about functional programming; the final point looks at what might be regarded as some of the cultural objections to declarative programming.

The first objection comes from those who regard languages like Prolog and Miranda as "toy" languages for toy problems which do not scale up to applications in the so-called "Real World", often coupled with the assertion that these languages are too slow for real applications. In a sense this is really an objection to the newness of the fields of logic and functional programming, which inevitably means that there may not yet be a large number of reports of applications. It is certainly the case, though, that recent implementations of logic and functional languages now have speeds comparable to conventional languages, and there are an increasing number of reports of real-world usage.

The second objection comes from those who regard declarative programming as the complete antithesis of conventional imperative programming. Hudak argues that, on the contrary, it has continued the key evolutionary characteristic of programming languages – increased expressiveness. Just as structured programming was concerned with a disciplined use of control statements, declarative programming can be viewed as a disciplined use of assignment (or memory management).

The third objection comes from those who are happy with declarative languages for the expression of algorithms and data structures but are puzzled as to how to deal with interactive programming in languages that have no notion of state or memory management. The answer here is that while imperative languages deal with state implicitly (via the assignment statement), in declarative languages we must deal with state explicitly by passing it as a parameter to a function call. This turns out to have the advantage of encouraging the programmer to separate those parts of the program dealing with interaction, input/output and persistent storage from those parts dealing with other calculations.

Finally, there are some who regard a declarative style of programming as "too mathematical". This is probably a cultural perspective on the role and relevance of mathematics, which we will only be able to change slowly. It is certainly the case that declarative programming can have a mathematical flavour but it only requires elementary concepts of the sort that students encounter at secondary school. It is also the case that more formal methods of program construction and verification are being encouraged (see, for example, the Ministry of Defence standards 0055 and 0056 for software projects). The challenge we have to face is to convince management of the value of relatively new styles of programming when they themselves may have succeeded in spite of an early alienation from mathematics. As Birkhoff (1969) puts it:

> *Potential pure mathematicians tend to think of algebra as a game played subject to certain plausible rules, whose object is to manoeuvre x to one side of an equation, leaving only symbols for known quantities on the other. For potential applied mathematicians, algebra is a dull tool which enables him to find answers to interesting questions by non-obvious methods.*

If in the above quotation we substitute programmer, programming and end-user for pure, algebra and applied then we obtain some of the flavour of the debates about the successful use of IT.

In conclusion, our view can be summed up as:

- A declarative style of programming provides a better set of mental power tools.
- It is not hard to learn but it does require a reorientation of perception of what computing is about – this may require a culture shift.
- Declarative programming is emerging from the laboratory.

II | INFORMATION SYSTEMS AND IT STRATEGIES

Editorial Overview

This section adopts the perspective of senior management, who may lack both the technical background and the inclination to delve deep into the technology of IT. Indeed, it is maintained that deeper IT knowledge may not be necessary, because insights into business strategy are more important.

Robin Matthews and Anthony Shoebridge (Chapter 2) argue, on the strength of both academic and commercial experience, that Executive Information Systems (EISs) can provide an invaluable tool to aid management effectiveness and efficiency. To consider strategic management without the aid of such tools would now be unwise, and managers need the vision to see beyond monitoring and control, to the possibilities opened up by distributed processing, networking and electronic data interchange. EISs need to support both qualitative and quantitative decision-making.

Dr Walter Skok (Chapter 3) provides an overview of system development methodologies, which seek to apply the vocabulary and organizational structures of business to the development of complex systems. He gives particular attention to Euromethod, a European Community initiative, which may have added significance as the international dimension of business increases, and outlines future challenges for the information systems community.

Mike Chesher's (Chapter 4) account of electronic messaging draws on business experience of the rapidly changing world of communications to offer essential insights to senior management. Time and information are crucial to corporate survival and success, and electronic messaging has become an integral part of business, building on advances in international standards and open systems.

Professor Juliet Sheppard and Peijie Wang (Chapter 5) address the difficult issue of the strategic management of IT Investments, and explore approaches to investment appraisal. Their survey and analysis casts light on current confusion: whether IT should be seen as a cost or as an investment, and which techniques should be used to secure the best value for money.

IT strategy is an area of ferment, as the transforming nature of the technology, together with the fall in its perceived cost, can have radical implications for the future of businesses and organizations. Seminal texts of a decade ago now look outmoded, as the emphasis changes at the leading edge from administrative efficiency to competitive advantage and now to organizational restructuring.

2 | The Strategic Importance of Executive Information Systems

Robin Matthews and Anthony Shoebridge

Introduction

Many senior executives and directors of UK companies have difficulty with information technology (IT). This is because they have no direct experience of systems designed specifically for them, nor have they been given a convincing picture of how IT systems relate to their business and information needs. Shyness of computers for their personal use should not be explained by the hackneyed excuse, frequently suggested by technical people, that senior people suffer from "technophobia".

What is needed is a simple overview of the information systems of an organization which incorporates concepts that senior executives must be aware of and regard as part of their strategic armoury – an executive information system (EIS). The senior executive needs to know the following:

- What can and cannot an EIS do for the organization?
- How does the EIS relate to the information technology systems within the organization and to an IT strategy as a whole?
- What should be expected during the implementation, and what pitfalls should be avoided?

The EIS Paradox

Many executives, who might be expected to be reluctant to embrace new concepts, have been eager to use information technology to extend their effectiveness and have embraced the use of EISs. EIS sales continue to grow, despite setbacks such as the failure of some

EIS implementations. Nevertheless, the EIS concept lacks a secure place in the mainstream of academic literature on organizations.

Over the last four years the growth of EIS usage has been phenomenal. According to Romtech surveys, the EIS market is growing at over 30% per annum, despite recessions in its main markets, and now amounts to more than $100 million worldwide. Our own research (Matthews and Lowles 1990) predicts growth in sales of EIS products of around 40% per annum in the next few years (a somewhat lower rate than that predicted by EIS suppliers). Research from as far back as 1986 shows a surprisingly high level of awareness of EIS among senior executives. Awareness may, however, be mixed with scepticism, since research has shown a high rate of failure among implementations in both the USA and the UK (Matthews 1989).

The market-place thus presents a picture of strong growth of an established product, and of enthusiasm mixed with scepticism among users and potential users. No doubt, this pattern is not unlike the lifecycle of other major software products, such as databases, fourth generation languages (4GLs), computer aided software engineering (CASE) tools and expert systems. At first high success rates are achieved because systems are carefully introduced into a small number of businesses. Subsequently, the system is exposed to more organizations, where implementations are poorly led, ignore early lessons and have less top level support.

After an inauspicious start in the US, where the term EIS appears to have been coined as a software vendor's description of a product designed to give an executive all the data he needs, EIS then received the blessing of academics within the Massachusetts Institute of Technology (MIT). Rockart and others embraced EIS, relating it to management style and to important concepts such as *critical success factors* (Boynton et al. 1985). Surprisingly, this did not give rise to strong foundations. The MIT school widened the concept to include all the IT an executive might wish to use. Such systems, known as executive support systems (ESS), consisted of a bundle of software products, but avoided a systematic approach to what executives do.

Currently, there is no authoritative view about systems that provide the monitoring and control information needed by executives in running a business (traditionally what the EIS does). Additionally, while Drucker has pointed to the potential of *The New Organization* (Drucker 1988), which focuses on information, no one has attempted to make the obvious connection in detail between this vision and of how to get there using modern technology (see also Kanter 1989). In practice, EIS provides the basis for the creation of an information organization, and such systems have come to incorporate other management tools such as decision support systems (DSS). This development came about as a result of a wider use of EIS within organizations and a demand for them to meet the needs of managers at different levels in the organizational hierarchy.

The Demand for EIS

Before defining EIS, it is important to identify the forces behind their growth.

First, there is the executive's need for information. As one chief executive puts it:

> there is a drive to decentralization in many organizations, but in the modern financial climate, with intense pressure from the stock market in particular, chief executives dare not delegate without the appropriate financial information (Matthews 1989).

Two further issues add substance to the use of EIS, concerning the need for more than just financial information and the need for systems to reduce dependence on other people for information. Management reports are typically inadequate as a source of information because they are insufficiently forward-looking, often too late, too financially orientated and not entirely relevant to the task of running the business. Systems then become more important because they reduce the executive's reliance on what other individuals are prepared to reveal.

The EIS thus has a magnetic attraction to the go-ahead, dynamic executive who wants to have an impact on the organization. It appears to offer a solution for the senior executive in a multi-layered hierarchy, who feels isolated and vulnerable to a highly competitive business environment.

Secondly, there is the attraction of the EIS to information professionals. Here, it is important to distinguish data from information and knowledge. Possession of data is not knowledge; indeed, data overload is a perennial problem for executives and threatens their ability to function. Information is that subset of data that is relevant to organizational and managerial goals and can be used to guide action. The role of the EIS is to transform massive amounts of data into controlled and understandable information, and to deliver that information rapidly to those people who can act on it. The EIS enables the executive to select, analyse, aggregate and present information, and is thus pivotal in the transformation of vast amounts of data from disparate sources into usable information that he or she can act upon.

The third aspect of the demand for EIS arises from the limitations of software systems. Software is not "soft" and malleable as such; in reality it is often rigid and brittle, and it achieves high performance in one respect by sacrificing performance elsewhere. The massive relational databases in which the organization will increasingly store data are ordered and flexible in their output. In practice, they are also difficult to operate and are only used by system experts; further software is required to provide easy access to relevant information and to present data to executives in a meaningful way.

The EIS thus has a strategic role in the organization as the delivery mechanism for information to executives who are not computer literate and who are not experts on the data structures within the organization.

Definition of an EIS

An EIS has traditionally been defined as:

> *a computer-based information delivery and communication system designed to support the needs of top executives (Paller and Laska 1990).*

This definition, however, tells only half the story. Most executives, especially those in the UK, are perfectly happy with their human delivery and communications systems – their secretary in particular. With this limited vision of EIS, there is, therefore, some justification in dismissing a computer for senior executives as merely the latest in a long line of executive toys, ranking alongside the executive jet as an optional extra to buy when times are good and shareholders' control is weak.

In practice, there are two aspects to EIS. One concerns the qualities and characteristics of a piece of software sold as an EIS, and the other concerns the information needs of executives.

EIS: The Software Product

EIS are software packages, used directly by non-expert users, which provide easy access to large amounts of complex data and which have facilities to analyse, present and communicate that data in a timely fashion. Key attributes of the software are, therefore, ease of use, ease of access to data, and facilities to analyse, present and communicate data. These attributes are achieved by the three elements of an EIS, namely:

- A multidimensional database to allow ease of access to complex data.
- A 4GL with which a system containing typical EIS facilities can be developed.
- A human–computer interface.

Distinctive characteristics of the EIS include:

- "Drill-down" from "hot-spots" using touch screen or mouse to allow the user quick access to related information.
- Presentation of information in graphical and pictorial form for greater impact and understanding.
- Flexible reporting, for example, of exceptional performance against various criteria.

Tables 2.1 and 2.2 provide a list of products currently available in the UK and a more complete EIS specification.

These characteristics are all obvious ways of making information more usable, which the power and flexibility of the EIS software is designed to exploit. Some of the functions listed are not unique to EIS: spreadsheets now have some graphics ability and can utilize macros to access data in a third dimension. The EIS, however, is distinctive in its multidimensional structure and its ability to create different representations arising from its powerful 4GL. Graphics and access facilities of spreadsheets are relatively clumsy in comparison to the elegance and efficiency of an EIS, and will remain so unless the spreadsheet shifts from its two-dimensional structure.

The trade-off in achieving flexibility and extreme ease of use was that

Table 2.1. The principal EIS products available in the UK

Product	Company	Architecture
Commander	Comshare	Collaboration Mainframe/PC
Pilot	Pilot	Mainframe
Lightship	Pilot	PC
EIS-Epic	Planning Sciences	PC, UNIX
EIS II	Information Resources	PC
Focus-EIS	Information Builders	PC
Acuity	Acuity	UNIX
InPhase	Eurosoftware	PC, UNIX
EIS-TRACK	Intelligent Office Company	OS2 PC

Table 2.2. Typical features of EIS

Feature	Meaning
Briefing book	Standard set of reports and graphs highlighted as important to key executives (also called Review Book)
Enquiry	Ability to scan interactively the entire database looking at all dimensions, and often incorporating figures in more than two directions at any one time
Hot-spot	Locations on a display that can be selected by the user for additional action. Selection is usually made by mouse or touch screen
Drill-down	A means of calling another level of detail while looking directly at a report or graph
Security	Access to information by individual managers is subject to security considerations within organizations
Exception reports	Report showing unusual performance against norm of budget, last year's performance etc., often using colour code to indicate degree of severity and allowing drill-down to detailed analysis.
Trend analysis	Graph showing set of hourly, daily, weekly, monthly or yearly data points to show trend, often using moving averages to smooth variations
Graphical user interface	Use of icons and pictographs that respond to user selection by mouse or touch screen
What-if analysis	Automatically generated extrapolations and extensions of sets of given figures

EIS packages were originally very expensive. Hence, they could only be used by a small number of senior personnel, who were prepared to accept a high cost per workstation. This gave rise to a vision of EIS as being restricted to top executives and directors.

The use of EIS technology has now been greatly extended so that some UK companies are now considering implementations with as many as 1,500 users (Matthews and Lowles 1990). Here, the EIS acts as a front end to a very large database, which needs to communicate with and be analysed by a large number of managers. Elsewhere, price deterioration of software costs has led to the widespread use of software at different levels of management. Consequently it can be said that EIS technology, providing access, analysis and presentation facilities, is now being used for wider purposes than those for which it was originally designed.

EIS: The Executive System to Monitor and Control

An information system implemented for and with executives concentrates on management's need for information to monitor and control operations, and to assist in policy formulation.

Such a system is not, however, simply an amalgam of products; it is a process. The quality of the information system is dependent on its implementation, how the system is used and its ongoing development. These human issues determine the success and nature of the system.

Fortunately, there is now a corpus of consultants, specialists and academics who have implemented EIS and developed their concepts and understanding of top level information needs. EIS implementations have successfully involved chief executives and their top management teams, and as a result have focused on genuine high level issues. Theories have, therefore, been tested in real life.

The relevance of information to an organization is that it assists the executive to achieve the organization's and his or her own objectives. This becomes apparent when dealing directly with senior executives, rather than in the "boiler room" of the organization (i.e. the data processing and finance departments) where data is the main concern.

Typically, EIS implementations in the private sector have concentrated on the information required to monitor and control operations. At the heart of such systems are two simple ideas:

- The importance of hard numeric information, e.g. profits, sales and activity levels, on the grounds that what gets measured gets acted on.

- The need to know one's performance on those critical issues that determine the company's success, i.e. concentrate your forces on what really matters.

In a complex organization, the information required by executives invariably has a number of features:

- Information is selected from large volumes of data. Data in itself does not inform; only when it is selected according to what the executive wants to achieve does it become meaningful.

- Information is aggregated to show how an organization is performing, with the possibility of drilling down to a lower level of aggregation.

- Internal information is usually multidimensional. It is expressed according to different criteria, such as by region, by product or activity, by responsibility, by financial or physical measures, and representing actual, desired or forecast states.

- Information is normally time dependent, both in the sense of needing to be recent to assist with decision making, and also being presented in a time series to show trends.

- Information must be perceived to be reliable, consistent and have a known degree of accuracy. It is especially important to clarify definitions and to avoid several versions of the "truth".

- The more senior the executive, the greater the orientation to the world outside the organization.

- Information includes both numeric (e.g. financial figures) and text (e.g. descriptions of what has happened or is expected to happen) data relevant to the executive.

This concept of executive information should be distinguished from what is traditionally referred to as a management information system (MIS). An MIS is usually a data system which encompasses all transactions within an organization. Unlike the EIS, it is comprehensive and vast. Typically, an MIS is only used directly by data experts, is difficult to access and does not present data in the flexible and interactive ways demanded by the executive user.

The MIS is thus a *data* system; there is a need for another system which will, utilizing both EIS software and other software solutions, provide usable information to executives.

Information requirements of this kind demand that the executive system should have a wider framework and specification than EIS software developers have traditionally allowed. The executive system should embrace more than monitoring and control of internal and mainly numeric information. Text processing, information for policy formulation and selection of external data, therefore, need to be added to the wider information system. Figure 2.1 illustrates the orientation of these information needs.

The information system thus depends on data reduction. There is a need to select from and aggregate existing data for the information system, which therefore needs to be linked to other data systems within and required by the organization. The information system required by the executive will also comprise more than simply EIS software.

Relationship of EIS to Data Systems within the Organization

The relationship of the EIS to the other systems of the organization explains why the EIS cannot be ignored by the top executive. The chief executive is the recipient of key information that is crucial to her vision of the organization. She determines the shape and content of the information; the data systems must then feed that demand.

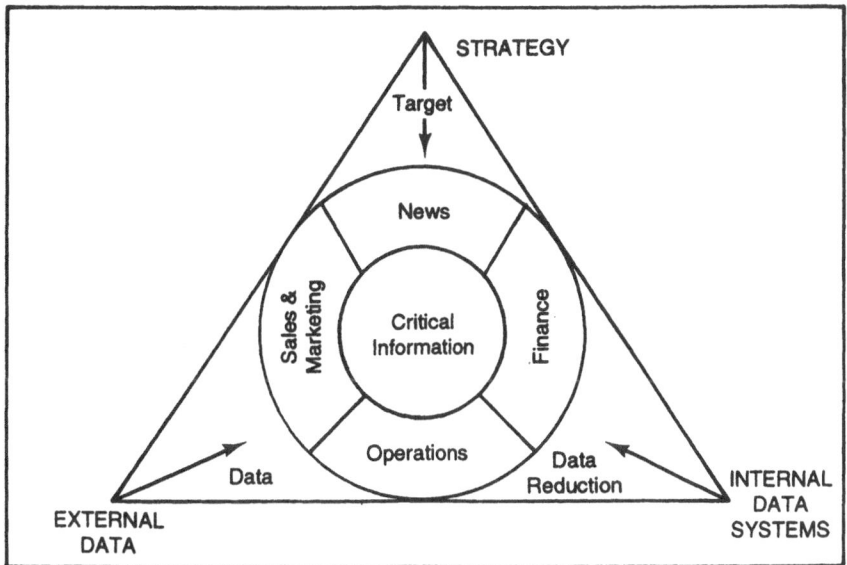

Fig. 2.1. The information needs of executives. Source: EIS Consultants.

Most organizations have extensive data systems that have been built up over many years and adapted to their needs. Wholesale replacement by better, more flexible, relational databases is usually out of the question. Moreover, while the relational database might claim to be able to provide answers to every imaginable question that one could ask, it does not provide a tool that is directly usable by the untrained executive and that gives information in the form in which the executive needs it.

Typically, organizations are moving towards the hybrid solution described in Fig. 2.2, although we are not aware of any organization that has yet achieved this state.

The paradigm separates systems into two areas:

1. *Data systems:* major data systems are vitally important to businesses, but their organization and control needs to be left to experts. This environment is what some hardware manufacturers refer to as the "data warehouse", which often comprises mainframe databases of varying age, containing comprehensive data about every transaction of the organization.

2. *Executive systems:* systems required by executives to assist their work are different in nature and content from data systems controlled by data experts. They focus on information, as opposed to data, and rely on non-expert executives using a range of connected systems. Typically, at the core of the executive's systems is the EIS, which will have the following features.

It will be designed to link efficiently with different types of data both within and outside the organization and contained on different hardware platforms;

(a) For numeric data, it will have a modified relational structure, allowing fast access to time series data.

(b) For text information, it will seamlessly link to a text retrieval system, which will add value to underlying text data by organizing it into concept hierarchies that enable users to search approximate areas more effectively.

(c) The EIS will link to other software systems required by the executive, typically via a graphical user interface (GUI).

The information contained in the EIS database is selected according to its relevance, a process which requires participation and discussion among the management team of the organization. The selection and

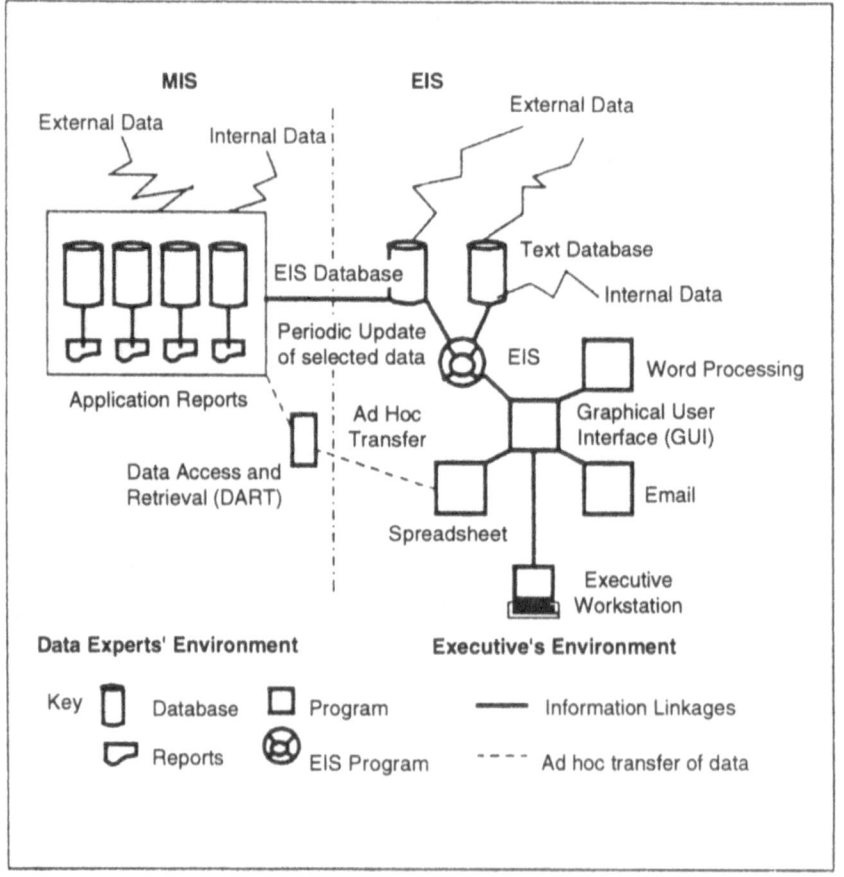

Fig. 2.2. Data and information systems within an organization. Source: EIS Consultants.

transfer of data provides an opportunity to vet, check and agree definitions, i.e. to improve its quality.

This architecture has been given added strength by other trends in the use of technology. The move to "downsize", i.e. to use smaller machines to perform the functions previously performed by the large mainframe, and the introduction of distributed data processing enable the organization to cope with the large volumes of information required by all the executives scattered throughout the organization. The rational organization might well retain its central mainframe databases (the data system), and download selected and aggregated data to regional locations using PC local area networks (LANs) and client servers (the executive system). Most of the interrogation and analysis then occurs within the executive system.

Interestingly, although much of the software in the data and information systems is different, there is some technical convergence. Because the EIS is adept at accessing relational databases, EIS packages are being used increasingly by accountants as a front end to the MIS. However, because the data is typically complex, vast and open to misinterpretation, the MIS front end is used only by executives who are expert in data, database management and information issues.

Executive Involvement

The above model is compelling for the chief executive and financial director: not only does it demystify the use of information technology, it also provides an effective route to improving systems. The executive can demand to use EIS immediately, thereby gaining the ability to influence information and data systems from the top down.

It is not the purpose of this chapter to describe how to run an EIS project or to list factors critical to the success of EIS projects. Researchers all emphasize the same or similar factors. The best description of key factors in operation is Cottrell and Rapley's account (1991) of the implementation of the first EIS at British Airways.

New Expectations

The executive should be forewarned of what to expect from an IT information project, which differs from traditional data processing projects. There is a need to set new expectations.

1. *Top level involvement:* personal involvement of senior executives is necessary if the project is to have the support it needs, and if corporate objectives, priorities and needs are to be reflected in information systems. This involvement may not be time-consuming, but should be sharp and focused at key issues.

2. *Emphasis on objectives and goals:* the emphasis of information system implementation has shifted from gathering data to understanding issues, such as what the business wants to achieve, how it intends to achieve its aims, and progress should be measured. The IT team must have an understanding of business issues and should discuss strategic and tactical matters with executives.

3. *Time scales:* the necessity for quick results is paramount, because senior executives are highly pressured people. The nature of their work causes them to move rapidly from one concern to another, while also being responsive to a changing world. We find that our implementations need to show definite results, in terms of new access to information, within six weeks.

4. *Evolutionary projects:* modern EIS projects have a different profile from that of the traditional data processing project (see Fig. 2.3). It is impossible, and indeed fruitless, to try to specify the eventual contents and format of such an information system at the outset. After obtaining strategic guidelines, it is much better to build the system and then modify it in the light of subsequent feedback from users. This requires confidence in those implementing the system but is effective, whereas sitting in committees discussing screen design is not.

Figure 2.3 describes the evolutionary nature of EIS projects. Usage commences and results must be demonstrated in under six weeks (Phase 1). The value of the system also increases after the official end of the project, as more users are attracted to the system (Phase 3).

All authorities emphasize that personal involvement, in one form or another, is a necessary condition for a successful project. There is, however, some dispute about what form this involvement should take, an issue that is pursued in later chapters. Our observation, from experience gained from responsibility for more than 50 implementations, is that personal involvement should happen in a manner consistent with the style of the organization and the personality of the senior executive. Practical ways in which this may occur include:

- Acting as chairman at the project team's progress meetings.
- Personally testing the prototype system before it is released to a wider team of executives.
- Formally presenting the new system to the management team.

The very minimum contribution requires interviews to determine corporate objectives and targets and information needs. Because the

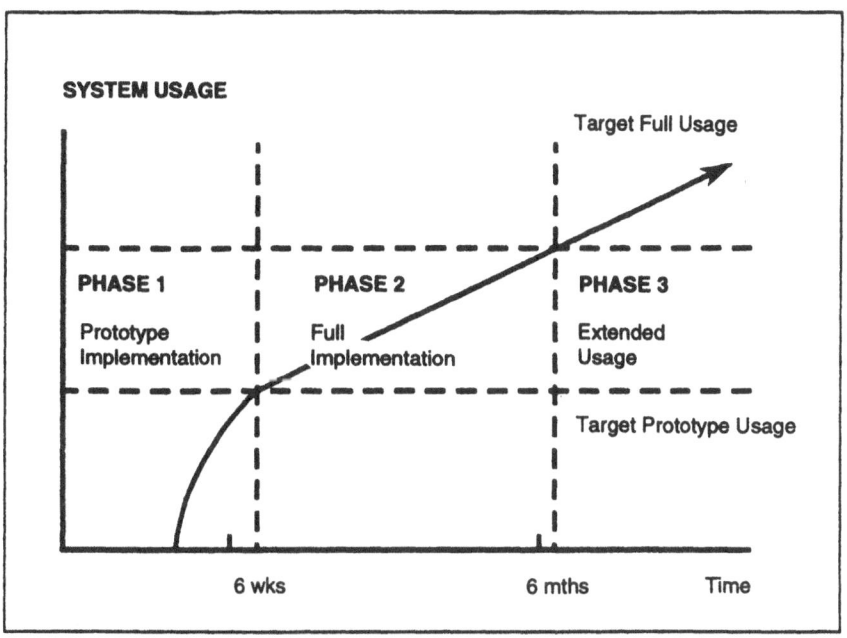

Fig. 2.3. Fast results of an evolutionary project. From Gilb in Finzi (1988) (Ed), *Principles of Software Engineering Management*, Addison-Wesley Publishing Co. Inc.

introduction of an EIS and the provision of relevant usable information to executives is a process, its success is dependent on very human factors – namely executive support and the calibre of the implementer.

Conclusion

The real barrier to the use of EIS by senior executives is not technophobia; it is the false belief that computing power can replace the intelligence of managers. Once top executives are aware of what they can realistically obtain from their organizations, they can achieve great success in extending their effectiveness and efficiency through information technology.

The change in terminology from "data processing" to "information technology" is symptomatic of a change at the heart of how computers are used. Data processing automated simple repetitive tasks; information technology applies technology to more complex processes, where information, judgement and selectivity are required.

An EIS is both a software package that helps an executive to cope efficiently with large amounts of data, and an information system that concentrates on the interactive use of information to monitor and control operations. In both respects, the EIS is an important step in the transformation of the computer to a sophisticated tool that assists complex and imaginative tasks.

Note: An earlier version of this chapter appeared in *Long Range Planning*, **26**, No. 6, pp.94–101 (1992).

3 | Information Systems Methodologies

Walter Skok

Introduction

The development of large-scale computer based information systems (IS) is a complex process. It needs to address strategic planning, systems analysis, systems design, programming, implementation planning, project management and user training. Within the context of an IS department, this chapter discusses how IS methodologies offer a variety of approaches to the stages of IS development, and outlines possible future standardization benefits, particularly from a European perspective. Finally, some proposals are made and issues raised concerning future directions.

Information Systems Development: The Current Position

Historical Perspective

In the 1950s computer systems development was centred around the programming task, which involved the use of languages understood only by specialists. The 1960s saw the growing use of computer based data processing systems, particularly at the operational level. This widespread use of computer systems throughout a company led to recognition of the need for analysis and design stages prior to programming. This usually meant that a systems analyst from the data processing (or computer) department would go out to the user department in order to establish requirements and form a communications link during system development.

The problems voiced during this period appear very similar to those of today, and centred around the gap between user expectations and results. Typical observations were that users' needs were not adequately fulfilled: systems were unreliable, slow and unnatural and difficult to use. Commentators wrote:

> *the full benefits of this important new tool have yet to be realized (Eason et al. 1974).*

> *there is widespread belief by users that computer-based systems are yielding less than the promised benefits to the organization (British Computer Society 1978).*

> *Implementation of data processing systems often causes unexpected disruption; the disruption often results in inadequate utilization of the new resource; and often systems fail to provide the type of analytic information most useful to management for longer-term planning (Demb 1979).*

A number of factors that influenced the successful implementation of computer systems were identified:

> *The level of top management support*
> *The degree of operating management involvement (McKinsey & Co. 1968).*

> *Organizational contingencies, such as the stage of an organization in its life cycle (Rubinstein et al. 1967).*

> *Attitudes toward and perceptions of computer systems which users have developed as a result of prior experience with EDP systems (Lucas 1973).*

> *The amount of the user's time he or she believes is necessary for development of the system (Manley 1973).*

> *Education provided to all parties (Heany 1972).*

> *The existence of well-defined and measurable objectives (Huysmans 1973).*

This final factor illustrates one of the perennial problems confronting systems development. During this period, communications between the user and the data processing department were very poor. The user might have been very good at undertaking the required job tasks, but often had difficulty in explaining the job needs clearly and unambiguously. It was also difficult for the systems analyst to specify the user requirements precisely, in order to proceed further with system development and implementation. This is still the major problem in the development of business information systems.

System development was said to proceed through a number of stages, known as the system development lifecycle (SDLC):

- Feasibility study
- Systems analysis
- Systems design

- Programming
- Testing
- Implementation
- Documentation
- Review and maintenance

However, in many cases, the boundaries between these stages were unclear. The above terms also had different meanings in different organizations, so it might be difficult to decide when the feasibility study was over and analysis had begun.

The early stages of the lifecycle, particularly systems analysis, were very often very frustrating, involving prolonged discussion and debate between different parts of the company. These user relationships could be difficult to maintain and often led to hostile reactions, if the user had political and/or emotional fears about the introduction of a computer based system.

Land (1980) outlined a number of possible outcomes if a system was not approved by its users:

1. *Active resistance:* "At the most extreme those who have the power will withhold approval for the implementation of the system in question. If those who do not approve have the power they will prohibit its implementation via the threat of sanctions such as strikes. If they do not have the power to prevent implementation, resistance can take the form of industrial action or even sabotage."

2. *Passive resistance:* "Symptoms of passive resistance include misuse or misoperation of a system. Typical examples are lack of attention to procedure manuals, lack of care regarding accuracy, and low levels of usage where use of the systems components are not compulsory. The systems tend to operate at a degraded level."

3. *Development of alternative systems:* "One of the most common symptoms of distrust or non-approval of a system is the development of unofficial informal substitute systems. At the best, unofficial systems can be used to complement and enhance the effectiveness of the formal system. But if the informal systems are the results of non-approval of the formal system, they can make it redundant and destroy the economic case for its implementation."

4. *Opting out:* "For those who have the opportunity, one of the most likely effects of non-approval is to leave the job or ask for a transfer to another area. And it is often the most highly skilled or most needed personnel who have the opportunity to indicate their disapproval in that way. Absenteeism is a further symptom of disaffection."

The problems described led to proposals for a significant change in approach to system development in the 1970s. This change involved the adoption of an IS methodology by the IS department.

Avison and Fitzgerald (1988) give the following possible objectives of a methodology:

- To record accurately the requirements for an information system.
- To provide a systematic method of development in such a way that progress can be monitored effectively.
- To provide an information system within an appropriate time limit and at an acceptable cost.
- To produce a system that is well documented and easy to maintain.
- To provide an indication of any changes that need to be made as early as possible in the development process.
- To provide a system that is liked by the people it affects.

Strictly speaking, the term "methodology" means a study of methods, but common usage in the IS development field has led the term to be used synonymously with "method". Avison and Fitzgerald also present an excellent and full discussion of the "methodology jungle". The most important points in this discussion are that the methodology (or method) has some underlying philosophy from its originator and that it offers a framework or policy for IS development. This usually consists of defining (and expanding) stages in the development process and indicating appropriate procedures, techniques, tools and documentation requirements.

The methodology is almost always a formalized set of procedures that are usually adapted by an organization to suit their particular requirements. It is unusual for every single step of each phase or sub-phase to be undertaken by the systems developers as directed, because a measure of human judgement is always present. The methodology should also be teachable. A suggested (top-down) view of this situation is shown in Fig. 3.1.

The criticisms often levelled at methodologies are that they:

- are bureaucratic
- are often led by documentation preparation
- contain too much jargon
- require experienced practitioners for effective use
- have no mathematical underpinning
- do not address the maintenance problem

However, the historical trend for commercial IS development has been one of movement away from just programming to the wider analysis of the business problem, and, more recently, to incorporation of strategic planning. This begins by examining why an IS is necessary to the organization, e.g. the business implications, the undertaking of a feasibility study, user requirements analysis etc., and then leads to program design and construction. The emphasis is on business and systems analysis/modelling, rather than on software development, which is mostly concerned with the quality of the final software product. Furthermore, the people involved in the development process, e.g. users, analysts, programmers, management, have a variety of backgrounds and knowledge, necessitating the introduction of standard procedures and practices to aid communication and understanding. IS development must be independent of individuals, facilitate teamwork and be sympathetic to user needs. This change in the roles of IS staff is illustrated in Fig. 3.2.

The pressing problems that need to be overcome by such procedures are:

- Application backlog
- Lack of human resources
- Need for standards for communication
- Difficulties with large-scale development environments

The intellectual challenge is one of analysing the business problem, determining user requirements, designing a new system and managing its implementation within time, budget and resource constraints. This is a complex activity, which is not easy to undertake and which certainly requires a disciplined approach.

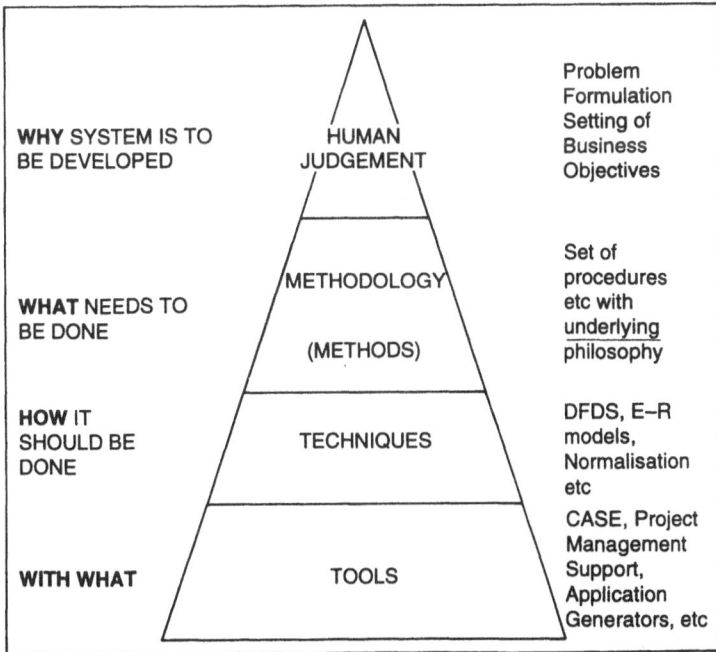

Fig. 3.1. Top-down view of information system development.

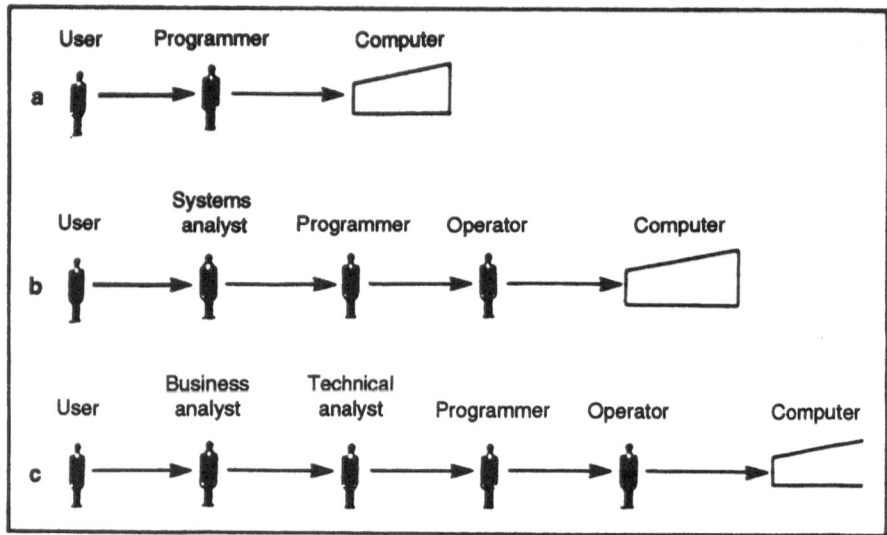

Fig. 3.2. Changing roles of people in data processing. From Avison and Fitzgerald (1988) *Information Systems Development*, Blackwell, Oxford.

Over 300 methodologies have been identified (Fitzgerald 1990) and they are often divided into two camps:

- Hard, emphasizing data structures, processes and temporal events.
- Soft, emphasizing human activity, participation and systems theory principles.

Over the last decade there has been what might be described as an "avalanche" of hard methodologies, which form the basis of this chapter. This rapid growth was a result of commercial, political and economic pressures. It is far easier to introduce a "new" methodology than, say, a programming language, which necessitates appropriate compilers.

More recently, a wide range of automated support tools have been introduced to improve software quality and productivity and to reduce maintenance costs. The acronym CASE (computer aided software engineering) is generally used to cover the automated support for the commonly used techniques that form the basis of most IS methodologies. The support involves a graphics capability throughout the SDLC, but the key characteristic of a CASE product is the construction of a design database (also described as a repository or encyclopaedia) to hold system meta-data.

The background and development of this rapidly changing field is fully described by Hewett and Durham (1989), Senn (1989), Gane (1990) and Fisher (1991).

CASE tools are usually divided into three categories:

- Front end, covering strategic planning, analysis and design.
- Back end, covering program design and coding.
- Integrated, covering the whole of the SDLC.

The major problem in this area is the lack of standardization, which means that it is difficult to integrate tools used at different stages of the SDLC. However, a number of tool integration developments, such as IBM's AD-Cycle and Softlab's MAESTRO II, are being undertaken to overcome these problems.

Although an extremely wide variety of hard methodologies and corresponding support tools are currently available, it has been possible to observe a harmonization of ideas. This harmonization has led to the following features being incorporated into the SDLC:

- Extension to include strategy planning
- Use of automation aids throughout the lifecycle
- Code generation

It is interesting to note that only one of the methodologies to be described, Information Engineering (Finkelstein 1989), had all three of these features in its original form.

The development of methodologies has resulted in a movement away from a somewhat parochial view of systems development to one encompassing a wider lifecycle, including business strategy planning. Three key philosophies in this development are discussed and a possible classification system is outlined.

Structured Systems Analysis and Design

This top-down, graphical approach is suitable for well-structured one-off applications, for which a specially tailored computer based information system is required.

Yourdon, the pioneering methodology, has now been extended to include development of real-time systems. This was one of the earliest approaches to emphasize user involvement in the systems development process.

In 1980 the UK Government carried out a study in order to decide on a structured system development approach, which could be adopted as the standard for all projects in UK Government departments. A survey was undertaken and the final choice was a method that integrated a number of techniques into a complete analysis package. The method chosen was designed with the help of a UK consultancy, Learmonth and Burchett Management Systems (LBMS), and is known as the Structured Systems Analysis and Design Method (SSADM) (see Downs et al. 1988).

The Central Computer and Telecommunications Agency (CCTA) took over responsibility for further design and development of the method, which is constantly being improved in the light of user experiences. SSADM is now a registered trademark and external consultants may obtain CCTA accreditation in order to run approved courses on this non-proprietary method.

SSADM has been used on a number of large projects involving many analysts and programmers, particularly in the area of government data processing. The results from live projects have shown that the quality of systems analysis and design has been improved.

Information Engineering

Information Engineering is one of the more recent approaches to system development, and it considers all aspects of the SDLC. It also provides automated software support for the analyst during the development process. This support comes in the form of:

- PC-based diagramming aids for analysis.
- Powerful mainframe-based code generation facilities.

The approach is based on the ideas and work of a number of researchers, including Martin and Finkelstein (1981) and Macdonald and Palmer (1991). It is currently marketed by James Martin Associates and the Ernst & Young Group (see Arthur Young 1987). This type of automatic generation of working programs has been generally available for a number of years; however, the Information Engineering methodology integrates this feature into the complete SDLC. Information Engineering is a fourth generation approach, which aims to model the business closely, rather than imposing technical constraints on the users. It is more than a checklist of tasks and deliverables. It provides a toolkit of techniques, which may be selected as required by the circumstances of a particular project.

The main features of Information Engineering are:

- It concentrates on the business issues rather than on technical design.
- It starts from strategic planning in order to incorporate the business plan of the company.
- It automates the technical design process.
- It enforces the view of data as a valuable corporate resource by emphasizing data structures.
- It is based on the use of automated software tools.
- It encourages user participation via diagramming techniques.

One of the later approaches to system development, starting from a strategic view of the whole business and aiming to express the users' requirements in business terms, Information Engineering uses modern automated software as an essential guiding tool in its development and implementation. It is often discussed in terms of "application development without programmers", implying a business approach to computer system development rather than a technical one, and is appropriate for the development of strategic and management information systems.

Strategic Planning for IT

Recent literature (Earl 1989; Martin and Leben 1989; Porter and Millar 1985), discusses the importance of strategic information systems and their role in providing competitive advantage. Information systems should be examined from a high-level strategic viewpoint, since their use can not only improve the running of the business, but actually change the nature of the business itself. They can often change the products, services and style of the organization, and may also give the organization a competitive advantage in the market-place.

Strategic planning methodologies have a much wider ranging and radical effect on a company's activities than the previous system development approaches. They go to the very heart of a business considering its very nature and basic goals. It is often useful to gain an independent view of the current business operations in order to make valuable forward projections. Strategic planning methodologies are appropriate for high-level strategic planning, evaluation and systems development studies.

Butler Cox Foundation (1987a,b) have proposed a classification for methodologies, which is shown in Table 3.1, alongside examples of some modern methodologies.

Overview

We have examined the historical development of IS methodologies and some of the leading methodologies currently available. We have also seen one classification scheme for comparative purposes. There are other key issues that relate to and impact on successful methodology use. They include:

- The size of the project
- The flexibility of use
- The type of development, e.g. rapid, package, end-user
- The experience of the systems development staff
- Project management

Table 3.1. Categories of information systems development methods

Method	Example	Supplier
Management Specify the various phases of the development process, stating the objectives of each phase together with what is to be done. Management methods deal with management of the process rather than its execution.	BIS Modus Method 1 Prism	BIS Arthur Andersen & Co Hoskyns Group Ltd
Single phase development These methods concentrate on how one phase is to be executed. For example, some deal with user involvement, e.g. Ethics, some with the programming, e.g. Jackson structured programming	Core Ethics Jackson Structured Programming	British Aerospace plc Prof. E. Mumford, Manchester Business School Michael Jackson Systems Ltd
Multiphase development Similar in approach to the single phase methods, but concentrate on more than one phase; e.g. on the analysis and design stages, or on the programming and testing stages.	Merise Soft Systems Yourdon	Cap Gemini Sogeti, Sema-Matra Prof. Checkland, Lancaster University Yourdon Europe
Integrated These are methods which attempt to cover all the development stages. They are integrated in the sense that they provide the project management techniques, development methods and tools used in the different development phases.	Information Engineering SSADM SUMMIT CASE*METHOD	James Martin Associates LBMS Coopers & Lybrand Oracle Corporation, UK

- Quality assurance procedures
- Methodology support and training
- Maturity of IT practice within an organization

This subject area is a relatively new, developing field. Often, theory is ahead of practice, and companies must not underestimate the change in working practices and culture that IS departments face. The management of change in IS departments is no less a challenge than in user departments.

Information Systems Development: Harmonization

Euromethod

The objective of the Euromethod project is to harmonize IS development procedures in European government administrations. This includes strategic planning, requirements analysis, design, implementation and project management. The original idea came as a result of an ESPRIT project – Method 92 – involving CCTA, Datacentralen (Denmark) and CESIA (France).

In January 1989 the first meeting of the project steering committee was held in Madrid, with representatives from the EC countries and the European Commission.

Hopkins (1990) and McDonnell (1990) of the CCTA describe the project background and current status, noting the current diverse range of IS planning and development methodologies used in Europe, with differences in notation, theory and culture. As a result, they argue, procedures tend to be localized in style and intellectual content, suiting local needs but limiting communication between governments and restricting the movement of IT expertise. Furthermore, markets for the provision of products and services which support the IS lifecycle, such as consultancy, training and software tools, are also locally specialized, which has the effect of limiting competitive opportunities for both suppliers and users.

They see Euromethod as seeking to address these problems by stating common procurement requirements for services and software tools which support the IS lifecycle. This should help in the contracting process, on both sides, and also reduce long-term maintenance costs, improve productivity, stimulate the development of tools and further open up the market for IS services.

They go on to argue that:

> The common specification of requirements for information systems planning and development will enable current methods and tools to be used after user assessment by associated conformance schemes for products and services.

The project is being carried out within the framework of the European Commission's Public Procurement Group, members of which are senior officials from EC administrations responsible for the definition of public procurement policy for IT systems and for the application of standards in this area.

The plan contains four project phases:

Phase 1: Requirements definition
Phase 2: Project feasibility study

Phase 3: Develop structural model

Phase 4: Consider options for populating the model with techniques and carry out further work to maximize harmonization.

By 1992, attention was turning to Phases 3 and 4. Although it is too early to address Phase 4 of the project in detail, possible deliverables include conformance schemes and the specification of techniques to populate the structural model.

A number of benefits have been claimed for Euromethod, including:

- Users of the structural model will have a single project architecture to plan, monitor and undertake work programmes.

- Suppliers of methods will be able to demonstrate how the methods they offer will fit the framework.

- Procurement bodies will be able to specify requirements and identify how the offered services and approaches conform.

- Methods developers will have templates for their future planning.

Euromethod should offer powerful mechanisms for encouraging convergence of products, and stimulating growth in the commercial market by providing a common base for methods development ,to which suppliers can add specialist skills. Most importantly, but with an accompanying set of political implications, Euromethod is intended to provide opportunities to lay the foundations, aligned with a range of international standards work, for facilitating the movement of experts and expertise around the single market of the future EC.

The feasibility study, which was funded by the European Commission, was carried out by a consortium of companies led by Sema Group. Other members of the consortium were British Telecom (UK), CGI (France), Datacentralen (Denmark), ERIA/CENINSA (Spain), Instituto Nacional de Adminstracio (Portugal), Softlab (Germany) and Volmac (Netherlands).

One of the deliverables of Phase 2 of the project was a State of the Art Report (Euromethod Public Procurement Group 1990) on IS development methods. This report did not survey CASE tool usage, which was left for a later phase.

The report identifies the main methods used in Europe, by examination of secondary survey data on method usage. It then undertakes a theoretical survey of the subject to identify gaps and convergences between the methods. Finally, it summarizes IS development methods and makes recommendations for future work.

The points made in the summary include:

1. *Organizational and technological context.* Companies are faced with a dramatic increase in computer supported systems (e.g. strategic,

decision and operational systems) and rapidly evolving technologies (e.g. new user interfaces, distributed systems and new storage systems). However, the problem remains that these developments are not fully understood and integrated, i.e. there is a gap between what technology can bring and the business value that is really added. The concept of strategic planning of IS demonstrates the importance of IT being more closely linked to business needs and plans.

2. *The role of methods.* There is a consensus view that methods should help in bridging the gap between business needs and IT. There is also a feeling, which is difficult to prove, that they contribute to more efficient and better controlled production of quality information systems. Although methods facilitate communication during IS development, it is still difficult to assess them and to evaluate the benefits that they bring to companies.

3. *The usage of methods.* The usage of methods across countries is difficult to evaluate because data is not always consistent and reliable. Although there are clearly significant differences, there is an increase in current and predicted usage of methods throughout Europe. Currently only SSADM in the UK, MERISE in France and SDM in the Netherlands have a significant impact in their respective markets. Many organizations use in-house methods, specifically adapted variants or no method at all.

4. *Evaluation of methods against their objectives.* The surveys undertaken have shown the failure of methods to fulfil their objectives. This does not mean that they have "missed the point", but that they can be improved. The main weaknesses identified are:
   (a) they are not sufficiently user friendly.
   (b) they do not fit the variety of systems encountered in IS development (e.g. DSS, strategic systems, uncertain applications etc.).
   (c) they have not assimilated the new technologies.
   (d) they do not cover all development activity types.
   (e) they are not adaptable and flexible.
   (f) they do not take sufficient account of human and social factors.
   (g) they are not sufficiently goal orientated.

5. *Convergence, divergence.* There are more similarities than differences between the most commonly used methods. Confusion arises because of the diversity of terminology and the commercial bias of the method vendors. Historically, one can identify a convergence between the methods, and this should continue as they focus on the same problems and attempt to provide the same solutions.

6. *Harmonization, standardization.* European method users are faced with a confused market situation, which is overcrowded with too many methods and tools. They are, therefore, strongly in favour of harmonization and standardization.

7. *Scope and nature of Phase 3.* Euromethod is concerned with providing an overall framework for information systems methods

usage. The context in which it will operate is shown in Fig. 3.3.

Its primary aim is to devise policies at the technical level (front plane of the cube) of the contextual model. This will be achieved by examining the IS characteristics (side face of the cube), which are:

(a) Organization and business needs. The overall approach to the development and maintenance of information systems should be within a business context. It should reflect the type of organization, e.g. public administration, retailing, service or manufacturing sector, and its information needs.

(b) Type of application. The approach should also reflect the type of application encountered, e.g. by examining the different data, process and intelligence characteristics of the application.

(c) Type of project. Projects may be classified as new developments (specially tailored package solutions) or maintenance.

(d) Style and extent of lifecycle. The lifecycle model used may be prototyping, user driven, waterfall etc.

The specific aspects of these characteristics with which Phase 3 will be concerned are:

(a) Full coverage of IS lifecycle, i.e. from strategy planning to implementation.

(b) Business systems applications with knowledge based systems as an option.

(c) Strategic and operational support systems developments, with office automation as an option.

(d) Development of specially tailored applications and package solutions, with re-engineering as an option.

(e) The established guiding principles must be mapped onto the needs of users. The top plane of Fig. 3.3 shows the agents and goals to achieve this.

8. *Technical direction and design.* This covers the areas of software engineering and systems analysis, including requirements and cost/benefit analyses, and performance, usability, security and reliability criteria.

9. *Infrastructure and configuration management.* This covers planning, monitoring and control of IS development and installation.

10. *Project management.* This addresses the preparation of plans, assignment of tasks and resources, and procurement skills, e.g. policy making, negotiating terms, conditions and standards, setting requirements, which may be evaluated, monitored and reviewed.

11. *Quality management.* This ensures that systems development and maintenance meet business criteria such as cost, timeliness and flexibility.

12. *Information service programme management.* This provides the link between business planning and project management. A key feature will be the development of a Euromethod Dictionary, which will unify the terminology in the IS field.

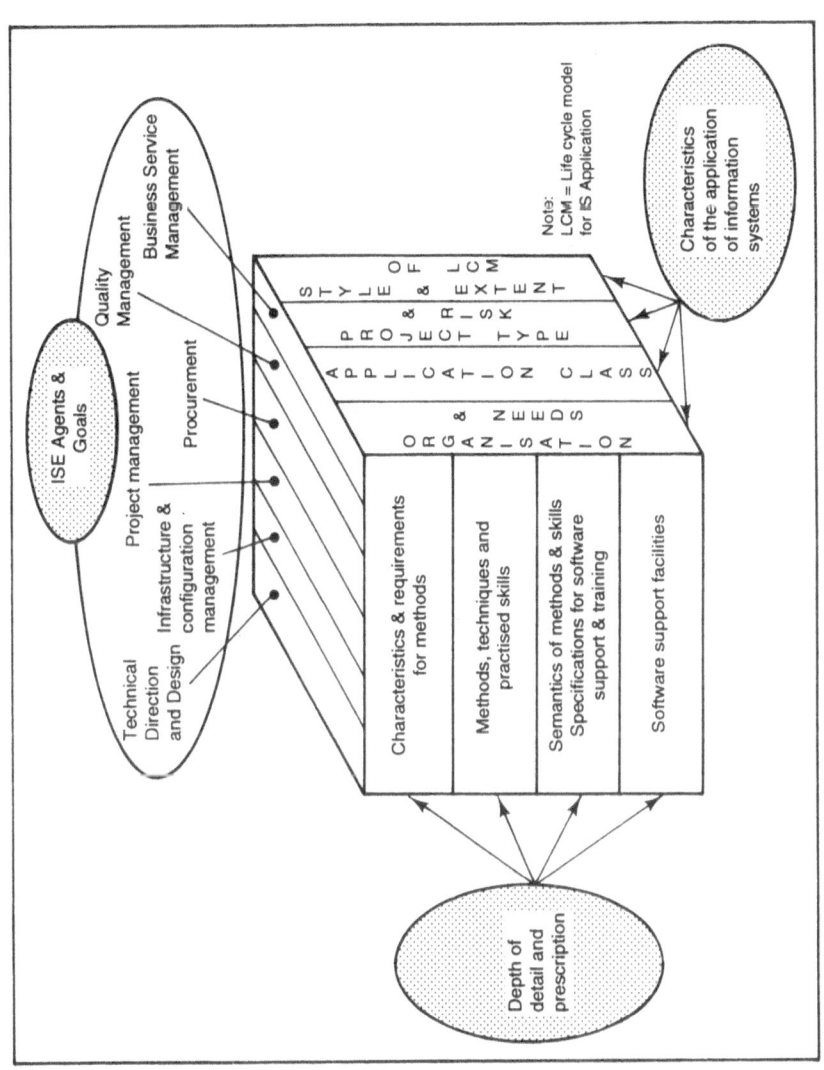

Fig. 3.3. The context of Euromethod.

Clearly, the scope of Euromethod is far-reaching and therefore subject to possible risk. Figure 3.4 shows the breadth and depth of the problem domain that Euromethod addresses.

The horizontal plane shows the full development lifecycle that Euromethod seeks to address. The vertical plane addresses the depth of knowledge in the Euromethod domain, and is the same as that described in the German *Vorgehens Modell*.

Phase 3a (1991–1993) will develop the initial version of Euromethod and will look at the central lifecycle component. The deliverable will be documentation, perhaps in computer supported form. Phase 3b (1993–1994) will develop a full version of Euromethod, covering the complete lifecycle.

The approach is not a replacement method, but a unified framework for IS development, which will provide benefits to:

- Customers (public and privately)owned organizations)
- Suppliers (in-house and external IS service providers)
- Community market (EEC, legislative, standards bodies, academia, public etc.).

Summary

Euromethod is a significant project in the field of information systems development which will have a major effect on participants undertaking transnational projects.

In their introduction to *Information Systems Methodologies*, Olle et al. (1991) pose the question:

> *Are there really so many substantially different ways to design a computerized information system?*

There are certainly advantages to be gained by innovation and the introduction of new methodologies. However, a balance needs to be set: at present, the multitude of approaches offered to users is causing confusion. There is an urgent need for a strong harmonizing force to redress this balance.

The Euromethod project has two important roles:

- From an academic viewpoint, to examine the wide variety of approaches to IS development and to identify the underlying principles (or techniques) that are used.
- From a commercial standpoint, to produce a structural model, which can be used as a reference point for IS development and for related commercial activities.

Phase 2 has been completed satisfactorily and has surveyed and compared methodologies currently in use throughout Europe. Planning for

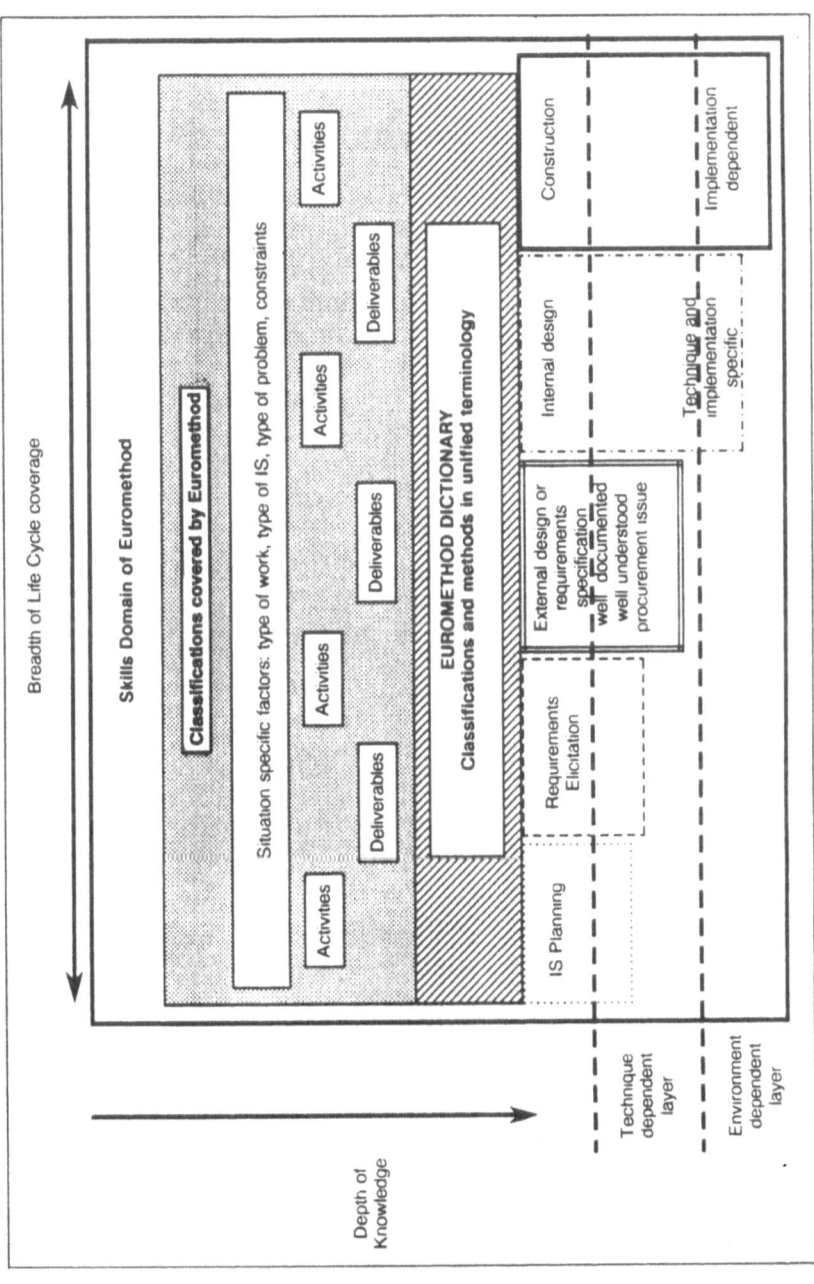

Fig. 3.4. Euromethod breadth and depth.

Phase 3 has now begun. These plans are currently very broadly based, merely indicating in outline the areas that need to be addressed and developed further.

Information Systems Development: The Way Forward

IS development is a relatively new discipline, which has a long way to go to reach the maturity and stability of say, civil engineering. Often practice is ahead of theory, which is usually derived from empirical methods. Companies have seriously underestimated the issues relating to management of change raised by introducing methodologies and supporting tools. The corresponding cultural change in working practices has met with the same sort of resistance as that found when clerical staff were faced with automation of their tasks. The learning curve for IS departments is steep and often insufficient planning and preparatory work is carried out.

Against this background, we have seen that there are a multitude of methodologies, causing confusion to companies and users. What, then, is the solution? What is the best way forward? The author believes that the critical issues discussed in the next sections must be urgently addressed if satisfactory progress is to be made.

Management of the Introduction of IS Methodologies

We have seen the importance of introducing an IS methodology into an organization to overcome the following problem areas:

- poor communications
- little or no strategic planning
- lack of top management support
- poor project management

The considerable management of change issues surrounding the introduction of IS methodologies and supporting tools must also be addressed in a formal manner. IS methodologies are often introduced after a short intensive course by consultants, with little or no support once the analyst returns to the office.

Similar problems arise with CASE. Too often a company might

purchase a CASE tool and present it to an analyst, who is somehow supposed to make the best use of it. The result is usually for the tool to remain in its glossy packaging on the shelf.

A formal programme for changing working practices should be established, which covers:

- exploratory discussions
- staff awareness programmes
- management and staff commitment
- comprehensive training
- full back-up and support

Methods are new and many staff are "doing it for the first time" in the rapidly changing world of IT. Problems need to be identified and addressed as a matter of urgency, before the benefits proclaimed by the vendors can be achieved.

Integrated IS Development Approach

In the field of corporate information systems development, there are three major areas of concern and activity:

1. *Strategy planning for IT.* A relatively new area of study, which aims to integrate IS/IT planning within the overall business plan, strategy planning for IT is an extension of the traditional and respected field of strategy planning, which was studied long before the dawn of the computer age. It is certainly a vitally important subject area, given the way in which modern IT developments are changing the nature of many businesses. IT can no longer be regarded as just another resource – its influence is all-pervasive within the organization.

Much academic work has been published recently which emphasizes the necessity of linking IS strategy to business strategy. This is also a growing area for management consultancy activity.

2. *Information analysis.* The area of information systems analysis has already had a major impact in the commercial world, leading to the widespread adoption of information systems development strategies and methodologies.

The emphasis here is on feasibility studies, user requirements analysis, user participation, automated support and project management.

3. *Program construction.* This area deals with the design and writing of the program code, with the emphasis on software quality. There have been many developments in this field, ranging from structured programming to formal methods approaches. Recent renewed interest in object-oriented methods has indicated possible benefits in program re-use. The human–computer interface is also receiving more careful

examination than before. An emphasis on ease of use has resulted in the widespread adoption of GUIs.

Each of the above groupings has a large body of followers with their own pet theories, success stories, sub-cultures, literature, working practices and prejudices. Each area is insufficient on its own. The areas must work together in order to produce a coherent and integrated IS development route within any major organization, as shown in Fig. 3.5.

The above is a high level generalization of the whole process, but it provides a framework for beginning to understand what the fundamental process really is. The main problem will be to clearly establish and define the linkages between these three major and distinct cultural groupings. The key point remains, that IS development should be business rather than technology driven, and the major challenge in the future is to link business strategy to IS strategy in practice as well as in theory.

The Toolkit Approach

Given the wide variety of approaches available, Fig. 3.1 provides a useful framework in which IS development takes place. Control passes from top to bottom, i.e. human judgement is applied in problem formulation and selection, methods chosen, suitable techniques and tools applied, while each level in the hierarchy supports the level above. The emphasis is on selection for the given project or application under discussion. As mentioned earlier, it is unusual for every step of each phase/sub-phase to be undertaken as directed. This provides the analyst with a toolkit of techniques to be tapped as required.

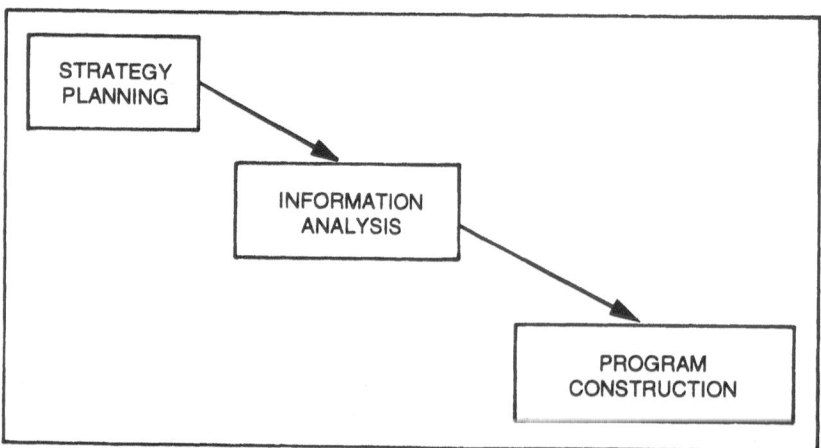

Fig. 3.5. Integrated IS development approach.

Consider the following examples, where this approach is relevant.

1. *Soft systems.* A soft systems method (SSM) might be appropriate in the early stages of a situation, where purposes and missions are more likely than specific goals. The SSM would help in understanding problems, rather than providing a scheme to solve them. One of the "harder" methodologies may then be adopted to proceed further.

2. *Using CASE experience.* Within the IS department, there may already be expertise in a particular technique or CASE tool. Therefore, it is advantageous to make use of that, even when new methods and techniques are introduced.

The wide range of approaches adopted at present shows that the real process of IS development has not yet been fully understood or universally agreed. The author believes that by following through on the issues raised in this chapter, the IS community will go some way towards clarifying this confused situation. Perhaps by the turn of the century it will be seen that IS methodologies played a pivotal role in gaining an improved understanding of this complex process.

4 | Electronic Messaging

Mike Chesher

Introduction

Messaging is the nervous system of business. Hardly any business activity can take place without messages: progress reports, requests for help, instructions to co-workers, purchase orders, delivery notes, invoices and so on.

Until a few years ago, most business was conducted at a fairly leisurely pace over restricted geographical areas, and messages could be written or typed on pieces of paper and distributed by internal or external mail. For urgent messages, or for communications where a degree of interaction between the parties was necessary, electrical devices have been available for about a century. The telegraph and the telex, its descendant, provide for expensive, rapid, long distance delivery of short written messages, and the telephone enables two people to communicate, providing they are both available at the same time and have a language in common. The remarkable degree of co-operation between national telephone companies allows telex and telephone messaging to take place, simply and without the intervention of operators, on an almost worldwide basis.

However, during the past fifteen to twenty years, this cosy world has changed:

- Business has become much more international in nature; for example, a computer may be designed in America, assembled in Taiwan using components bought from a dozen countries around the world, and then packed with its peripherals into a complete system back in America, ready for worldwide distribution.

- Competitors are no longer just the companies up the road; they are often from other continents and intent on extending their markets across the world.

- Customers have become more demanding, expecting immediate response to their requests, whether for goods or for information.

- The regulatory environment has changed, and will continue to change, as consumer protection and environmental issues become more important. To keep pace with these changes, messaging systems have had to adapt. The laboriously typed letter or memo, carried from place to place by the postman, has given way to electronic or digital messages, created in a computer and distributed by electronic means to other computers. Some messages are still typed by, addressed to and read by humans, but another class are created, addressed, received and interpreted completely automatically.

In this chapter we consider both types of message and the infrastructure being put in place to enable electronic messaging to be used as naturally and easily as traditional mechanisms.

Electronic Mail for People

Soon after mainframe computers gained the ability to service communities of remote users, each with a simple terminal, users realized that the computer itself could provide a personal messaging system. All that was necessary was for the sender to type a message and leave it as a file with the recipient's name attached. At some later time the recipient could retrieve the message and, if need be, relabel the file to pass the message on to another reader or initiate a response to the original sender.

Such an informal mechanism will work perfectly well for a small, close-knit group of users who can agree a simple file naming convention for

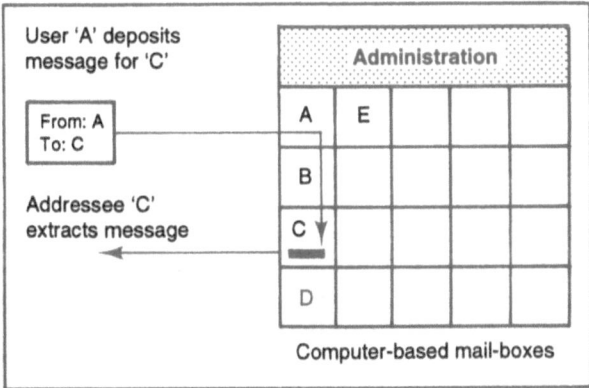

Fig. 4.1. Traditional "store and retrieve" electronic messaging.

message addressing, but can descend into chaos as the user community grows. The result was the creation of simple electronic mail systems built around a "rack" of "electronic pigeon holes" or mailboxes. Each user is allocated a mailbox by a central administrative function which can prevent duplication of names and handle message counting and billing activities (see Fig. 4.1).

Simple security mechanisms were added to prevent users from peeking into other users' mailboxes, and the outcome was the direct precursor of the "private" or in-house electronic mailing systems available today from computer vendors and third party software suppliers. IBM's PROFS and DISOSS systems and DEC's ALL-IN-1 system are three well-known examples.

The next step came when the regulatory environment changed, first in the USA and subsequently in many European and other countries – in Europe a major milestone was the publication of the CEC Telecommunications Green Paper in 1987. The new rules relaxed PTT monopolies on certain telecommunications services and permitted "service providers" to offer commercial electronic mail services. Within a few years a host of such services were available, some aimed at the intersite internal mailing requirements of major corporations and others at intercompany mail. GE Information Services' QUIK-COMM System is representative of the first group, and British Telecom's GOLD Service of the second.

The Standards Issue

The success of these "second generation" mailing systems demonstrated that businesses had a real need for the flexibility and power of electronic messaging systems to complement conventional telephone and paper-based mechanisms. To begin with, growth was simple; user communities grew by adding more and more "dumb" terminals to the supplier's data network. The widespread availability of desktop and portable microcomputers was handled by providing software packages that enabled the micro to act like a dumb terminal, albeit with sophisticated message creation and display facilities.

However, all of the in-house and third party systems were different. They had different message formats, different addressing conventions and used a wide variety of underlying communications protocols; the introduction of local area networks (LANs), providing simple electronic messaging services for co-operating groups of micro users, merely added another level of complication. Two types of problem arose:

- How could work-group messaging systems be connected to in-house or third party company-wide messaging systems?

- How could corporate messaging systems be connected to intercompany messaging systems?

When numbers are small, *ad hoc* solutions are both possible and practical. It is not particularly difficult to write a program for, say, a PC, which can connect to one mailing system, extract messages destined for another system, reformat them and re-address them, then connect to the "target" system as a sender and pass them on ("refile" them, in telex jargon). This approach was taken, with considerable success, to allow corporate users of GE Information Services' QUIK-COMM System to connect work-group users of popular proprietary messaging systems to the corporate community. A similar approach may be used to connect small numbers of corporate systems to each other or to a common intercompany service (see Fig.4.2).

However, as the numbers of both "islands of users" and of "target systems" grew, chaos again threatened and it became clear that *ad hoc* solutions merely delayed the inevitable.

The computer industry and the related service companies had made a virtue of "own brand" solutions since their inception in the 1960s. In the 1980s, the users of mailing services made it very clear that, whatever the opinions of suppliers, interconnectivity of mailing systems was now a necessity. Or, put another way, whatever the internal standards

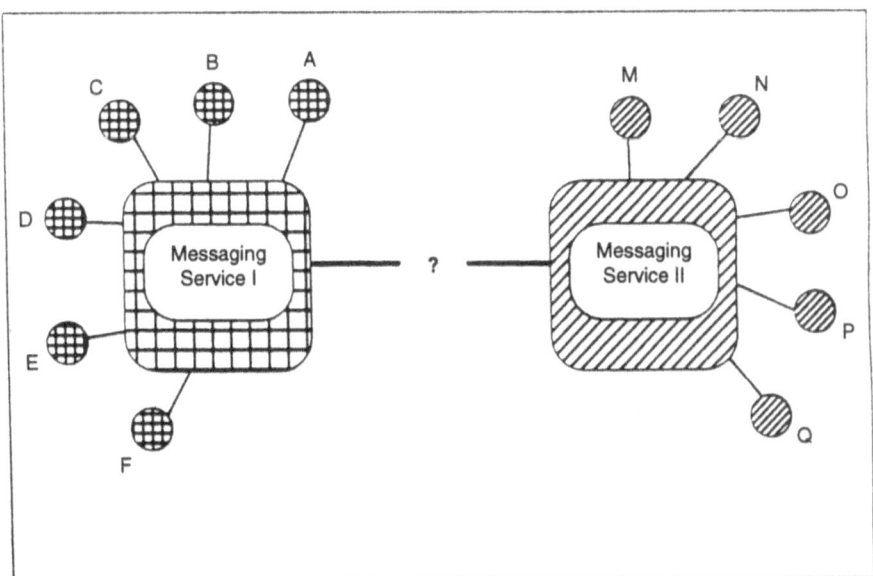

Fig. 4.2. The standards problem – how do members of different messaging communities communicate?

used within any given system, that system must also be able to communicate through a standard interface to any other system.

Meanwhile, in the mid-1970s, noting the increasing use of public telephone networks to connect terminals to computers, the telecommunications administrators saw an opportunity to offer new digital services, which became known as packet-switched public data networks (PDNs). To maximize the national and international potential of PDNs, the Comité Consultatif International Télégraphique et Téléphonique (CCITT) and the International Organization for Standardization (ISO) began to develop standard communications protocols for networked applications.

This activity was complemented by the Open Systems Interconnection (OSI) initiative, which was aimed at allowing users of a "Brand X" mainframe or minicomputer to attach equipment from a wide range of independent suppliers, who, in turn, no longer had to tailor their products to a large number of different central processors. A natural extension was to enable disparate open systems to co-operate, and the OSI X.200 Reference Model provided a means by which communications between computer applications are standardized through a seven-layer model (Fig. 4.3).

However, it was the telephone companies that provided the solution to the messaging problem. By their nature, telephone companies are standards-minded, and for many years have been able to interconnect

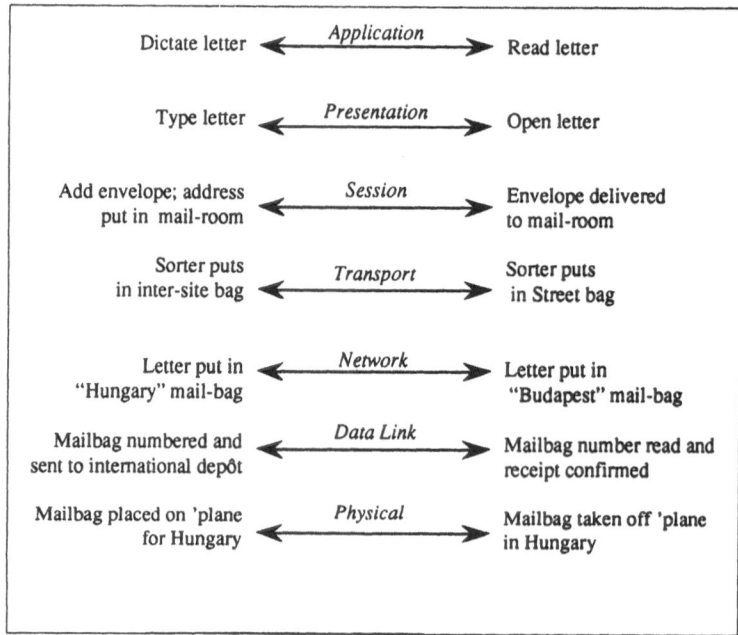

Fig. 4.3. Letter post interpretation of the ISO open systems Reference Model.

disparate local and national systems to provide a more or less unified worldwide international direct dial capability. They saw electronic messaging as an attractive service offering, and the CCITT designed a set of messaging recommendations which built upon the OSI Reference Model. In the short and medium term, any messaging system or service able to format and process messages according to the new X.400 recommendations, first ratified in 1984, would be able to exchange messages. More importantly, each messaging system or service would henceforth need just one interconnect mechanism to bring most of the world's messaging communities into reach.

The X.400 recommendations have a second important attribute. Most messaging systems started from small beginnings, with options and facilities being added as user needs dictated. The CCITT began from the opposite premise:

How do we interconnect the world?

Telephone companies are big and they think big! They are also used to taking a long-term view, and therefore took care to avoid boxing potential users into obsolete technology by segmenting their standards into distinct functions with well-defined interfaces. This approach, which is common to the OSI Reference Model, enables individual parts of the system as a whole to be redefined without impact on other elements. Thus, for example, the introduction of fibre optic communications implied new ways of handling the interface between the computers and the communications medium. The segmentation implicit in the "layer" approach means that a user can slot in a new "driver" for handling the machine-to-medium interface without affecting, say, the routing or error control layers.

This segmentation produces a solution with a lot of components, which can therefore look extremely complicated – not helped, it must be said, by the proliferation of acronyms used to identify the components. In fact, the entire X.400/X.200 complex of recommendations has the same underlying simplicity as the conventional mailing process used to send a letter across the world.

There are two major components:

- Inside the sender's computer, where the message is formatted and addressed ready for transmission.

- In the outside world, where the message is transferred from the sender's computer either directly to the recipient's computer or to an intermediate message store from which the recipient can collect it later.

The message transmission or data network component is placed under an administrative umbrella which ensures uniqueness of addresses and provides a variety of operational, security and accounting facilities.

Not least among these is the directory services facility, which is still in its infancy (the X.500 standards).

How Does X.400 Work?

We explain the X.400 message handling system by following a message from generation to ultimate destination, and, for the sake of simplicity, we assume that both users are equipped with microcomputers, each with a software package and communications capability which conform to the appropriate standards (otherwise one or more additional interfaces will be needed).

First, the sender puts together the outgoing message. This used to be one or more pages of text and text alone. However, many computers now have spreadsheet processors, drawing packages, scanners able to capture graphics and photographs, or devices to capture and digitize sound or images from video, and a message can contain any or all of these. It is, in the jargon, made up of one or more "body parts", which, between them, simulate whatever we might place in a conventional envelope: a tape recording, a computer disk containing spreadsheet data or software, a photograph or drawing, and so on (see Fig. 4.4).

The message body (made up of body parts) is then given a heading. This will typically include the address list, message identification and a line of text describing the contents. The headed message is called the

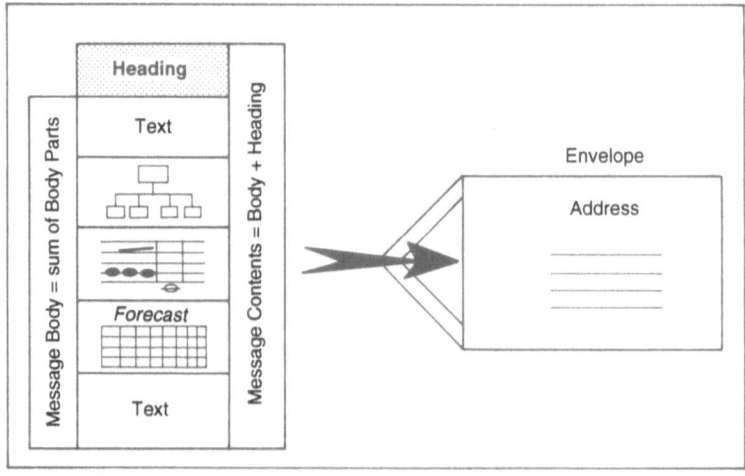

Fig. 4.4. The message and its envelope.

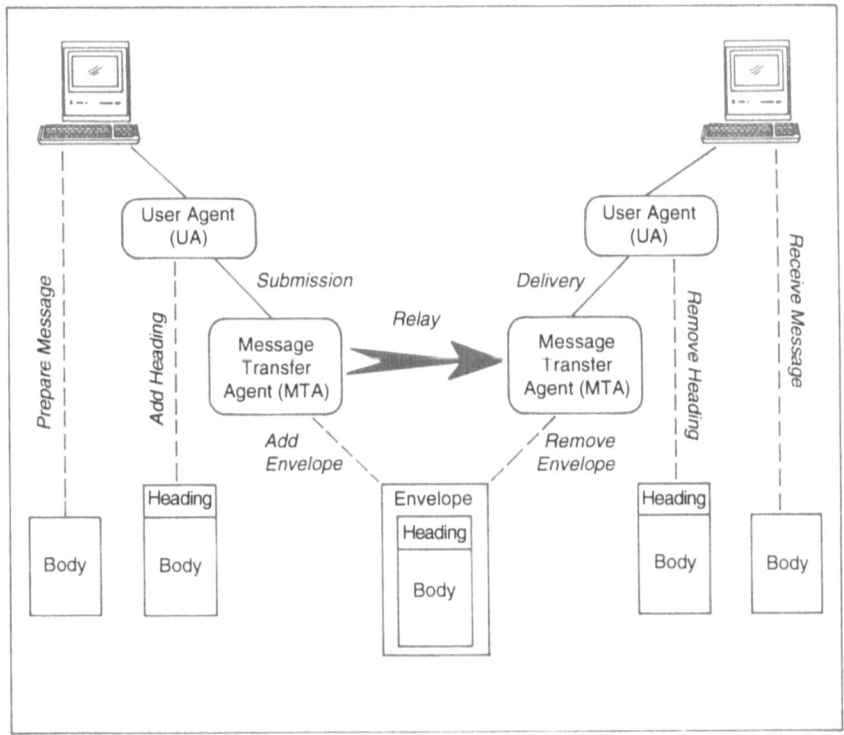

Fig. 4.5. Active entities in X.400 interpersonal message transfer.

message content, and will, in the fullness of time, be delivered to the recipient's machine.

The application or device used to make the message transfer service (MTS) available to the user is called the user agent. In our example, this will be a software package in the user's PC. The user agent also receives and holds incoming messages addressed to the user (see Fig. 4.5).

The next step is to put the message into an envelope. For an electronic message this means taking the file containing the message and adding a "top" and a "tail" to indicate where the message stops plus check information so that any subsequent process can detect missing, added or changed contents and call for retransmission. The envelope is then given an address, together with other control information needed to relay the message through the MTS. X.400 addressing looks immensely complicated, but in fact follows ordinary postal addressing procedures very closely.

X.400 addressing is, like ordinary addressing, based on "lines" or "layers" of organisational structure (Fig. 4.6):

• A memo travelling within an office needs only the recipient's name.

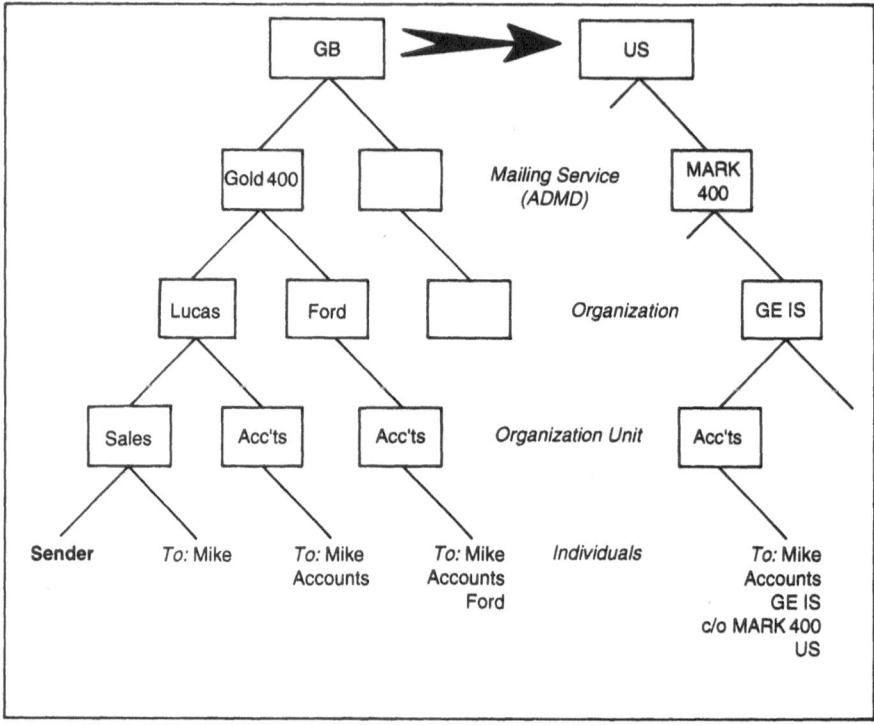

Fig. 4.6. Simplified addressing scheme. The length of the address is determined by "distance" from sender.

- If the message is to travel to another department within the same building it requires two layers: the name and the department.
- If the recipient is in another company in the same country then three layers may suffice.
- The most lengthy address will usually be on international mail.

Within this basic structure a wide range of options is provided to allow for particular circumstances. In a small organization the individual may be found by giving his name and that of the company, possibly with a forename if two employees share a surname. This would be impossibly unwieldy in General Electric Company, which has nearly 300,000 employees located all over the world. So optional organization unit layers may be interposed to enable the mailing system to locate the correct recipient.

X.400 Address Components

The normal X.400 address structure, central to the operation of an X.400 messaging system, is perhaps most easily explained back to front, with the largest "community" first:

c = *country code*. A two-letter code (as in ISO 3166) has been allocated to every country; for example US = United States of America; DE = Germany (Deutschland).

a = *Administration Management Domain (ADMD)*. ADMDs are allocated to telecommunications administrations or independent service providers. The former provide electronic mail services for individuals or small businesses, the latter for whatever their customer base is made up of. Thus, the German public telecommunications operator has an administrative domain called DBP (Deutsche BundesPost Telekom) and GE Information Services has an administrative domain called MARK400.

p = *Private Management Domain (PRMD)*. These are allocated to corporate user communities spread all over the country, and enable a country-wide, and in some cases international, internal messaging system to be treated as an entity by an outsider sending in a message. For example, Esso, the oil company, would have a PRMD within GE Information Services' MARK400 ADMD: C = GB; A = MARK400; P=ESSO; . . .

o = *organization*. The name of the organization to which the addressee belongs; this may in some instances be the label of its electronic messaging system.

ou = *organization unit*. An operating company within a major corporation or a department within a company; there may be more than one level of organization unit, numbered ou1, ou2, ou3, etc. to enable a complete address to be created. Note that organization units do not necessarily have anything to do with geography, so, for example, Field Service Engineers might belong to ou1 = FSE, and cover all of Europe.

s = *surname*. Messages go, at least in principle, to people, and we know their names.

g = *given name* (in most organizations there are at least two people with the same surname).

I = *initial* (to distinguish Mike C. Chesher from Mike G. Chesher; in some cases a "generation identifier" might be used to distinguish Mike C. Chesher Sr from his son Mike C. Chesher Jr).

Any given message needs only that addressing information required to ensure that it goes to the correct addressee. If the two parties are on the same LAN then only the name (with or without given name and/or initial) is needed; if they are within the same organization then only the name and organization unit are needed; and so on. The whole panoply of address components is needed only for an inter-administration message to an individual working in a large organization. These more complex addresses may be stored with a simple alias in a Local Directory, so you can write to, for example, MIKEC@GEIS; the user agent process will look up this address in the directory established by the user and replace the shorthand form by the full X.400 address.

Individual private users and small businesses without mailing systems themselves will, of course, not need the address elements concerned with organizational structure, and will use a mailing service made available by the ADMD of their choice, using its standard user agent interface.

There are some other considerations concerning the X.400 addressing scheme that illustrate the amount of creative thought that went into its design:

- The complete address is unique *in the world.*

- Responsibility for naming is pushed down to the lowest possible level of system administrator. The administrator for a LAN-based mailing system in a low-level organization unit is responsible for adding, ensuring uniqueness of, updating and deleting names within that OU. The administrator for a corporation has to deal with only those OUs reporting directly to the top. Only at the highest level of ADMD is there a need for an international peer-level naming consensus.

- The converse of addressing is routing: the message has to find its way from sender to recipient. It is clearly unreasonable for every electronic mail terminal to have to know how to send a message to every other terminal in the world (e.g. by keeping the terminal's telephone numbers), and it is equally unreasonable for any central body to have to keep such a directory up to date. The X.400 mechanism means that any given node in the worldwide electronic mailing system needs to know only the next node "up" or "down" in the hierarchy, apart from the ADMD nodes, which need to know how to send a message to each of their peers.

This brings us to the next step in delivering our message. The *message transfer agent* (MTA) is the X.400 element responsible for addressing the message and passing it out of the user's environment into the data communications network for transit to a corresponding MTA in the recipient's environment. From the address structure we already know how this is done:

- The MTA either knows where the recipient is (since it is "in" the same machine) or it passes the message "up" to the next level, for example to an organization unit.

- The OU either knows where the addressee MTA is (since it is another user within the same organization unit) or it passes the message "up" to the organization node.

and so on, until:

- The ADMD knows where the addressee ADMD is (since it knows where they all are), and relays the message accordingly.

- The addressee ADMD passes the message "down" through its structure to the addressee MTA (or directly to the UA in the case of a private user associated with the addressee ADMD), where the envelope is removed and the message is stored in the user agent awaiting the attention of the addressee person (Fig. 4.6).

In the real world, the various nodes have three other jobs to do:

- They must check that the message has not been truncated, lengthened or scrambled; this is done within the OSI data communications environment using the checking information built into the layered protocols.

- They must check that the address really exists and return a status message to the originating MTA, and thence to the sender if it cannot be delivered (the use of local alternate addresses or automatic message forwarding can ensure that some messages are rerouted within the target organization); senders may also request notification of delivery (the message has been placed in the recipient's MTA) and/or notification of receipt (the addressee has listed the message).

- They must measure the size of the message and record its passage through the global X.400 system to ensure that the sender is correctly billed and that in future intermediaries receive their correct apportionment of the charges for handling the message.

However, these administrative details, though important, are outside the scope of this chapter.

In summary, X.400 messaging services enable a message, either of simple text or more complex combinations of text, graphics and binary files, to be delivered to an addressee anywhere in the world. The onus on the user is quite light and generally consists of a simple local software package which handles formatting and enveloping, plus a communications package which knows where to find a small number of contiguous X.400 nodes and is able to share their communications protocol. Since these messages are sent between people, little is required in terms of confirmation of receipt, except an indication that the message has been correctly delivered to the appropriate MTA and subsequently listed by the user.

Electronic Mail for Computer Applications

We have seen how electronic mail is evolving from a myriad of little local user communities with a need for a certain amount of intercommunity messaging into the global X.400 community. While this was happening, a second form of electronic messaging came into being and followed a roughly parallel path. Electronic data interchange (EDI) was invented as a means for business forms, such as purchase orders and invoices, to be passed directly from the sender's application to the complementary application in the recipient's computer.

The driving force was a need to reduce costs and improve customer service. By transferring a purchase order, for example, through some form of electronic messaging system, several benefits would arise:

- The order would be available to the vendor's computerized order entry application within a matter of hours rather than the several days taken by conventional mail.

- Opportunities for orders to be misdirected or simply lost would be virtually eliminated.

- The expense, delay and opportunity for the insertion of errors associated with keying the order into the recipient's computer would all be eliminated, since the information would already be in computer-readable form.

- The customer would receive better service, and, over time, the frequency of ordering could be increased without significant addition to overheads.

The last of these points is perhaps the most important because it has permitted the introduction of "Just in Time" inventory philosophies, which have in turn allowed purchasers such as automobile assemblers or High Street stores to phase out their Goods Inward stock-holdings and move incoming goods directly to point of use or point of sale, with replenishments on a daily or shorter cycle. Successful implementation of such systems provides order-of-magnitude improvements in end-user service, enormous one-off savings, and improved flexibility in production planning, giving the ability to make what is actually needed rather than what a planner thinks might be needed, resulting in improved cash flows.

EDI was first used on a large scale in the automotive assembly industry and has spread to virtually every industry sector, as well as to areas such as customs documentation and payment services through links with clearing banks. From the outset it was clear that, while some of the underlying mechanisms of interpersonal messaging might be used for EDI, EDI messages had some additional characteristics needing special treatment.

The most important point is that the recipient is not human, but a computer program, and, unlike humans, computer programs are highly inflexible. If you send me a paper purchase order, I can rekey the information into my order processing application in the required format, whether you have your name at the top of the form or at the bottom or running up the side. I can unscramble an order line regardless of the sequence in which you present the information, and can even make sense of one that reads:

Please send me six dozen cans of spray lubricant in the economy size, and can I have the ones with the red tops, since those with yellow tops won't fit into my spray guns.

It is necessary to take your order, in the format in which it is presented by your replenishment application, and, having relayed it to my order processing application, persuade the latter to read and understand it. Ten years ago, when these problems were first presented, it was virtually impossible to find any complementary pair of applications capable of accepting one another's output. It was unreasonable to expect all of one's customers to recode their applications to present orders in the format used by the supplier (and, even if they would do it for one supplier they could hardly do it for twenty), so the need for standards soon became apparent.

Unfortunately, the CCITT and ISO were not ready and waiting with proposals for global standards, so each industry invented its own, predictably with different forms in different countries, and a new electronic Babel sprung up in just a few years. Within each "island of users" this did not much matter, since each user had merely to translate outgoing documents from the internal format into the industry format and translate incoming documents back into (usually a different) internal format. However, the manufacturers of commonly used products such as paint sold to every industry and it soon became clear that proper cross-industry standards were necessary.

In the USA the American National Standards Institute (ANSI) developed their X.12 family of standards and the Transportation Data Co-ordinating Committee (TDCC) developed a different family for communications between shippers and carriers. In Europe and the Far East a number of independent standardization bodies developed more or less compatible standards under the Global Trade Data Interchange (GTDI) banner. It soon became clear that universal standards were necessary and the Joint EDI (JEDI) Committee was set up to produce harmonized standards for global use. There are now a large number of these completely agreed or on their way through the agreement procedure; they are known as the EDIFACT (EDI for Administration, Commerce and Transportation) standards.

In summary, companies today can exchange a large number of types of business document by translating internal formats to and from a single, universally agreed format. It remains only to relay the EDI-standard format document to the intended recipient. There are two commonly used mechanisms:

- Direct machine-to-machine transfers. Given the level of electrical and protocol incompatibility between machines, and the difficulty of scheduling message exchange sessions, this mechanism is appropriate only in situations where small numbers of trading partners have regular high volume interchanges.

- Using a mailbox mechanism like that used for interpersonal messages (Fig. 4.7).

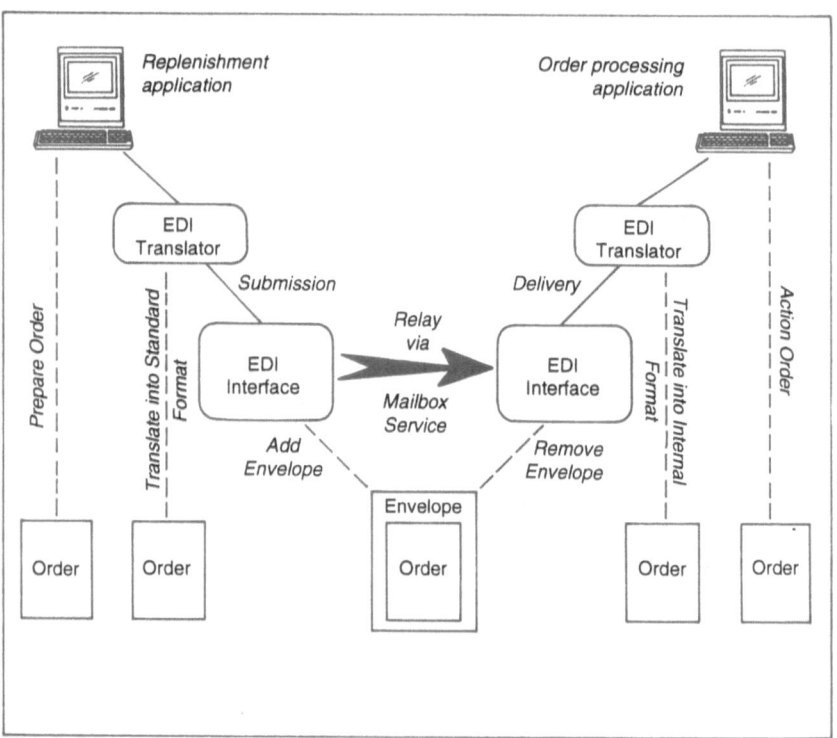

Fig. 4.7. Active entities in conventional EDI message transfer.

A number of service providers, including GE Information Services, began to offer message transfer systems specialized to the requirements of EDI users. These differ in some respects from interpersonal messaging systems, and the differences are important if we are to understand the issues that arise when we try to extend the X.400 messaging mechanism to embrace EDI messages.

First, there is a broad area of "security", which we may break down to include:

- *Trading relationships.* It is clearly vital that a pair of trading partners do not start trying to exchange EDI messages until both are ready to do so (have their internal systems and message translators in place, for example); some EDI messaging systems refuse messages unless the recipient has previously signalled that he is ready to receive messages of that type, thereby preventing messages from being delivered into an electronic "black hole".

- *Exclusion of interlopers.* The integrity of a business depends on messages being delivered intact to the intended recipient – unlike interpersonal messages, many EDI messages have a real monetary value, and incorrect delivery could result in loss of trade (for a retail store) or loss of output (for an assembler). This means that third parties should be unable to tap into a message stream and, for example, extract messages and throw them away, or change messages and re-insert them or simply replay them time and again. This area is receiving considerable attention as EDI methods are adopted by payment systems and the messages act as electronic cheques or money transfers.

- *Message integrity.* The system must not alter or truncate messages, and if this does happen as an artefact of the transfer process it must be detected and damaged messages must either be retransmitted automatically or marked as suspect and the parties to the transaction informed immediately.

- *Message acknowledgement.* The sender cannot feel secure until he has received a positive acknowledgement that each individual message has been received by the intended addressee; a second level of acknowledgement indicating that the message has been read and understood is also needed in some cases (a purchase order needs to be acknowledged line by line, while there is little requirement for, say, an invoice to be acknowledged except as a message).

A second group of EDI service facilities extend the message transfer offering to include a level of sorting and batching of messages. Thus, a sender might make up a bundle of messages of many different types, but all to a single addressee, and send them as a batch. The addressee will typically have a number of different applications involved in EDI transactions and will wish for incoming messages to be bundled by type, each bundle including inputs from many different sources.

A third type of service provides for automatic en route translation between different EDI standard formats (or, indeed, between private internal formats and EDI standard formats). Fortunately, the need for this type of added service will diminish as the EDIFACT standards gain ground.

Finally, some services permit a wide range of payment options, ranging from "sender pays" to "equal shares for sender and recipient" or flexible terms agreed by each pair of trading partners.

EDI and X.400

The X.400 recommendations were originally devised for interpersonal messaging and have, at least so far, shown that they can cater for, or be extended to cater for, the needs of this user community. The needs of the EDI community are rather more stringent, and there are also differences in the make-up of an EDI message (or interchange) that impact upon the suitability of the X.400 message relay mechanism for EDI messages.

An X.400 system is just a relay system, with no provision for the "value added services" such as standards translations, checking on "trading relationships" or sorting and re-bundling groups of messages. If such services are genuinely needed in the future then it is likely that they will continue to be provided by third party service vendors. This will be possible if they act as the recipient for outgoing messages, which they can collect (as though they were an ordinary user), process and then retransmit to the originally intended addressees. Indeed, CEFIC, a consortium of European chemical companies, use just such an approach. Messages are sent to GE Information Services' EDI*EXPRESS system using an X.400 relay mechanism, and GEIS then retransmit them to the ultimate addressees, again through X.400 links.

A more difficult point is raised by the need for positive acknowledgements. A standard EDI message (sent through a conventional EDI system and based on EDIFACT standards) consists of three major parts:

- A header (referred to as record type UNB), which contains information about the following interchange; this information is more comprehensive than an IPM header and, in particular, allows for "intelligent" acknowledgements to be generated automatically and sent to addressees (which need not be the same as the sender).

- A body or interchange, which may contain many different types of document (at least in some implementations of EDI systems) as well as multiple documents of the same type.

- A trailer record (called a UNZ record), which refers back to the header, contains additional control information and acts as a positive marker that the message is now complete, thereby fulfilling part of the requirement for message integrity.

The header, or to be more precise, acting upon the information contained in the header, is what causes the problem. The basic X.400 process will merely indicate that the message has been delivered to the recipient's MTA, whereas the EDI users want to know precisely which message, as identified by the EDI reference numbers rather than X.400's message serial numbers. An additional difficulty is that once the file of EDI messages delivered in the message body is accessed a further application process needs to take place. This will either mailbox the EDI messages or attempt to pass them directly to the relevant end application (such as the order processing application in Fig. 4.7). If format errors are detected at this point, completely outside the X.400 environment, the return of error messages has to be handled by a separate application rather than being integrated into the MTS.

It will come as little surprise to learn that different groups of EDI/X.400 users or service suppliers have devised a variety of solutions to this problem! The simplest, referred to as the "P0" approach, is to define a new message content type called "Undefined", and deliver it in the usual X.400 envelope without X.400 headers or other information. It is then up to the EDI application to create and send acknowledgements and process the message contents in the appropriate way. This approach was developed in the United States. The European approach was to treat the entire EDI transaction as the body of an IP message, and deliver it with the X.400 header to the recipient user agent (Fig. 4.8).

Clearly, these approaches do not solve the underlying problem of handling EDIFACT addressing and acknowledgement procedures in an "EDI-aware" manner – they just push the problem into an envelope and pass it to the interchange recipient. A more promising approach has been made under the aegis of the CCITT, through the definition of a new message content type called "Protocol for EDI" (PEDI, also known as P35). This is distinguished by a redesigned header which contains some of the information from the EDIFACT message header (UNB) as well as the information required by the X.400 relay mechanism. The EDI users will need an uprated version of MTA software to recognize the new message content type, but can then exchange information along the lines envisaged by the designers of the EDIFACT standards. It is equally suited for processing messages formatted according to ANSI and UN-GTDI EDI standards. The additional X.400 recommendation for PEDI is numbered X.435.

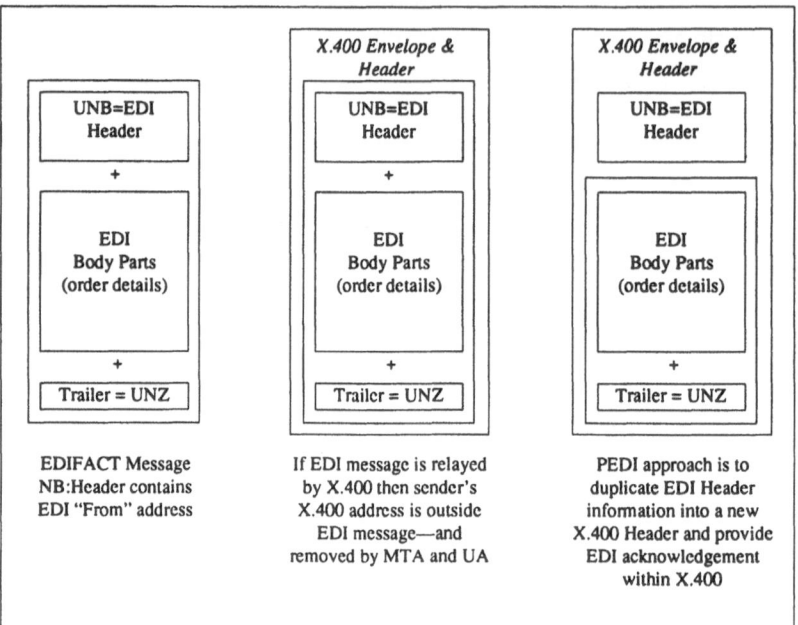

Fig. 4.8. EDI and X.400.

PEDI brings some new features to X.400 functionality, including clear end-to-end acknowledgement rather than relay level acknowledgements, additional security features to cater for the special needs of EDI users, the ability to send positive, negative or forwarded acknowledgements to users other than the original sender and the ability to interface with a wide range of "gateways". Gateways are frequently installed by EDI users to protect their existing investment in hardware and software, and simply act as interfaces between in-house applications and the X.400 delivery mechanism. From the X.400 viewpoint the EDI message is delivered to a user's application; the gateway delays the time when this in fact becomes the case but still allows the user to adopt X.400 message delivery standards.

Where We Are Today

The majority of national telecommunications administrations in the developed world have, or are actively creating, the infrastructure required to provide X.400 messaging services. Major third-party service providers, including GE Information Services, have installed gateways and appropriate software to enable their well-established messaging services (IPM or EDI) to be accessed by X.400 users. Most vendors of computer hardware and their software suppliers are able to support X.400 messaging.

So the components are more or less in place. The caveat is necessary, because very little of the equipment was designed in the first place for use in an X.400 environment, and the X.400 recommendations are not one hundred per cent crystal clear over every possible detail. As a result, most implementations have an element of customization to overcome difficulties encountered in retrofitting the new protocols and procedures to existing equipment. In addition, implementations can differ slightly depending on the way in which the implementors have interpreted the standards, and the extent to which optional service elements are included.

The effect is that, taking into account the internetwork connections now planned or in place, a company or a group of companies can realistically implement a corporate interpersonal messaging strategy based on the X.400 approach. While a few work-groups with obsolete equipment may have difficulties, the way is open for companies to move rapidly towards the use of EDI and so gain the benefits made possible thereby.

Some of the events described earlier in this chapter demonstrate the truth of my remark that the CCITT "thought big" and "thought long term" when they first laid out the X.400 recommendations back in 1984. A major revision was made in 1988 and the X.435 PEDI recommendation was added in 1991; additional recommendations for directory services (the X.500 group) were agreed in 1988 and a further revision took place in 1992. The original foundations have proven themselves strong enough and flexible enough to adapt to changing needs and changing technology, giving every reason to believe that, as new possibilities evolve during the 1990s and into the next century, the X.400 "family" will grow to accommodate them. In short: X.400 is safe. By implication, if messaging communities standardize on the X.400 approach, they will safeguard their investment against obsolescence.

5 | Strategic Management of Information Technology Investments

Juliet Sheppard and Peijie Wang

Introduction

The Shift of Business Focus

Since the 1980s there has been a shift of focus for information technology (IT) applications, away from improving efficiency and towards achieving competitive advantage, thus increasing the importance of IT to the business. Roger Tomlin (1990) describes this shift in a report prepared for Amdahl Executive Institute:

> IT is now targeted increasingly towards adding value to the internal and external activities at the forefront of improving competitive positioning and management effectiveness. In many instances, it is also an active agent in restructuring whole organisations and industries.

Authors like Earl (1989) distinguish the changed perception of IT's role in terms of the data processing (DP) era and the IT era, and summarize the criteria that characterize the differences (Table 5.1).

Table 5.1. The changing perception of IT

Distinctor	DP era	IT era
Financial attitude to IT	A cost	An investment
Business role of IT	Support	Often critical
Applications orientation	Tactical	Strategic
Economic context	Neutral	Welcome
Social impact	Limited	Pervasive
MIS thinking on IT	Traditional	New
Stakeholders	Few	Many
Management posture	Delegate	Involved

Ward et al. (1990) develop this typopology into a three-phase model that describes the prime objectives of using information systems (IS):

1. Data processing to improve operational efficiency by automating information based processes (from 1960s).

2. Management information systems to increase management effectiveness by satisfying their information requirements (from 1970s).
3. Strategic information systems to improve competitiveness by changing the nature or conduct of business (from 1980s).

The recognition that IT may have worth as a strategic weapon has implications throughout the organization for the appraisal of IS and technology investments.

Increasing Expenditure in IT Systems

Price Waterhouse (1991) report that actual IT expenditure per installation in the UK was £3.813 million in 1991. The annual increase was 11.3% from 1988 to 1991. The forecast UK average IT expenditure in 1991 as the percentage of turnover was 1.3%. This expenditure is not confined to the private sector:

In the public sector the Department of Social Security is committed to spending in excess of £2 billion on its 15 year computer strategy; the Department of Health is currently committed to spending hundreds of millions of pounds on IT based systems (Willcocks 1991).

The size of these investments requires managers to be concerned with the appropriateness of the decision process and their expected return.

Management Satisfaction with IT

The strategic management of IT, which focuses on sustainable competitiveness and long-term corporate development derived from IT investments, is still under consideration. A significant proportion of IT investments failed to achieve their objectives or to integrate with business needs. The CBI survey (1991) concluded that:

a significant 44% reported feeling less than satisfied with their current (information) systems, despite the high level of monetary investment by many companies in IT.

Recent research by Willcocks and Lester (1991) suggests that:

at least 20% of such spend is wasted, and that between 30–40% of IS projects realize no net benefits whatsoever, however measured.

Excellent IT practices do exist, but they are not easy to apply. A review conducted by the Butler Cox Foundation (Chang 1991) concluded that organizations had to design business-oriented measures for appraisal, and manage the investment and the achievement of benefits to ensure they were receiving value for money from IT investments. Recent research at Kingston Business School into the appraisal of IT investments yields further quantitative and qualitative data.

Key Questions

The focus of IT decision making for organizations within the business sectors is moving towards the alignment of IT investments with corporate business objectives using more formalized appraisal and post-evaluation of investments, while for government agencies the imposition of new legislative requirements within short time-scales denies them the opportunity to plan strategically and in many cases forces them to be purely reactive. The dynamic opportunities offered by technology development stimulate investments, the size of which increases concern regarding the methods by which these decisions are reached. The research at Kingston Business School surveyed 500 organizations to investigate specifically:

- The amount spent on IT.
- The perceptions of monies spent on IT: expenditure or investment.
- The perceived importance of IT.
- The decision makers involved in these decisions.
- The decision making procedures: consistent strategies.
- Evaluation: measures of "success", explanations of "failures".

Profile of the Respondents

The research was based on a questionnaire survey. The questionnaires were sent to organizations in all sectors: business, higher education, research and public administration. The number of organizations in each sector in the total sample was chosen to be proportional to the IT spending in that sector. There were 135 participants in the survey, representing a response rate of 27%. Institutions in the public administration sector accounted for nearly a quarter of those who replied, and, considering the business sectors alone, finance accounted for the largest proportion (32%).

The Amount Spent on IT

Total Spending

The survey indicated that the most frequently selected size of IT investment under consideration was in the range of £2–£10m and that half the organizations spent more than £2m. An IT spending of between £2m and £10m in 1990–1991 was reported by 34% (46) of the organizations. Nearly a quarter (23%, 31 organizations) of the organizations investigated spent less than 0.1% of their revenues on IT; and more than half spent less than 0.5%. Only 13% (17) of the organizations spent more that 1% of their total revenue on IT.

IT Spending Categories

The composition of IT spending was explored by eight items:

- Hardware
- Software
- Installation
- Maintenance
- Direct staff costs
- Telecommunications
- Training and development
- Security

Hardware and direct staff costs accounted for the major part of the total spending across all sectors, followed by software, telecommunications and maintenance. In the accounting year 1990–1991, 36% of the organizations reported hardware spending of over £2 million, while 32% spent more than £2 million on direct staff costs. The increasing size of software costs is of note. Training and development accounted for relatively small percentages of the overall expenditure, and the spending on security was the smallest proportion.

IT as an Investment

Organizations harbour different attitudes towards spending on IT. Is IT spending a capital investment or an operating expense? Earl's (1989) criteria for characterizing these differences are listed in Table 5.2.

Those managers who consider IT spending as a capital investment hold an attitude consistent with capital planning and the management of benefits, while a focus on IT as an operating expense highlights cost management and the requirement for self-financed projects (Earl 1989). There is evidence that strategic thinking contributes to the successful application of IT in organizations. In a survey of 635 organizations

Table 5.2. Earl's criteria for differentiating attitudes to IT

From expense	To investment
Small numbers	Large numbers
Tactical outlook	Strategic outlook
Do we have to?	Can't afford not to!
'Stop–go'	'It never stops'
Cost analysis	Investment appraisal
Self-financing	Capital planning
Manage the costs	Manage the benefits
Expense accounting	Asset accounting

(Tomlin 1990) 79% who had implemented very successful IT applications agreed that:

> planned IT developments clearly relate to the strategic goals of the business.

It has been argued that the management of benefits requires attention (Chang 1991), and that the justification for monies spent on IT that relies on understated costs and notional benefit calculations needs to be replaced by formal appraisal methods (Willcocks 1991).

The respondents were asked to give their views on eight statements that were used to discriminate between attitudes that consider money spent on IT as an investment and as an expenditure. Most organizations had an attitude to IT spending consistent with IT viewed as an investment. Fewer organizations held the shorter term view that IT spending was an expense.

It has been argued that strategic management of IT requires organizations to view money spent on IT as an investment and an asset rather than as an expenditure and liability. The research identified that there was a division of opinion, with some organizations believing that projects should be treated as an investment to be financed by capital planning, while others thought such projects should be self-financed.

The Importance of IT to Organizations

McFarlan and McKenney (1983) suggest that:

> Organizations need to identify how critical IT is to their business prior to making investments.

Cash et al. (1989) argue further:

> *Within (an) industry context it is increasingly clear that good manage-*
> *ment of IT varies widely in different settings. For some organizations,*
> *IT activities represent an area of great strategic importance; for other*
> *organizations ... one distinctly supportive in nature. A complicating*
> *element in some organizations is that while today's existing IT*
> *applications are not critical to the firm in meeting its goals, the*
> *thrust of its new systems applications portfolio has great significance*
> *for the future. Understanding an organization's position on these issues*
> *is critical to developing an appropriate management strategy.*

Strategic Impact of IT

Based on the strategic impact of IT applications on future development and the importance of IT applications to existing business
operations, McFarlan and McKenney categorize four quite different
IT environments: strategic, turnaround, factory and support. Their
IT applications quadrant of future impact and existing importance is
shown in Fig. 5.1.

Strategic

> *There are companies for whom smooth functioning of the IT activity*
> *is critical to their operation on a daily basis and whose applications*
> *under development are critical for their future competitive success.*
> *Appropriately managed, not only do these firms require considerable*
> *planning but the organizational relationship between IT and senior*
> *management is very close. In fact, in some firms the head of the IT*
> *function, broadly defined, sits on the board of directors.*

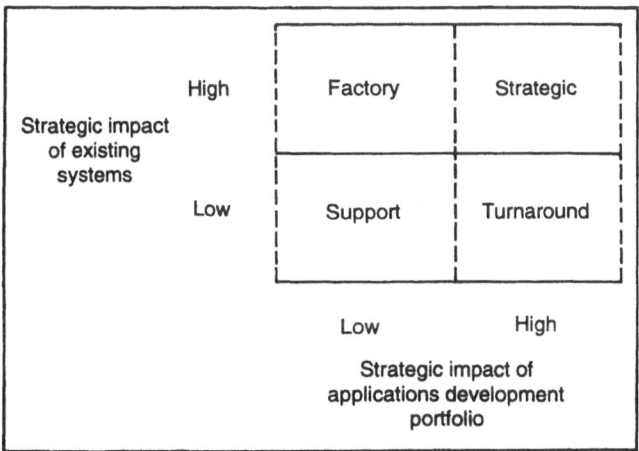

Fig. 5.1. IT applications quadrant.

Turnaround

> Some firms may receive considerable amounts of IT operational sup-
> port, but the company is not absolutely dependent on the uninterrupted
> cost-effective functioning of this support to achieve either short-term
> or long-term objectives. The applications under development, however,
> are absolutely vital for the firm to reach its strategic objectives. ...
> Enhanced IT leadership, new organizational placement of IT, and an
> increased commitment to planning are all steps being taken to resolve
> this situation.

Factory

> Some firms are heavily dependent on cost-effective, totally reliable IT
> operational support. Their applications portfolios, however, are domi-
> nated by maintenance work and applications that, while profitable and
> important in their own right, are not fundamental to the firm's ability
> to compete ... even a one-hour disruption in service from existing
> systems has severe operational consequences on the performance of
> the business unit.

Support

> There are firms . . . that are not fundamentally operationally dependent
> on the smooth functioning of the IT activity nor are their applications
> portfolios aimed at the critical strategic needs of the company. . . . IT is
> at a significantly lower organizational level than in other settings, and
> the commitment to planning – particularly at the senior management
> level – is quite low.

Our research investigated the match of organizations with the strategic
quadrants. The following questions were posed to describe the importance of IT to organizations:

- How substantial are the IT planning requirements?
- Is there integration of IT strategy with business objectives?
- Is there commitment to IT activities at senior management level?
- What degree of business awareness and understanding of IT
  requirements exists?
- To what extent do the existing business operations involve IT
  applications?
- Will IT enhance competitiveness or change the way in which
  organizations compete in the future?
- What is the size of future IT budgets?
- What is the size of current and past IT expenditures?
- How effective is the communication among top management,

general line management and the IT function during IT investment decision making?

- Who makes key IT decisions?

The survey indicated that reported management views on the role played by IT revealed recognition of the strategic importance of IT within their organizations; overwhelmingly, respondents "strongly agreed" or "agreed" with those statements that implied a high impact of IT on future developments and existing business operations.

The finance to support future investments in IT activities is not expected to increase; the inference is that developments within the IT industry will decrease the costs of hardware and application software; users will get more from their pound of investment.

Key IT decisions were made mostly at board level (51%). Although respondents indicated high commitment at senior levels, there was little suggestion that this has, as yet, been communicated throughout the organizations.

In general, organizations appreciated the importance of IT for their overall business activities; IT is not a matter for which single departments can take responsibility. As one respondent remarked:

> securing consensus (the best platform for change) is difficult for systems which cross internal boundaries. "Good IT" equates to beneficial change and managing change continues to be difficult. Hence IT requires substantial senior level sponsorship.

Decision Making Procedures

It has been argued (Cash et al. 1988) that organizations need to consider the strategic impact of IT on both existing and future business operations to identify the importance of IT to the organization (Table 5.3).

Parsons (1983) puts forward six linking strategies, representing different approaches to managing IT activities (Table 5.4).

The prescription, then, requires organizations to adopt IT strategies that are consistent with their view of the importance of IT to their organizations. This research investigated whether there was coherence across the following four areas of decision making with the respondents' perceptions of the importance of IT analysed in the previous section:

- Linking with business needs.
- Deployment of IT activities.
- Expectations for IT.

- The way of doing business through exploiting IT.

Table 5.3. The impact of IT on business operations

Strategic impact of IT	Importance of IT
Low currently and expected to be low in the future	IT has a *support* role, valuable but not critical
High currently but expected to be low in the future	IT's role is like a *factory*, a tightly run unit for day-to-day operations
Low currently but expected to be high in the future	IT's role is in a *turnaround* stage, important for future success
High currently and expected to be high in the future	IT's role is of *strategic* importance, critical for future success

Based on Parsons, Earl and other researchers, structured linking strategies were constructed for these four aspects. Hence, agreement with the statements under each of the following headings signified that strategy's adoption.

Table 5.4. Different IT strategies

Appropriate IT strategy	Importance of IT
Scarce resource Necessary evil Free market	Support
Scarce resource Monopoly	Factory
Free market Leading edge Centrally planned	Turnaround
Leading edge Centrally planned	Strategic

Centrally Planned

- IT capabilities are centrally integrated with business needs.
- There is a proactive approach to promoting competitive advantages;

the requirements for exploiting the competitive opportunities are well understood and systematically incorporated into planning procedures.

- Planned developments in IT create and develop competitive advantages.
- IT creates the means by which "we do the business excellently".

Leading Edge

- State-of-the-art IT is developed to create business opportunities.
- IT systems are established through prototyping.
- Risk taking with IT developments is encouraged to achieve strategic change.
- IT allows us the means by which "we do the business differently".

Free Market

- Users determine their own IT needs.
- Internal providers of IT compete with outside vendors for their business; they interact with their internal clients and are reactive to users needs.
- Explicit financial goals have to be achieved by IT investments.
- IT allows us the means by which "we do the business efficiently/effectively".

Scarce Resource

- The management of IT requires, most importantly, cost containment and resource rationing.
- IT investments are subject to capital rationing in line with other capital projects.
- Resource productivity is the key issue.
- IT allows us the means by which "we do the business efficiently".

Monopoly

- IT services are provided to all users from a single internal source.
- Abilities need resource planning to meet the demand within reasonable cost.

- Emphasizing users' satisfaction.
- IT may be the means by which "we do the business effectively/efficiently".

Necessary Evil

- IT is only used if there are no alternatives.
- IT investments require very strict cost justification; and are accepted/rejected on that criterion alone.
- Very risk-averse.
- IT is not seen as the means of changing the way we conduct our business.

Some 80% of the respondents indicated views of IT as strategically important. To be consistent with viewing IT as a strategic weapon, Parsons argues that central planning would be a coherent strategy for an organization that regarded IT as critically important both now and for the future. None of the respondents followed this paradigm exactly (as might be expected); rather, the majority of views supported both a centrally planned and monopolistic strategy: the latter implies a view of IT as critically important but not yet as strategic.

Organizations mostly adopted centrally planned and monopolistic approaches to linking IT with business needs, and monopolistic and scarce resource strategies for the deployment of IT activities. Their expectations for IT and the way of doing business were described by free market. IT had not yet been considered as a strategic weapon to fundamentally achieve leading edge.

The analysis accumulated responses; hence, all that can be said is that the preponderance of views in agreement with the centrally planned strategy is consistent both with the majority response that IT is strategically important and the normative models. The agreement with a monopoly strategy in this section implies operational decisions that discount the future impact on business operations. This view is supported by such comments as:

> *Previously, inadequate attention to a clear definition of intended benefits and insufficient reviews undermined the whole process of strategic importance.*

Although the theory is not targeted specifically at local authorities it may have application. As one respondent noted:

> *Competitive edge is not on the agenda as yet ... however the implications of the single tier local government proposals strongly suggest it will be important in the future.... Quality and speed of service linked to productivity may provide a competitive advantage for a district prior to reorganization and potential merging.*

Evaluation of Information Technology

The survey sought to gain a view as to the definition of a "major" IT investment: who initiated it, and what methods of investment appraisal and evaluation were used?

The Definitions of Major Investments in IT

Respondents were asked for their definitions of "major" IT investments within their organizations. The figure was given in absolute terms by 72%, and of these a value of £100,000 was most often adopted to describe a "major" investment; 26% gave the figure as a percentage of their turnover; and 13% outlined some other definitions in their organizations.

The Appraisal of IT Investments

Almost all studies on IT management emphasize the strategic importance and competitive use of IT, but the identification of competitive advantage and its exploitation remains unresolved. The appraisal procedures used need to be appropriate for the search for competitive advantages and business opportunities; and match the requirements of the perceived benefits from the IT investment. There is an extensive literature in the area of objectives and benefits of IT investments. Ward (1986) states that the overall, implied objective can be broken down into three particular objectives, as follows:

- to improve the efficiency of operations
- to increase the effectiveness of management
- to improve the competitiveness of the business (directly)

Peters (1988) reports from a review of some 50 IT projects:

> Benefits fall into three categories on a continuum. At one end of the continuum benefits are associated with enhancing productivity. . . . At the other end of the continuum benefits are associated with innovative ways of creating new products or ways of doing business, or providing services. . . . Between these two extremes is the category of risk minimization.

Enhancing productivity includes:

- Headcount reduction
- Working capital improvements

- Processing economies
- General efficiency improvements

The benefits under risk minimization are:

- Minimizing the risk of litigation
- Minimizing the risk of loss of profitability
- Variability in business profile
- Minimizing the risk of loss of market share

The benefits associated with business expansion fall into the following areas:

- Consolidating existing markets
- Creating new opportunities

In summary, the literature suggests that the benefits derived from IT investments exist in four broad areas:

- Operations efficiency (cost savings)
- Management effectiveness
- New business opportunities (differentiating product/service)
- Competitive advantages

As the business focus of IT applications changes, so do the perceived benefits from IT investments.

Characteristics of IT Benefits

IT investments include benefits that are intangible, subjective and integral to the organization. As IT applications move from "back office" cost savings to investments capable of creating business opportunities and competitive advantage, the contribution of intangible benefits to organizations has increased considerably, making IT projects more difficult to cost-justify. Tate (1990) summarizes the issues of measuring benefits as follows:

> New ways are needed of identifying the value of different sorts of information to a company ... traditional cost/benefit analysis criteria are becoming increasingly inadequate in today's technology based industries. ... Justifying investments in corporate-wide networks, ergonomic user interfaces or distributed databases is much more difficult, and requires new criteria based on overall potential value.

He quotes Silk (1990):

> The trouble with information is that it is not readily quantifiable. Unlike the other types of assets a manager deals with, its value is both intangible and subjective.

The integration of information technology into an organization's operation makes it increasingly complicated to track the return on investment. According to the chief executive of a major UK supermarket chain:

> the new service and the computer system that went with it were so interwound that it made no sense to try and separate them. . . . We came to the conclusion that we couldn't cost-justify the new system.

The Research Findings

The survey sought to identify how benefits were perceived by the respondents. The questionnaire listed 14 categories of perceived benefits, and the respondents were asked to assess the importance of these benefits to their organizations.

"Improved services" was considered to be the most important benefit from IT investments, with 50% of the respondents ranking this issue as "very important". Other highly ranked benefits were "improved product quality", "faster delivery", and "better communication". These three categories are consistent with an overall objective of "increasing market share and/or revenue". However, "lowered product prices" within this area was not seen to be as important as the other three benefits, with only 17% giving their assessment of "very important" to it.

Summing the "very important" and "important" rankings indicated the top three benefits, which accounted for 87% of the responses, as "increasing labour productivity", "improved services" and "better communication".

The most important benefits perceived from IT investments reflected a desire to achieve greater business effectiveness through improved services and better communication, and to achieve improved operations efficiency through increasing labour productivity. Further, lowered prices, decreased inventory and optimizing production programmes were comparatively unimportant aspects of the perceived benefits. The proportion (60%) of the organizations who judged IT investments to yield competitive advantage was more modest.

Models for the Appraisal of IT Investments

Extensive studies have been completed on the appraisal and evaluation of IT investments. The results suggested that the methods used in practice varied considerably and were far from satisfactory. The critical issues remain to identify appraisal approaches that match the needs of IT strategic planning and its alignment to the overall business strategy, in different business settings across industrial sectors and over time.

In a survey by Hochstrasse and Griffiths (1990) they prescribe:

> *the primary objectives of IT initiatives can be evaluated by matching specific evaluation techniques to specific application areas.*

They summarize:

> *IT systems that are introduced to increase accuracy of information, to enable management to take on additional tasks . . . are best evaluated by well understood techniques of cost benefit analysis based on cost elimination and on increased data volume.*
>
> *IT systems introduced to increase staff productivity, to utilize resources better, or to offer better information sharing within a company can be evaluated by Value Chain Analysis, Value Linking and Value Acceleration.*
>
> *IT systems introduced to improve product quality or to offer better services to customers can be evaluated by methods derived from the Customer Resource Life Cycle.*
>
> *IT systems introduced in order to strategically exploit the potential of the new technology to do things that were not possible before, can be justified by risk evaluation techniques.*

One of the main purposes of our research in this area was to investigate the appropriate investment appraisal methods to be used in relation with the IT environment, in particular the strategic grid proposed by Cash et al. (1988). The IT strategic grid provides some clues about the strategic management of IT investments. Some results indicated that there were no universally best approaches applicable to organizations, and the investment methods used were contingent in nature. In developing the strategic grid analysis, Ward et al. (1990) suggest ways of relating benefit evaluation to application types.

Research Findings on Appraisal Methods

Approximately 16% of the respondents did not use financial methods for the appraisal of investments. The majority of respondents (58%, 103) reported that they used financial methods to evaluate IT investments, 29% (52) used non-financial methods, and 13% (23) used both financial and non-financial methods.

Within the category of financial methods, cost–benefit analysis was the method selected most often for the appraisal of IT investments (34%). Net present value was used by only 17%, and internal rate of return by 12%.

The most widely used non-financial method was informal judgement (56%), and when all financial and non-financial methods are considered together, the methods were ranked as follows: cost–benefit analysis, payback, net present value, informal judgement, return on investment, internal rate of return, and multi-factors.

It would appear that of the methods of appraisal, cost– benefit analysis remains the method used more than traditional investment appraisal methods (net present value, return on investment and internal rate of return), despite its limitations in reflecting the qualitative and quantitative factors relevant to strategic business needs.

Who Initiates Major IT Investments?

Major IT investments could be initiated by several different people within the organization. IT managers were identified by 26% of the respondents; the second biggest category was financial managers, chosen by 18%; followed by managing directors (17%); other members of the board (12%); marketing managers (11%); and production managers (9%). IT managers, with their specific responsibilities for IT activities, contributed not only to the everyday administration of IT, but also to the initiation of IT investments leading to new IT applications in business operations. The involvement of managing directors and other board members in the initiation of IT investments implies a more corporate perspective, rather than specific application areas.

The Success of IT Investments

Having considered the perceived benefits from IT investments and their methods of appraisal, the survey went on to seek an overview of the track record of IT investments within responding organizations: were they generally "successful"? In what ways was the investment performance evaluated? To what did the organizations attribute the lack of success in the event of an unsuccessful IT investment?

A General Outlook

The organizations surveyed were generally satisfied with their information technology applications. A majority (70%) thought that the IT applications in their organizations were successful, while 17% perceived them as very successful. Only 10% were less successful, and 1% failed to achieve most main objectives.

It would appear that post-evaluation for these investments was still in its infancy. Such investments, involving new technology, were not all evaluated in terms of the outcome of the investment against intended benefits. Approximately two-thirds (64%) of the organizations did some kind of evaluation (although in some cases at an informal level only). There were, however, examples of "best practice" where:

At the outset of each project a systems proposal is prepared that identifies critical success factors, and both qualitative and quantitative benefits. On completion a post-implementation review establishes mechanisms to ensure that the predicted benefits are accrued. These activities are conducted in conjunction with an internal IT consultancy (a free service).

The benefits perceived at the feasibility stage are reappraised at each subsequent stage of development and via post-implementation reviews.

End-user satisfaction was consistently quoted as an ingredient of post-implementation review.

Most organizations (70%) reported that they had made IT investments that had not been successful in some sense. The following section gives their explanations as to the lack of success.

Lack of Success

Explanations included:

- Technical problems:
  - Specifications poorly defined
  - Incompatibility of equipment
  - Other technical problems
- Lack of commitment:
  - Poor communication
  - Organizational structure constraints
  - Inappropriate sponsorship
- Project objectives did not match key issues for the organization

The biggest single cause for lack of success remained a technical one: "specifications poorly defined" (25%). In addition, answers to the open questions revealed that poor project management was consistently cited as a further explanation. The second reason chosen was "poor communication" (18%) within the category of "lack of commitment". However, when the three categories ("technical problems", "lack of commitment" and "project objectives did not match key issues for the organization") were considered as a whole, "lack of commitment" seemed to explain the major single area of concern for the lack of success in IT investments.

Summary

Content analysis of several open questions yielded qualitative data for the explanation and further expansion of the quantitative results. They additionally indicated that the high response rate from the public administration sector reflected their interest focused by legislative changes forced upon them. Given the complexity of the questionnaire (and the time needed to complete it) the response rate indicates that this area of enquiry is of significant importance to managers in all sectors.

Across all sectors, although not all of the organizations have a formalized post-implementation review, many are actively seeking methods based on factors in addition to purely financial ones. The theory has not yet been generally applied, despite the overwhelming evidence that these investments have strategic importance for organizations. The application of theory to practice is inhibited by the difficulty of managing the change inherent in the implications of applying the new technologies.

Managing IT investments successfully requires the successful management of new ways of conducting different businesses: the appraisal of the investment at the feasibility stage requires measures related to the performance of the business and appropriate to the business objectives; the investment needs to be project-managed during its development to achieve predicted benefits, and reviewed after completion to learn from mistakes and to continue management of the organization's changed behaviour. Further, although the term "business" has been used, the requirements are equally applicable to the public sector.

III

ARTIFICIAL INTELLIGENCE AND KNOWLEDGE BASED SYSTEMS

Editorial Overview

Artificial intelligence (AI) is presented as having come of age in business terms, with competitive advantage now being secured by organizations that have developed an understanding of both the power and limitations of knowledge based approaches. In some cases companies have identified new resources of expertise, which have transformed the orientation of their business.

Dr Chris Hutchison (Chapter 6) provides an illuminating insight into the history and state of the art in AI, with an account of systems whose technical development now makes them amenable to commercial exploitation. AI draws on a breadth of intellectual background which may appear daunting to managers, but offers exciting potential for those who are prepared to think, and not always expect instant results.

Dr Gail Swaffield (Chapter 7) reports on experience in the commercial worlds of management consultancy and commercial law, where knowledge based systems are proving invaluable in support of knowledge professionals. She offers practical advice on how to proceed in an area where extravagant claims from vendors have often been followed by disappointment from poorly informed users. Business strategy needs to be combined with a grasp of new concepts in knowledge based systems.

Chris Tompsett (Chapter 8) focuses his attention on the automotive industry, in which many successful applications of knowledge based systems have been developed. Again, success depends on a mix of expertise in operations management in manufacturing and openness to a knowledge based approach to problems that may previously have been considered in exclusively mechanical terms.

David Browne and Ara Yeghiazarian (Chapter 9) offer
a review of work in the fast-moving world of business
and finance with the new technology of neural networks:
learning from experience rather than following rules. As
Japanese and American companies are developing powerful systems that rapidly recoup their costs, more cautious
managers need to investigate the practical benefits of this
new extension to intelligent technology.

The challenge for managers from AI and knowledge
based systems is to approach their problems and organizations with open minds and fresh insights. Leading edge
systems can be implemented on affordable technology,
but depend on a culture where new ideas are considered,
prototyped and evaluated.

6 | Artificial Intelligence in Business and Industry

Chris Hutchison

Why Is Artificial Intelligence Important to Business?

The "White-Collar Overhead"

Not so long ago introducing "intelligent systems" into the industrial context would have been equated with the replacement of blue-collar labour by some form of unwearyingly complaisant "mechanical man". Automate your factory with machines that will grab, move, shape and weld things, and you will produce high quality goods in bulk at low cost.

At least in theory: the costs of initially "robotizing" the factory are high, and the increase in productivity and cost saving has turned out to be disappointingly low. Blue-collar work in the manufacturing process accounts for as little as 25%–30% of costs; even if factory automation were cost-free and all blue-collar work could be done by robots, this would represent a saving of only around one-third of a company's production costs.

It has been estimated that value-added operations are being performed for as little as 2% of the time an order is in a factory, and that white-collar labour accounts for as much as 50%–75% of production costs in the manufacturing cycle (Machine Tool Technology 1980). The bulk of the costs are consumed by white-collar knowledge based tasks such as procurement, design, quality assurance, management coordination and control, marketing, sales and distribution, service, and financial management. If the productivity of personnel involved in knowledge intensive work – in planning, problem solving and decision making – can be enhanced, then costs fall, and the company becomes more competitive.

The potential business benefits of artificial intelligence (AI) and knowledge based systems (KBS) are inestimable: AI systems can give economic leverage to companies through their ability to find fast and often novel solutions to complex problems that are either time-consuming for human beings, difficult to solve, or perhaps not solvable at all using alternative, more traditional, computing techniques. Many hundreds of organizations, large and small, including American Express, British Telecom, Coopers and Lybrand and the New York Stock Exchange, are using AI systems for a wide range of knowledge based tasks – from the interpretation of international tax laws, through fault diagnosis, identifying ships from satellite pictures, mineral prospecting and machine translation, to the allocation of landing gates at airports.

The principal aim of AI is to endow machines, not with shop-floor muscle, but with the ability to perform tasks requiring the application of types of general intelligence and often specialist knowledge that one associates uniquely with the human mind. The last decade has brought unprecedented levels of funding, interest and expansion to the field, so there is now probably no definition of the discipline that matches more than a subset of the contents of contemporary AI journals, conferences and courses. The classic definition offered by Marvin Minsky was:

> artificial intelligence is the science of making machines do things that would require intelligence if done by men (Minsky 1968).

This chapter outlines what AI is, then surveys some of the applications of AI and KBS in the white-collar sector.

What Is Artificial Intelligence?

The Emergence of Machine Intelligence

The most efficient, innovative, and "user friendly" of all intelligent systems are human beings: good at using common sense yet also having valuable and scarce specialist knowledge; good at finding inventive ways of solving "hard" problems, usually good at explaining what they do and why they are going about things in a particular way. Learning from experience, they can apply that learning to novel situations, and may be friendly, helpful and co-operative.

If we can automate these abilities on computers, then are human beings just Psion Organizers writ large? Far from it! There is a *qualitative* difference between the processing done in conventional computing and the kinds of reasoning that distinguish us as human. Unlike calculating machines, humans think symbolically rather than numerically: they organize and manipulate structured concepts and ideas rather than numbers. AI technology, modelling human information processing, is also based on symbol manipulation; in this resides the intelligence of AI systems and their ability to reason in a human-like manner.

The argument is stated by pioneers of AI, Allan Newell and Herbert Simon (1975), in their discussion of the so-called "physical symbol system hypothesis":

> *A physical symbol system has the necessary and sufficient means for general intelligent action.*

A physical symbol system is a rigorously organized set of symbols designating objects, properties and relations in the world, together with a collection of processes which, operating upon the organized symbol structures, will generate new structures. Symbols may be, for example, atoms in a programming language like LISP or PROLOG. A symbol identified by the character string "widget" might then represent the concept widget; the symbols "splange-nut" and "has-part" the concept splange-nut and the relation has-a-part, respectively. From atomic symbols one might then build symbol structures such as:

> *(widget has-part splange-nut)*

and from such simple expressions, more complex expressions.

Imagine a system defined in terms of such complex symbolic structures. Imagine that the mutual relations between its constituent symbol structures parallel perfectly the mutual relations that define our own knowledge states, such that its internal states are functionally isomorphic with our own. The internal states of the system are causally connected to inputs, to each other, and to behaviour in such a way that its performance in some task domain mirrors the performance of a human being in that task domain. We might be willing to say that, in spite of its differences from a human being in terms of the "hardware" in which these functional states are physically realized, the system has the means for human-like intelligent action.

The business of the AI researcher is to construct good theories about the knowledge structures and cognitive processes of human beings. A good theory of how a subject went about solving a problem may then be viewed as a model of the problem solver's activities in tackling the task, and can be translated into a computer program. In this sense, Newell and Simon claim, "the theory performs the task it explains":

> *A good information processing theory of a good human chess player can play good chess; a good theory of how humans create novels will create novels; a good theory of how children read will likewise read and understand (Newell and Simon 1972).*

More traditional computing technologies – including data processing and word processing, where the input may appear to be words or concepts or symbols – do not manipulate symbols: although they may handle text, they do not "see" characters but rather ASCII codes. Even apparently "clever" operations such as word search and replace, data retrieval or spelling checking are basically "dumb" number-crunching operations.

Building Models of Mind

AI distinguishes itself as an intellectual and engineering enterprise in its concern with simulating the cognitive skills that make us human: the ability to reason and solve problems, the ability to see and interpret what we see, the ability to speak and understand the speech we hear, the ability to plan and to execute those plans in an intelligent manner, the ability to learn, and so on. These are summarized in Fig. 6.1.

The AI scientist will have to address himself, in the first place, to questions regarding how human intelligence works:

- How do we understand language?
- How do we give explanations?
- How do we perceive the world?
- How do we reason from evidence to conclusions?
- How do we co-ordinate hand and eye?
- How do we solve problems?
- How do we learn?
- How do we make plans?
- How do we walk around without knocking into things?

He will then address himself to how computers can be made more useful through the implementation of the resultant theories. Where

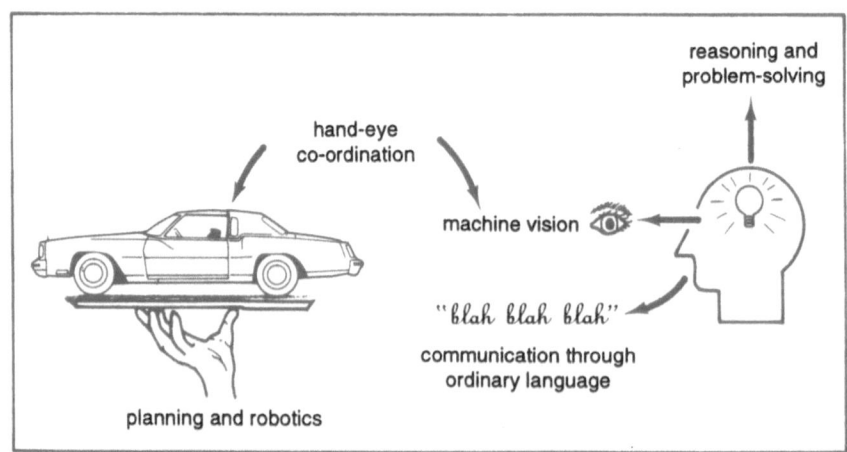

Fig. 6.1. Human cognitive skills.

will the answers have come from? With its aim of building models of mind functionally isomorphic with those of human beings, AI, though itself a comparatively young field of enquiry, has its intellectual roots in many more traditional academic disciplines. Psychology, linguistics, the biological and brain sciences, mathematics, logic and philosophy: academic division of intellectual labour may have forced them apart in the early years of this century, but all have valuable contributions to make to the study of human intelligence. As Gunther Kress and Bob Hodge perceptively note, in another context:

> *Disciplines exist for the sake of their subjects, not the other way round. If the boundary that has been drawn around a discipline proves a hindrance to the proper study of that subject matter, then it is the boundary that must change (Kress and Hodge 1979).*

The boundaries are now being redrawn around a field of endeavour that, with further inputs from more recent disciplines such as computer science and electronic engineering, is bringing together experts from each of these disciplines with the goal of forging new silicon-based brains that aim to perform as well as – and sometimes better than – human beings in knowledge based tasks.

From psychology, in particular, come models of human mental processing – of reasoning, perception, understanding, memory, learning, planning, perhaps even emotion – which may inform the design of artificial minds; from linguistics, precise models of linguistic knowledge and language use, which provide the theoretical basis for the design of systems that can communicate naturally with the outside world. Philosophy, in addition to providing us with the formal languages of logic with which to express our theories clearly and concisely, gives us the conceptual tools for reasoning about the nature of mental states and the forms of knowledge.

The intellectual forbears of AI are numerous. Rene Descartes, Gottfried Leibniz, Julien Offray de la Mettrie (author of *L'Homme Machine*), Charles Babbage and Augustus de Morgan, among others, all have their places in the intellectual genealogy. Particularly deserving of mention are the mathematicians George Boole, Alan Turing and Alonzo Church, who attempted to formulate "principles of reasoning".

George Boole (1815–1864) was a self-taught mathematician and the inventor of symbolic logic, with which he hoped to be able to give account of "the laws of thought". In "The Mathematical Analysis of Logic" (1847) and "An Investigation of The Laws of Thought" (1854), Boole formulated precise definitions of the connectives *and, or, not* and *implies*, and invented class-inclusion logic and the two-valued "Boolean" logic, which prefigure the basic principles of computer science and AI.

The twentieth century mathematicians Alonzo Church and Alan Turing may be jointly credited with demonstrating, independently, that in principle any well-defined mental operation can be performed by a suitably programmed machine – what we would now call a "universal Turing machine". (Turing and Church are difficult reading; see Penrose (1990) for a lucid discussion). Turing's career from the 1940s was closely entwined with the development of the modern digital computer. After setting out the theoretical foundations of computing in the mid-1930s, he worked during World War II at Bletchley Park as one of a team of academics who had been assembled by the British government to crack the coded messages broadcast by the German armed forces. To help in this task, they built what was arguably the world's first electronic computer. The machine, Colossus, was built two years before ENIAC, the first US computer, but it was cloaked in military secrecy and, designed for code-breaking, did not have a general purpose architecture. Turing also worked on the Ferranti Mark 1 in Manchester.

Computers – the vogue technology of the late 1940s – became the newest metaphor for the mind. Newspapers were full of articles about the "superhuman brain" and the "electronic genius". Swept up in the intellectual euphoria, Turing published, in 1950, an entertaining and highly readable paper entitled "Computing machinery and intelligence", in which he addressed the question "can machines think?". Turing opens the paper with what he calls the "Imitation Game" (later to be known as the "Turing Test"):

> Imagine a computer (C), a human being (H) and an interrogator (I) in separate rooms, with one teleprinter line from the interrogator to the human, another from the interrogator to the computer, and no other means of communication. The interrogator does not know which line goes to H and which to C. The object of the game is for the computer (C), in responding to I's questions, to fool I into believing that it is C and not H who is the human being. The ultimate aim is to effectively program a computer so that it can convincingly imitate a human.

The question and answer session, Turing suggested, might go something like this:

> Q: Please write me a sonnet on the subject of the Forth Bridge.
> A: Count me out on this one. I never could write poetry.
> Q: Add 34957 to 70764.
> A: (Pause about 30 seconds and then give as answer) 105621.
> Q: Do you play chess?
> A: Yes.
> Q: I have K at my K1, and no other pieces. You have only K at K6 and R at A1. It is your move. what do you play?
> A: (After a pause of 15 seconds) R-R8 mate.

Notice that the respondent gives a wrong answer to the sum in the dialogue above; imitating a person involves mimicking human errors and lapses. If, after a reasonable number of questions, the interrogator cannot tell which line is connected to the human and which to the computer, then the computer might be said to think.

In the second part of the paper, Turing raises, and dismisses, some of the reasons (such as the argument that computers cannot be creative) why it might not be feasible to program a computer to pass his test.

An annual contest is still held for systems to compete in attempting to pass the "Turing Test"; despite thirty-five years of boasts, promises and predictions, passing the Turing Test is still far beyond the capabilities of any existing computer program. It will be a very long time indeed before we ever see a system capable of displaying general intelligence comparable to that of any human being.

Applied AI has forged ahead with the more modest task of developing and producing, often in collaboration with government and industry, high-level tools to enhance the efficiency and productivity of knowledge processing personnel in the workplace.

AI and KBS in the 1980s and 1990s: Looking Towards the Future

New Initiatives

Until around 1980, the AI enterprise was largely confined within a small number of university departments and research laboratories. Although outstanding basic research work was, from the early 1960s, being carried out in prestigious institutions such as Stanford University, the Massachusetts Institute of Technology, and Carnegie-Mellon University in the United States, and Edinburgh and Sussex Universities in Britain, the work had had very little impact on the world of business and industry, had produced few marketable products, and had excited very little public interest or awareness. In Britain AI had suffered a severe setback in 1973 with the publication of the Lighthill Report, which drew attention, not entirely unfairly, to the "lamentable failure" of its actual achievements to live up to the predictions for the discipline that had been made in the previous 25 years.

The dramatic turn-around came in 1981 when Japan's Ministry of International Trade and Industry (MITI) announced the establishment of its Fifth Generation Computer Systems project – a 10-year programme of advanced research and development in knowledge information processing systems (KIPS), with industrial collaboration from Fujitsu, Hitachi, NEC, Mitsubishi, Toshiba, Matsushita, Oki and Sharp. The Japanese government would invest $450 million, with industry matching and maybe doubling that figure. The following year saw the establishment of the Institute for New Generation Computer Technology (ICOT) in Tokyo to guide the R&D programme, Phase 1 of which (1982–1985) was to be chiefly concerned with speech and picture understanding. Phase 2 (from 1985) was concerned with parallel computing, expert systems and expert system tools.

Still smarting from Japan's market successes in the automobile and electronics industries, and now fearing Japanese ascendancy in computer technology also, Britain and the United States were jolted into action. The US response came in the form of the Strategic Computing Plan (October 1983) of the Defense Department's Advanced Research Projects Agency (DARPA); the formation of the Microelectronic and Computer Corporation (MCC) to carry out collaborative research in computer aided design, image processing and expert systems, including the monumental 10-year CYC project; and heightened activity in major universities and in the research laboratories of such organizations as Bolt Beranek Newman, Stanford Research Institute and Xerox PARC.

The UK's response, following the recommendations of the Alvey Committee (chaired by John Alvey of British Telecom) in mid-1982 for a national programme for Advanced Information Technology, was a budget of £350m over 5 years for research in:

- Software engineering
- Man–machine interfaces
- Very large-scale integration (VLSI)
- Intelligent KBS

Government were to contribute two-thirds of the sum, with industry contributing the remainder, together with the costs of transforming the outcomes of the research programme into marketable products. Thus was born, in 1983, the Alvey Programme, and its AI component, Intelligent Knowledge Based Systems (IKBS). As well as a number of small projects in specific areas of AI, four large "demonstrator" projects were eventually established in the IKBS area:

- A voice-driven word processor and desktop workstation
- A knowledge based decision support system for the Department of Health and Social Security
- A range of mobile information systems, including a route guidance system and a mobile electronic office
- A "design-to-product" system to demonstrate the automation of the total production process, from inception through manufacture to field maintenance (see Oakley and Owen 1989)

Excitement was spreading throughout Europe; 1985 saw the launch of the European Strategic Programme for Research and Development in

Information Technology (ESPRIT) to promote European cooperation in:

- Software engineering
- Microelectronics
- Robotics
- Advanced production techniques
- Artificial intelligence

The programme, now in its third phase, is supporting major research projects in:

- IKBS
- Multimedia
- Intelligent databases
- Machine translation
- Intelligent full-text browsing
- Neural networks
- Intelligent information selection and delivery

and many other advanced IT areas.

The Key Technology Centre in Japan in 1986 invested more than $100 million in the Japan Electronic Dictionary Research Institute Ltd for a 7-year programme of research in natural language processing and knowledge-base inference. The principal application areas envisaged in the project were:

- Intelligent word processing
- Intelligent office automation
- Machine translation
- Speech understanding
- Expert systems
- Computer aided design
- Computer aided manufacturing
- Decision-support systems
- Computer-assisted instruction

In the area of expert systems there were, in 1984, less than twenty systems used in a real operational role; by 1988 over 1400 expert systems were in commercial use and a further 8000 under development; today, with good shells now commercially available for microcomputers, the number of systems in everyday use is beyond count. AI is big business, with annual turnover of over half a billion dollars.

Language Technologies

Probably the first non-numerical application for computer science, and certainly the motivation for the development and implementation of the first high level programming language, COMIT 1957, was the machine processing of "natural" (i.e. human) languages. Andrew Booth, a Nuffield Fellow at London's Birkbeck College, had discussed the possibility of creating electronic dictionaries with Alan Turing, in the context of Turing's work in cryptanalysis at Bletchley Park; Booth later met Warren Weaver, at that time a vice president of the Rockefeller Foundation, and from these meetings came the suggestion of machine translation (MT) as an application of the new computing technology. In 1948 Booth collaborated with Richard Richens on the first (French to English) MT system.

MT has developed into a thriving multi-million dollar industry. The use of – and indeed the perceived need for – commercial MT in business and industry has been limited, but for many years such systems have been used by governments and public bodies. The European Commission has, since the 1970s, been using the SYSTRAN system for in-house translation, while the Canadian Weather Service has been using a system – TAUM-METRO – to translate weather forecasts daily from English into French. Nearer to the interests of business and industry are the tools that, by enabling users to communicate naturally through ordinary speech or typed text, will bring advanced information technology within everybody's grasp. These include natural language interfaces to databases and expert systems, text editing tools, and documents contents scanning systems, which will skim and summarize the important points in texts.

Perhaps the most exciting innovation in language technology is the "talkwriter" – a dictation system that will translate spoken free format language input into machine readable text without the need for keyboard input; a typewriter or word processor that one can use to create documents quite simply by talking to it. A fully functioning talkwriter would need to be capable of accepting, without prior training, natural (continuous) speech from any speaker, with an ability to process unlimited vocabulary and grammatical structures and to produce high-quality textual output. General purpose free-text dictation systems of this kind, however, are still a little way off, although the current state of technology suggests that the first useful commercial continuous speech talkwriters will be available around 1995.

A number of tolerably good systems already exist. DragonDictate (manufactured by Dragon Systems, Boston), launched in March 1989, for example, has been successfully marketed to both general business users and to the disabled market (around 300 sales in each sector). Speaker-independent and capable of accepting unrestricted syntax, it has an active built-in vocabulary of 25,000 words, with space for 5000 more to be added by the user; it also allows access to a 50,000-word dictionary for retrieval when spelling words. "Writing" and editing are both voice-activated, and the system is always in "learning mode", so that a correction by the user (e.g. "choose five" from a list of alternatives offered by the system) causes the system to adjust its pairing of signal (digitized wave form) to word, and to "remember" the new pairing. User reactions to date have been impressive enough for a British insurance company to be considering giving portable versions of DragonDictate to their loss adjustors, thus cutting out the time-consuming process of getting dictaphone tapes typed, checked and corrected.

The "Electronic Brain"

When, in 1946, Lord Mountbatten, then President of the Institution of Radio Engineers, talked about the development of "an electronic brain, which would perform functions analogous to those at present undertaken by the human brain", he had in mind an architecture that would mimic the neural architecture of the brain itself:

> It would be done by radio valves, activating each other in the way that brain cells do. . . . now that the memory machine and the electronic brain were upon us, it seemed that we were really facing a new revolution; not an industrial one, but a revolution of the mind, and the responsibilities facing the scientists today were formidable and serious (The Times, 1 November 1946, quoted by Boden 1989).

Connectionism, parallel distributed processing, neural networks, neural computing and neurocomputing are all terms that are used to label an approach towards AI whose basic assumption is that intelligence emerges from the interaction of a large number of very simple processing units, similar to neurons. This is opposed to the alternative "algorithmic" approach to AI which, until the mid-1980s, had been the dominant paradigm in AI research.

Neural networks offer a number of advantages over standard AI systems. They can act as content-addressable memories; like human beings, they can access information in memory based on nearly any attribute, or set of attributes, they are trying to retrieve. They are resistant to low-level "noise"; they are robust and (because representations are distributed across the system, rather than localized) degrade gracefully when damaged. They can learn (or "be trained"). Learning is a matter of the network adjusting its "weights" in response to inputs, and many have learned to perform tasks that have proven difficult for traditional AI. They can make default assumptions in a natural way, by making rational "guesses", and they can produce spontaneous generalizations, beyond the training set instances, as a natural by-product of the memory retrieval process.

The range of potential applications is bewilderingly wide – from face recognition through speech processing to generating spontaneous profiles of a typical cocaine smuggler! They are still "new technology", having fallen into neglect as a research area for almost 20 years. Only since the mid-1980s has research funding brought about a renaissance in neural computing, and only in the past couple of years have real-world applications been studied. In 1986 DARPA launched a 6-year research initiative with a $390 million budget; by the mid-1990s we should see the commercial pay-off.

Expert Systems

The most important development in AI, commercially, at least, has been expert systems, computer programs encapsulating, in the form of hundreds or even thousands of rules, the knowledge and reasoning skills of one or more human experts such as to enable them to operate at the level of the human expert in some specialist domain. The technology arose out of a discovery that was probably first made around 1960, and that crept into AI around the mid-1970s, but the power of which was not recognized until around 1980. Marvin Minsky, of MIT, wrote:

> today's expert systems demonstrate a marvellous fact we did not know twenty-five years ago: if you write down if–then rules for a lot of situations and put them together the resulting system can solve problems that people think are hard (Minsky 1984, p. 244).

An "if–then" rule is simply a statement of conditions (the "if" part) followed by the conclusions or actions that follow if the conditions are satisfied. Here are some examples:

> if (1) determination how to acquire the asset is known;
>   and
>   (2) put any OBJRULES which meet the condition:
>   lease is to be a modifiable option lease is mentioned in the rule
>   into SET-1, and
>   (3) put any OBJRULES which meet the condition:
>   lease is to be a straight lease is mentioned in the rule into SET-1,
> then DOBEFORE is assigned the values: (VALUE-OF-SET-1)

> if CANNOT-BORROW and PRESERVES-CREDIT and PRESERVES-CASH,
> then FINANCE-IT = TXTG1; UTILITY: 5

Expert systems need not store information uniquely in the form of "if–then" rules. The PROSPECTOR system, which analyses geological data, codes much of its knowledge in a "semantic net" – a tightly structured network of concepts and the links between them; other systems have used "frames" or a computable form of predicate logic. As human knowledge takes many different forms, so there are many different ways of enriching rule-based systems to encode that knowledge in a computably tractable form.

Human beings by definition have specialized knowledge in their field, acquired both from extensive training and, more importantly, from years of practical experience of dealing first-hand with real problems. Experts tend to be scarce, expensive, invariably busy, and fallible; they are also mortal. In-house experts may move on or retire, and they take their expertise with them. Consequently, computer systems that are able to provide on-line expert assistance to people working in knowledge intensive tasks have an inestimable value. As "consultants" in management, finance, strategic planning, medicine, engineering, computer system configuration, and insurance and investment, such systems are capable of providing the support of expert knowledge that is relatively cheap (a full-time human consultant commands a much higher salary!), reliable (humans do make mistakes), portable (human experts are sometimes too busy to come on call), and untiring (human experts have to sleep sometimes; eventually they die). Because of the modularity of such systems, they can be extended to become more proficient than any single human expert whose knowledge has been "written into" the rulebase. Yet human experts do not simply apply their knowledge to problems; they can also explain exactly why they have made a decision or reached a particular conclusion. This facility is also built into the expert systems that simulate human expert performance: they can be interrogated at any moment and asked, for example, to display the rule they have just used or to account for their reasons in using that rule. That a system is able to explain its reasoning is in itself no guarantee that the human user will understand the explanation: if the advice is to be of use, it is important that the system justifies its reasoning process in a cognitively plausible manner, by working through a problem in much the same way as a human expert would. Expert systems can be made to reason either forwards, from initial evidence towards a conclusion, or backwards, from a hypothesis to the uncovering of the right kind of evidence that would support that hypothesis, or by a combination of the two. One significant factor that will determine whether a system will use forward or backward reasoning is the method used by the human expert. It is, as much as anything else, this flexibility and the consequent ability of the system to simulate human reasoning processes, that makes the expert system such a crucially important new technology.

When Is a KBS Appropriate?

Identifying Expert System Applications

What is an appropriate application domain for KBS? How do I get a feasibility and requirements analysis done? What kinds of knowledge are appropriate for what kinds of problems? Who are the experts?

An expert system may well be the appropriate technology for tasks such as configuration, fault diagnosis, intelligent data analysis, financial planning and analysis, and training. It may very well often be the case that AI techniques can also offer optimal solutions to non-AI tasks.

In more specific terms, Teknowledge Inc. suggest (1983, quoted by Rauch-Hindin 1987) eight common situations where a KBS can be of value:

1. *Excessive demands on human experts*. The knowledge required to perform a particular task effectively is available only at a central location. Requests for advice are channelled to a small group of people who are always in demand, e.g. a key product design team may be spending an excessive portion of their time on the phone advising repair personnel.

2. *Inaccessibility of expertise*. A written document or flowchart is intended to facilitate the use of a program, procedure or piece of equipment, but it is so long and detailed that it is useless in practice. The users develop folklore-like methods for accomplishing the task, and rely excessively on previous methods that were determined empirically to work, e.g. a flexible and sophisticated computer simulation program goes unused in favour of building expensive models because its user manual fills a shelf of three-ring binders.

3. *Experts involved in time-consuming routine work*. An organization turns away work or loses business to competitors because an overworked human expert is required to make judgements or recommendations, even in routine cases, e.g. to reduce unnecessary, expensive work, a locomotive repair centre requires a supervisor to approve all diagnoses and recommendations before work is undertaken. Although costs are controlled, the average downtime increases to a point where it is economical for customers to tow broken equipment to other repair centres.

4. *High (re)training overheads*. Because of turnover in equipment or personnel, an excessive amount of time is spent training rather than doing, e.g. a company updates its line of test equipment each year, and field engineers must spend an average of two months per year attending training sessions.

5. *Continuous routine monitoring.* A large amount of mainly routine data must be scanned by a highly trained expert on a continuing basis, e.g. a high-energy physics laboratory employs a crew of ten people to look for rare events in bubble chamber images.

6. *Monitoring/integration of diverse information sources.* A variety of information from heterogeneous sources must be monitored and integrated to determine the possibility of an important event, e.g. a government agency must constantly examine information from multiple sources to determine if a military threat is present.

7. *Fast rational expert judgements are essential.* A critical judgement must be made in a very short time interval to avoid a potential disaster, e.g. a nuclear power plant control centre must decide quickly to shut down or cut back a particular unit when a potential problem is detected.

8. *Optimal solutions are prohibitively expensive.* An optimal solution to a routing, planning or configuration task is too expensive or time-consuming to determine. Instead, a minimally effective process of guesswork has been substituted, e.g. a computer company has to configure orders for its equipment, with the proper cables, components and mounting arrangement, on an individual basis. Errors and delays in this process become a serious problem as orders increase.

Consider the case of project management, which is a knowledge based task that satisfies an important subset of the above criteria. The problem with standard project management techniques such as PERT and CPM is that although they indicate a theoretical critical path, they do not themselves manage projects. Projects are managed by people, and it is people who have to come to terms with the delays that may result from the often unanticipated complexity of a project and the interdependencies among its various aspects. Good project managers consequently command enviable salaries, and their skills are highly valued; yet it appears that many of their skills can be automated, thus both enhancing the performance of the manager and providing instant feedback to engineers and designers working on the project.

A pilot knowledge based project management system, Callisto, developed by Carnegie-Mellon University and Digital Equipment Corporation, has been designed to take account of the interactions that occur during different phases of the project lifecycle by scheduling activities to accomplish some task, monitoring the status of parallel activities to ascertain both plan and schedule changes required to meet project goals, and managing engineering change orders. This quite clearly distinguishes Callisto – an "intelligent" system with some degree of agentivity – from more passive conventional software such as, for example, Claris's CPM-based MacProject, which will neatly construct your schedule and spot the initial problems, but will do no more than that.

Conclusion

What else does AI currently offer? We summarize the basic approaches to using AI that are open to business and industry:

1. The simplest and cheapest solution may be the "off-the-shelf" KBS for supporting fairly routine judgements and decisions in certain types of generic task. Accountancy, taxation and tax analysis, assessing a company's financial future, and so on, are areas where the required knowledge is of a standard kind that can be built in to the system, the complexity of the underlying technology being hidden from the user.

2. There are also semi-custom applications. Some generic knowledge applicable to particular application domains is already built in to the system; but recognizing that most companies have quite specific personal requirements of the technology, it allows for the end-user to add the remaining knowledge specific to a company's problem.

3. A third option is application development tools – expert system shells such as XI Plus, Crystal, Instant Expert – available for microcomputers, and sensibly priced.

4. A more serious investment, in terms of cost and potential pay-offs at the end, is in knowledge engineering and development tools like ART, KEE and KAPPA, or environments such as POPLOG. These very often require the use of some AI-specific knowledge and skills to be used successfully.

5. The final option is to use one of the few AI programming languages (LISP, Prolog, POP-11, SCHEME, OPS5, Smalltalk etc.) to craft your own bespoke product. The advantage is that you have a unique application customized exactly to your personal needs. The investment is likely to be high, particularly if imported expertise is required.

In Britain, more than anywhere else, the platform for AI and expert systems development has been largely microcomputers. A broad array of good quality AI software is now available for IBM PC and Apple Macintosh computers, with most basic software sensibly priced below £1,000.

What will be the training needs? Will the company investing for the first time in KBS need to engage new skilled personnel? This will depend on its AI requirements. If a simple expert system shell will do the job, there are commercial shells, such as Crystal, that can be learned and used in a very short time. For more advanced technologies, the need for training of key IT personnel will increase.

We end on a quieter note. Writing in January 1983, in a book charting the emergence of "Fifth Generation" computing initiatives worldwide, Edward Feigenbaum and Pamela McCorduck (1984) soberly note that:

> *Britain is the only major Common Market country to have experienced a decline in privately funded research and development between 1967 and 1975 – down 11% in those years. It's largely thanks to this indifference on the part of private industry that the percentage of Britain's GNP spent on basic research also fell from 2.32% in 1964 to 2.09% in 1975.*

They conclude grimly:

> *No one expects any change in these trends . . . the British . . . have demonstrated how to turn a nation from a winner into a loser.*

This is a harsh judgement, but hardly unjustified. The economic future of any nation today depends crucially on its investment in the new technologies, since they will quite clearly have implications for every other area of the economy: telecommunications, retailing, manufacturing, agriculture – you name it. This often means taking gambles – such as the gamble the Japanese took 10 years ago when they announced their Fifth Generation project – looking not for the "quick and dirty" short-term pay-off, but with an eye to the future. Anyone can make a fast buck – there's usually nothing especially clever in that; only nations with vision, however, can seed the buck that will grow.

7 | Commercial Expert Systems

Gail Swaffield

Introduction

There is now sufficient evidence of the beneficial use of expert systems in business that they can finally be said to have come of age. To justify this statement, there are two main questions that need to be answered. What is the role of expert systems in a business environment, and what are the keys to successful expert systems development in order to achieve business benefits?

The Role of Expert Systems in Business

In examining the role of expert systems in a business environment, there are four main issues to consider:

- What can expert systems offer over other methods of expertise delivery?
- What type of expertise is applicable to expert systems development?
- How are expert systems used?
- How can the use of expert systems impact directly on the performance of a business?

Expert Systems versus Other Methods of Expertise Delivery

The three most commonly used modes of delivery of expertise other than expert systems are books, hypertext systems and human experts. Taking each of these in turn, we can see just what expert systems have to offer.

Books are a traditional method of delivering expertise. They suffer, however, from two specific drawbacks:

- They are static.
- They presuppose that the reader knows exactly what it is he needs to know.

If in need of advice of a procedural nature – for example, how to plumb in a washing machine – in most cases a book would satisfy that requirement, and the correct book, or portion of a book, would be easy to locate. If, however, the advice needed is more complex, then a book is less suitable. The reader may be faced with a mass of information, much of which is not relevant to the specific problem to be solved. How does the reader sift out just that information required to solve that problem? There will always be a chance of the reader being misguided. As an example, if we think of a book of diseases, it is easy for a reader to discover that he has 20 out of the 500 or so diseases described in a book – it is much more likely that he has none or at the most one!

Hypertext systems add a level of intelligence and remove the entirely static nature of the information presented. The reader can navigate through the text via a series of preset links between related pieces of information, thus removing, to an extent, the problem of irrelevancy. As with books, however, the reader still needs to know exactly what it is he needs to know in order to follow the correct paths through the text. Taking the medical example again, although the reader may be guided to the correct passages via the links set up between symptoms and conditions, it is likely that a whole network of links will exist, such that each symptom could be linked to many conditions and vice versa. Yet again, therefore, our reader could find he has 20 or so conditions to worry about.

So, how does an expert system overcome these problems? Whereas with books and hypertext systems the onus of problem solving rests with the reader, an expert system, like an expert, takes on the role of problem solver, either solely or jointly with the user. Whether the system acts as the sole problem solver or works with the user will depend on the level of expertise of the user as compared with that of the expert. The wider the expertise gap, the more the onus is on the system. The problem of irrelevancy is solved by the elicitation of only the necessary facts and the application of only the relevant parts of the expertise, in order to find a solution to a problem in the most logical manner.

Human experts, by definition, offer the best means of delivering expertise. However, also by definition, they are few and far between, and thus the availability of the expertise they hold is limited. Also, they do not, generally, have the benefit of eternal life, and are as exposed to the vagaries of human nature as any other human being, suffering from the common problems of inconsistency, forgetfulness and so on.

Using an expert system provides the same benefits as consultation with a human expert, or more often, a panel of experts. Where expert systems offer significant advantages over human experts are in the areas of availability, speed and consistency. It is not unusual for an expert to admit that an expert system encapsulating his expertise can, at times, outperform him. For straightforward problems, the expert may have complete recall and thus solve the problem as quickly as the expert system. For more complex problems, the expert may have to work from first principles, carrying out a large amount of problem analysis before reaching a solution. Once the expert system has been developed, however, as long as the problem it is faced with lies within its scope, solving that difficult problem will take very little extra time.

It must be said, however, that the ability of the human expert to work from first principles also gives a distinct advantage over expert systems – that of learning and solving new problems. An expert system will, in many cases, be able to solve new problems, but generally will not be able to learn, i.e. adjust its own role-sets or models. However, in most cases, an expert system is developed to liberate the expert for exactly that purpose – to work on the more complex problems and those that require the extension of existing knowledge, and thus this should not pose a problem.

The Expertise

The expertise that is usually incorporated into an expert system is high-grade expertise, resulting from years of experience in a specific field, and which is, almost by definition, scarce. The two important factors here are the scarcity of the expertise and the quality of it. Scarcity of the expertise must not, however, be considered in isolation. That expertise must also be in demand. Where scarcity of expertise leads to a demand that outstrips availability, this presents an ideal opportunity for the development of an expert system.

There are situations where it may be considered feasible to develop an expert system even where expertise is not scarce – for example, where human life is at risk.

Quality is, however, always a necessary precondition for developing an expert system. It is hard to imagine what benefits could be reaped from the dissemination of low-quality expertise. Although difficult, the assessment of the potential expert is therefore an important task to be carried out before the start of any expert systems project.

The Users

The mode of delivery and use of the expertise is generally dictated by the users who need access to that expertise. Where users are novices, the mode of use of the system will be as an adviser or even as a tutor, taking on the role of problem solver or teacher. Where the user has some knowledge of the area of expertise, or at least understands the context of it, then problem solving will be more of a joint exercise and the system can be described as an assistant. In a few cases, the users of an expert system may be expert in the field of application, in which case the system is most likely to be used as an *aide-mémoire*. Lastly, in certain cases, there may not be a user as such; the expertise may be delivered via an automaton, or may be working "behind the scenes", taking input from some form of data-feed, and itself feeding another application.

In some situations, the same expert system may be used in different modes by different users. As an example, VATIA (VAT Intelligent Assistant), an expert system developed by Ernst & Whinney (now Ernst & Young) (Susskind and Tindall 1989) is used both by auditors who have little or no VAT knowledge and by the VAT specialists who provided the expertise in the system. For the auditor, the system takes the place of a VAT specialist at the audit; for the VAT specialist, the system acts as reminder of the topics to be covered. Whereas the auditor simply enters the client's answers into the system and relies on the report produced at the end of the consultation, the VAT specialist will interpret those answers and, if necessary, investigate issues arising as the consultation progresses – there is much less reliance on the report produced at the end of the consultation.

The Impact of Expert Systems on Business Performance

In assessing the impact of expert systems on business performance it is necessary to look at just what part of the business they will support, and the benefits that are likely to be reaped from their use.

Because of the very nature of expert systems, they play a very different role to traditional IT systems. In, for example, professional service organizations, traditional applications such as word processing, accounting systems and corporate databases support the infrastructure – they are crucial to the operation of the business. Although achieving savings in time and cost, such systems cannot be considered to have a direct impact on business performance.Expert systems in the same environment, however, will support the day-to-day activities of the professional advisers, providing immediate benefits such as an increased quality of advice to clients, an increased speed of delivery of that advice, and a consistency difficult to achieve without the use of such technology. This positioning of expert systems at the cutting edge of the business makes them more able to contribute directly to the performance of the business.

As an example, the Latent Damage System (Susskind and Capper

1988), an expert system operating in the specialist area of latent damage law, allows lawyers access to scarce expertise, at the same time liberating the expert in latent damage law for more complex tasks. The application of this complex area of law can be delegated with confidence to lawyers who would otherwise have to spend a great deal of time getting to grips with it.

Using the expert system offers several advantages to the lawyer – exposure to only those parts of the law relevant to the problem being solved; a greater confidence in the advice given; and reassurance that that advice is correct, because of the quality of the expertise within the system and the access to relevant legal sources while using the system.

So, within the business, improvements are most likely to be seen in such areas as the reliable delegation of tasks, the freeing of experts to carry out more complex tasks and the reduction in the cost of service provision. Such cost reduction will result from the more efficient use of experts, the increased speed of offering advice and the use of lower levels of staff to offer advice only previously offered by expensive experts.

It should be expected that such internal benefits would result in an improved service to customers, who may see, for example, an increased quality of service, the provision of new services, a faster response or lower costs. With an improved customer service, it should follow that the performance of the business improves, either by quantifiable factors such as increased revenue or reduced costs, or by less tangible factors such as an increased competitive edge or better risk management.

Keys to Success: Organizational and Project Issues

Although we have seen that real business benefits can arise from the use of expert systems, there are, of course, both costs and risks associated with the pursuance of any new venture. In terms of an expert systems initiative, costs are mostly due to the need to acquire specialist skills and development environments and the high time commitment required from experts. A risk of any new venture is the change or fear of change which it may bring about, and this is particularly true in the area of technology. Experts may feel threatened by the dissemination of their expertise and users may react to possible changes in their working environment.

In addition, the question of liability may be relevant, particularly if developing expert systems for external clients. Where an expert system has given the wrong advice, or the advice given has had unforeseen repercussions, who is potentially liable? Is it the expert who supplied the knowledge within the system, the developer or the person who ultimately used the system? The question of legal liability of expert systems is covered in some depth in Susskind and Capper (1988).

The combination of these factors means that there will always be a risk of failure. There are a number of factors, both on the organizational and the project level, that can significantly affect the success of expert systems initiatives.

Management Commitment

The commitment of senior management is crucial to success both at the organizational level of setting up an expert systems initiative, and at the project level.

On the organizational level, there needs to be a representative group of informed management who can discuss IT at the business, rather than the technical, level. This could be either a specific group of senior management who discuss just expert systems, or the same group who discuss all IT matters. As expert systems technology matures and becomes another tool in the IT kit-bag, then it seems more sensible to take the latter approach. As projects are proposed, it is the role of this group to assess whether or not they meet the business goals of the organization, and if so, to prioritize them.

At the project level, the first requirement is a champion or sponsor. This will be the person who initiated the project, and whose business it will affect. The sponsor should sit on a steering group, the role of which is to oversee the progress of the project, though not on a day-to-day basis. Members of the steering group should be representatives, at management level, of all departments or functions within the organization which will be affected by the development and introduction of the expert system. The steering group should be kept informed of progress against time and budget and should take any decisions that will affect either.

Goals and Expectations

The success of an expert systems initiative or project will depend largely on the goals and expectations of those involved. It is always tempting for those on the technical side to launch into a new area of technology with the goal of exploiting it to the full. Similarly, sponsors and users, given a taste of what the new technology can do, can suddenly have quite incredible expectations.

The question is, how can we ensure that neither the technical goals nor the management expectations get out of hand? The answer is linked to the discussion above concerning management commitment and revolves around identifying and answering business needs. Technical issues and solutions should take a back seat until requirements have been identified. Only then should technology be considered, purely as a means to meeting those requirements. In this way, it is easier to handle the expectations of management and users.

Application Selection

Primary considerations when selecting expert systems applications are the perceived benefits and the user needs. As discussed by Taylor and Thomas (1991), the perceived benefits of an expert system project should exceed the costs such that an overrun will not cause the project to be pushed over the break-even curve. Too often, a project in a new area of technology such as expert systems is given a special budget, which encourages high spending without necessarily giving sufficiently high return. There is a temptation to test the technology, often producing a solution which passes the point at which the users would have been satisfied.

In the past, as a result of both the relative immaturity of the technology and the research nature of many expert systems initiatives, there has been a tendency to opt for high-cost workstations and development tools. Although these are ideal for developers, when it comes to delivering the solution to users, the cost may then be found to be prohibitive. Although the use of low-cost hardware and software – for example, the standard PC and an expert system shell – may not be considered adventurous, the cost of delivery is far more attractive, and this approach is therefore more realistic from a business perspective. If it is possible to deliver a simple solution which meets the requirements and business objectives, then regardless of the technology used, this is the right solution.

A sensible approach is, therefore, to select those applications that tend towards high benefits and low costs, concentrating more on the business benefits than on any technological considerations. Too much concentration on the latter may result not only in high costs but also in a lack of user focus. Equally important as the cost–benefit consideration is the issue of user focus. The first question should always be "What does the user want?"; only when this is answered should the best technical solution be considered.

In addition to looking at cost and user needs, there are a number of criteria against which a potential expert systems project may be assessed. It is important that there is a genuine business need, i.e. that the problem to be solved is one that is sufficiently recurrent such that dissemination of the expertise is required, and important enough to warrant the cost. Again, we come back to assessing the perceived benefits.

Once the business needs and benefits have been assessed, we then need to turn to the problem domain itself and consider whether, from a technical point of view, it is suitable for delivery as an expert system. The issues that need to be considered at this point concern the size and scope of the domain, i.e. its manageability and the extent to which it can be defined.

The nature of expertise is generally such that it can be fairly easily compartmentalized. However, there will be occasions where the expert also needs to draw on many other areas of knowledge. It is necessary, when developing an expert system, to be able to draw a line around that expertise which will be incorporated into the system. There may be many other related areas of knowledge, and if the incorporation of these is seen as necessary but would make the domain unmanageable, then the area is probably not suitable for expert systems technology.

In addition to assessing the size and scope of the domain of expertise, it is important to consider the extent to which that expertise has been explicated before, i.e. how well defined and how well understood it is. In the case of VATIA, prior to the development of the expert system there existed a paper checklist used by the auditors to carry out a VAT review. Although not pursuing the subject to the same level, and not making any interpretation of the client's answers, the checklist did, at least, define the scope of the domain and outline an approach. Similarly, before development of the Latent Damage System, the expert had written a book on the subject, and had also prepared and given many lectures on the subject. Although the final system took a different approach to the book, there was at least some form of model in existence for solving latent damage problems.

Having assessed the problem domain, it is then important to look at the nature of the expertise itself – not all expertise will be suitable for incorporation into an expert system. While assessing whether the problem requiring the application of expertise is recurrent, it is also necessary to assess the scarcity of the expertise – one without the other would generally not point to an ideal expert systems opportunity. A major problem with scarce expertise, however, and therefore with expert systems projects, is its availability. If the expert will not be able to devote time to the project (expert involvement is particularly high and should not be underestimated), then the project cannot possibly succeed.

Methods

Also at the project level, the use of methods can have a significant impact on the success of an expert systems project. Some of the more important method-related issues are: project management and planning, feasibility assessment, prototyping, user involvement and testing.

Planning for expert systems development is a crucial but difficult task. Although an overall plan can be devised, detailed planning and estimation is a different issue altogether. There are many unknowns and complicating factors, in particular concerning the relative immaturity of expert systems technology, and the potential complexity of the expert's domain.

Whereas in conventional systems development the capabilities and limitations of a language are known and understood, it is still likely that when developing expert systems, these factors will be, to a certain degree, unknown. The market for expert systems tools has not yet stabilized, and the tools themselves are still developing and, in many cases, have not been sufficiently tried and tested for performance statistics to be available. When selecting a tool for the development of a system, it is quite likely that, in order to gain the functionality required of the system, a tool will be selected that has not been used previously to any great extent.

Due to the nature of human expertise and knowledge, for example, the years of experience which the expert has at hand but cannot easily make explicit, the complexity of the expert's subject cannot easily be assessed during the planning stages of a project. Tasks which the expert can complete in a reasonably short time can explode into very much larger problems when made sufficiently explicit for inclusion into an expert system.

For these reasons, planning and estimation for expert systems needs to be a continuous task: as the project progresses, the plans need to be refined to reflect new knowledge about both the tool being used and the expert's domain.

A crucial stage in the life of an expert systems project is feasibility assessment. This involves the assessment of both commercial viability and technical feasibility, as previously discussed.

Prototyping is particularly widely used for expert systems development, and has many uses in this field. The two basic approaches to prototyping are "evolutionary" prototyping, where the prototype becomes the final system, and "throw-away" prototyping, where the prototype acts only as a research or design aid.

The first method, evolutionary prototyping, is also known as incremental development. In the case of a very small system, the prototype may, in fact, be the whole system, built, tested and refined as more knowledge is gleaned from elicitation sessions. For larger systems, the prototype is generally intended to represent the scope, depth and functionality of the final system. To this end, it will usually represent the structure of the whole system, but with only one or two modules completed in depth. The functionality, in terms of user interface, help and explanation facilities, reporting and so on, will usually be demonstrable in the prototype. Once this prototype is accepted by the users, remaining modules can be developed and integrated into the structure, thus forming the complete system.

Throw-away prototyping is generally used where different tools are used for prototyping and for full development. The prototype thus acts as the specification for the full system. Whichever method of prototyping is used, it should be viewed as the chance to experiment. Different methods of providing the desired functionality can be investigated and, in the case of evolutionary prototyping, the capabilities of the development tool tested. It is important, however, that the same quality considerations are applied to prototyping as to full development – in particular where the prototype is to become the final system. The issue of quality in expert systems development is discussed fully in Born (1988).

The main uses of prototyping in expert systems development can be summarized as:

- Concept demonstration (at the start of the project).
- Project planning and estimation.
- Establishing a system design.
- Assessment of tool functionality.
- Knowledge elicitation.
- User acceptance.

However, there are limitations of prototyping, which should be recognized.

First, the performance of a tool may change significantly as the system increases in size, and, by definition, a prototype will never test this aspect of the tool.

Second, although the portion of the system used for prototyping is usually selected on the basis that it is the most representative part of the whole problem, the complexity of other areas of the expert's domain remains unknown until detailed knowledge elicitation is carried out in these areas.

The involvement of a user group in expert systems development is of extreme importance, and should be considered at the start of the project. The criteria for selection of user group members should be strictly defined to ensure that those selected are representative of the target end-users. The same set of users should then be involved from the investigation stage onwards so that they have input into the definition of requirements of the system, right through to testing the final product.

Testing is one of the more difficult aspects of expert systems development. It can be divided into three distinct, but related, areas:

- Verification
- Validation
- User testing

Verification is concerned with assessing the performance of the system against what is expected, the criteria being completeness, consistency, accuracy and robustness. This is not significantly different from the testing of any software product, except that within an expert system there may be many paths through the logic. In many cases, exhaustive testing of all paths through the system will be too time consuming and therefore costly. In such cases, a modular approach to development and testing of the system can ensure that at least all paths within each module can be tested.

Validation involves comparison of the system against the human expert, looking at such issues as quality, approach, explanation facilities, degradation, scope and so on. The first test is whether or not the system addresses the type of problem it was intended to address, and, further, whether it knows when it is faced with a problem it cannot solve. Secondary to this is the performance as compared to that of the expert, in terms of the quality of the decision reached and the reasoning process used, the ability to explain and give help when asked and so on. This is a more subjective and difficult area of testing than verification, but equally important.

User testing is possibly the most neglected area of expert systems development. The principal concern is whether or not the system is usable by the specified set of users – too often, systems are developed with little user input, resulting in a system that is not, in fact, usable by those users. The system should fit into the users' working environment and be aimed at the right skill level in terms of jargon employed and interpretation of questions and answers required.

Although testing is usually not considered until towards the end of a project, it actually plays a part throughout the development cycle. During the knowledge elicitation phase, the expert and knowledge engineer will continually be testing and revising the model as it develops. A prototype system, if developed, will be tested both for verification and validation (though to a lesser extent than the full system) and should also be given to users for feedback on usability.

Conclusions

Expert systems have, in many cases, been shown to expand on the benefits already reaped from mainstream IT, while at the same time supplementing existing expertise. The incorporation of expertise into a computer system often places expert systems at the cutting edge of the business, enabling them to impact directly on business performance. Both initiatives and individual projects must, however, be business driven, and require management commitment for success. Individual projects should always focus on user needs as opposed to the achievement of technical excellence, and will benefit from a structured development approach.

8 | Expert Systems: Changing Perspectives in Applications in the Automotive Industry

Chris Tompsett

Introduction

Expert systems have been successfully applied in industry and commerce since the early 1980s. However, the number of expert system projects that become fully implemented systems remains remarkably small – of the order of 1%–5%. There is considerable variation between market sectors, and the field of mechanical engineering, including the automotive industry, has developed more slowly than most. Some notable successes have been achieved but the scale and scope of the projects varies considerably between the USA and elsewhere.

The widespread use of other computer integrated manufacturing (CIM) systems, coupled with the wide range of expertise required in design, has stratified approaches. Six projects from the diagnosis/maintenance and design fields are described. These illustrate a range of applications from islands of "expertise", for immediate benefit, to expert system technology integrated within a CIM framework, with the reward of longer term and more strategic benefits.

Background

Early Developments

A key feature of the historical development of expert systems has been the vast disparity between the number of systems that move from research design to prototype and those that are finally implemented.

Johnson (1984) provides figures from 1984 to illustrate the significant difference between the number of projects started and finished (see Table 8.1); subsequent figures do not suggest that projects begun become active.

Analysis of the current literature reveals that in the UK the vast majority of reported work is still conducted by researchers in universities, with very few systems being conducted in collaboration with commercial enterprises. A recent survey in Germany (Bullinger et al. 1990) found that some 1200 projects had been initiated, but it proved difficult to find any that had reached an implementation level. Only Japan reports a significant departure from this trend, with estimates of more than 45% of 400 expert system projects reaching full implementation (Motoda 1990).

Furthermore, the distribution of projects is not uniform across industry. Early industrial development has been concentrated in particular sectors, with computing and telecommunications, defence and aerospace generating some 500% more expenditure in the UK than other manufacturing areas (DTI 1988). Programmed work in the automobile sector was not initiated until the mid-1980s, with the establishment in several companies, including General Motors and Ford Motors, of AI groups aimed at high value applications.

However, all applications of expert systems in manufacturing must be viewed within a framework of CIM. During the 1980s there was a significant shift in the management and control of manufacturing within the automobile industry. The introduction of new approaches, and the increasing power of computer and telecommunication systems has engendered some major changes in the design field. Similarly, changes in production management, whether towards MRP II or JIT, have radically altered the ways in which work is carried out and computers are applied.

These changes alone have created problems within the CIM field. Piecemeal development of systems that offer short-term local advantages has created environments in which integration is not possible without first simplifying the existing systems and formalizing their interrelationships (for example IBM's 36 different production facilities used 45 different work-line control packages). It is against this shifting

Table 8.1. Comparison of the number of expert system projects in the UK and the USA

Status	USA		UK	
	Major	Minor	Major	Minor
Begun	70	700	12	125
Active	5	100	1	20

background that expert system projects have to be planned and developed.

Typical Projects

Wills (Ford Motor Company) characterized the company's policy on identification of potential expert system developments as having the following features (Wills 1986):

- The task should take between 5 and 8 hours.
- The project should be economically valuable.
- There should be at least one friendly expert, and no experts should oppose the development.
- The development time should be approximately 2 years but there should be an acceptance of a high failure risk.

Consideration of these features suggested that initial development could be carried out in the following design areas:

- Design critique
- Material selection
- Matching specifications with existing designs
- Geometric packaging
- Extremes analysis
- Selection of manufacturing steps or processes

The criteria for success varied between applications. Work on diagnosis might be acceptable with an accuracy rate of 80%, but work on design would need to achieve a higher level of accuracy consistently.

Although these criteria provide a guideline for identifying projects, it is useful to place these suggestions within a more general framework. With all applications of information systems, the benefit of a new implementation is dependent on three factors: the added value of the "decision" that is supported by the system, the frequency with which the decision is taken, and the extent to which the new information is used throughout the organization. Added value can be gained in many ways, for example through higher accuracy or more timely decision taking. However, some projects can be considered appropriate that normally take many man-months of analysis and are only considered once or twice a year, if the payback is sufficiently high (for example, selection of circuits to include in new application specific integrated circuits (ASICs) in the computer industry). Decisions repeated many times during a year, which normally have a high possibility of being taken incorrectly, could also form the focus of a suitable expert system project if consistency of response is needed.

From Research to Implementation

The majority of expert system projects, those that do not mature into implementations, fail for various reasons. The most typical characteristic is that the systems are established to demonstrate that a particular form of expertise, whether in diagnostics, configuration, scheduling or design, can be represented and reproduced on a computer system. It is possible to achieve this on relatively small problems and to consider the research successful or not on this basis. This approach ignores the problem of integrating intelligence into a manufacturing environment. The possibility of "capturing" a fragment of reasoning is only of value if this information can be used elsewhere in the enterprise.

The significant steps that are required to move beyond this "proof of concept" are therefore focused on the environmental issues that arise when the system is to be embedded into an executive, economic, business, social and computing environment. At the executive level there must be a concern that the project addresses a strategic issue for the enterprise, enhancing the enterprise's ability to compete, as well as being economically viable. With limited financial resources, selection of development projects must be justified on more than purely economic grounds.

At the business and social levels, the systems must integrate with the existing workplace environment. Each project will become a single element in a wider business activity, with personnel necessarily integrating the new competencies supported by the system into an existing structure. Failure to do so will lead to either misuse or non-use of the expert system. A critical aspect of this level of analysis focuses on the reaction of the experts to the proposed system (as noted above), but similar consideration must be given to situations in which the "users" of the system are not necessarily expert themselves.

Finally, the expert system will need to integrate with the computing environment of the company. If the expert system cannot integrate with the existing CIM strategy and available systems, then it is likely to be inefficient. Furthermore, it will be isolated from future strategic development of computing and information systems within the enterprise.

What Is Correct?

Before specific systems are considered, one particular difference between research and implementation systems must be identified.

Within research and development there is a "natural" sense of what is a correct response from an expert system and what is not. Within an implementation environment, although it is important to retain a notion of what is theoretically possible, the critical comparison of system performance is not between the system and the expert or experts who contributed their understanding to it, but rather between the users applying the system and the users continuing in their current manner, with the potential for an equivalent sum invested in improving their performance through some other means. This emphasizes far less the need to produce "correct" answers and highlights the importance of ensuring that the system is "usable". It also accentuates the importance of analysing the cost of errors as much as the cost benefits of correct decisions.

Framework for Expert Systems Assessment

The systems that are reviewed in this chapter represent a cross-section of applications for the automotive industry drawn from work in the UK, the USA and Japan. They illustrate the differing scale and design of systems in two major areas, diagnosis and design. They have been selected to illustrate the importance of integration as a controlling factor in system design. Where appropriate, these systems are contrasted with a selection of projects drawn from a wider range of problems and application domains.

Some expert systems developed within the automotive industry have demonstrated the potential of such systems, but do not reflect issues central to this sector (for example ANALYST in financing (Hudson 1989) and YES/MVS II in computer operations (Chekaluk and Hofziger 1989)). Scheduling, a third major category of expert systems applications, is not considered specifically. Scheduling is particularly complicated by the need to integrate with existing scheduling systems and practice, and the proposed analysis applies equally well to this category (see, for example, Ford Motor Corporation's Mold Scheduling System (Meszaros 1988)).

The systems that are considered also represent two different modes of expert system application: expert duplication and expert assistance. In expert duplication the aim is to reproduce the performance of the expert but in a transposed environment. This raises two problems. Firstly, the system is not being used by the expert, which raises the possibility that the user and the expert do not share the same understanding of the concepts and issues used to discuss a problem and prescribe a solution. Further, as the user is normally working beyond their own level of understanding, they will lack an appropriate framework within which to critique the solutions provided by the system. However, if this model is acceptable, it may only be necessary to duplicate the decisions of the expert and not to mimic all aspects of the decision making process (for example, C-P-C STACKER/DESTACKER (Pudar and Harper 1988)).

Expert assistant systems do not aim to replace an expert, rather to remove some of the more routine work. In this model, the expert remains the arbiter of the solutions. He/she spends more time considering the complex aspects of the problems and has the possibility of contrasting information from the expert assistant with expertise from other sources. It is essential to mimic the decision taking process of the expert. As experts are able to critique the performance of the assistant, and also concentrate on more complex issues, this model includes the essential feature of a feedback system to monitor and develop the performance of the expert assistant.

Repair/Maintenance

Traditional repair and maintenance requires the attendance of an expert technician rather than an operator. With increasing engineering sophistication in automotive technology, whether in the vehicles themselves or in the machinery used for production, the required level of knowledge is also increasing. Within the domain of expert systems, such problems have been routinely tackled either as diagnosis or closed classification systems. At the least sophisticated end of the spectrum, systems have been created for individual items of machinery.

Creating an expert system for an individual item of machinery allows specific expertise to be captured, ensuring that the most efficient methods of problem identification can be exploited, but simultaneously reduces the applicability of the system. Expertise is focused on experience, and benefits accrue either from greater accuracy in diagnosis, use of less expert staff (or the same staff in an area where complexity is increasing), or more timely diagnosis.

ATREX

ATREX, an automobile troubleshooting expert system, is under development by Toyota Central Research (Takahashi 1989). Maintenance by experienced operators combining several areas of "expertise" – heuristic knowledge, previous case histories, characteristic patterns, understanding of the mechanism – is considered. However, the increasing sophistication and complexity of current vehicles and machines has placed greater demands on the level of understanding of those performing diagnosis. New knowledge is required to understand the systems under test, typified by an increase in the level of on-board monitoring and off-board diagnostic systems.

The requisite knowledge is straightforwardly represented in a rule-based system. Interestingly, the implementation is based on a central computer linked with local PCs at individual sites. A central computer provides knowledge based processing. The PCs support the user interface and additionally control an interactive video disk to provide pre-recorded explanation and demonstration of both repair techniques and diagnosis.

This system enhances the field support of vehicles that have been sold, and thus falls into the expert duplication model. The use of a mainframe reasoning system allows maintenance of the "expertise" but also requires that the mainframe system provides a reliable service. Each variation will require a separate representation, both because the statistics of failure rate will vary and because the video disk will need to show the different components. This aspect limits the possibility of updating the knowledge.

It would seem that an approach using more powerful PCs and CD technology to distribute software and video material together might offer an alternative distribution mechanism in the future.

Strategic Aspects

Increasing competition in the mass market from developing nations has concentrated production in Europe into the area of high quality wide-scope manufacturing, offering the customer a wide choice and fast delivery of a customised product. This places increasing emphasis on short lead times and total quality approaches, requiring guaranteed production.

The same application of expert system technology can also be used to tackle more strategic problems within the automotive industry. Production line failure triggers additional chaos in production, whether production is controlled by MRP II or JIT methods. Planned preventative maintenance provides a partial solution but increases the "cost of quality" and often requires downtime for planned maintenance when it is not essential.

The potential for condition monitoring to support JIT maintenance has advanced considerably through the development of sensor technology, and several commercial systems now support data collection. However, analysis of these reports is time consuming and requires expertise to provide a formal assessment of the large volume of data. Viewed as an expert decision, the level of expertise is not high but is complex, requiring identification of key response signals, attribution of particular responses to aspects of machine function, and then identification of responses that are beyond acceptable limits.

One commercial system to address this problem is AMETHYST.

AMETHYST

AMETHYST is a rule-based expert system constructed with the CRYSTAL expert system shell (Milne 1990) with a specific interface to a commercial condition monitoring system produced by Mechanalysis. The condition monitoring system has two components: a hand-held data collection system and the software. The software manages the data from the hand-held equipment, displays it in a variety of formats and provides a collection cycle for the set of machines to be monitored. Computer analysis of the results is limited.

Human expertise is required both at the data collection level, to ensure that the sensors are correctly sited for accurate measurement, and at the interpretation stage. Some straightforward checking of the measurements is carried out at the data collection level but output is limited to untagged warnings, without giving any indication of what is out of condition. Thus, an understanding of the effects of the poor condition cannot be determined until after the analysis has been completed. This will typically take place at the end of the day's collection cycle, when the data is transferred and expert analysis is carried out.

As a commercial system, shipping started in May 1989 and more than one hundred copies have been distributed within the UK and the USA. Although AMETHYST cannot provide expertise, it supports intelligent analysis of the data, producing reports on error conditions in minutes as opposed to several hours. It is a general package that is able to cover a wide range of errors on all rotating machinery, either fixed or variable speed, such as motors, pumps, gear drives and spindles. The additional input from the user, over and above data input from the database, requires only 30 seconds on average.

In addition to the higher strategic value that this system offers in comparison with ATREX, it demonstrates two aspects of integration that raise its potential long-term value. Firstly, the system is generic – it is able to cope with a wide variety of machines with the same general structure. Secondly, the system is integrated with other computer systems. It is not possible to solve this problem without a direct interface to the source data.

However further levels of integration are possible, as illustrated by CHARLEY.

CHARLEY

CHARLEY is a generic expert system diagnosis for manufacturing plant equipment used by General Motors Corporation. It was created by Advanced Engineering Staff and Saginaw Division and has been in operation since 1988.

It covers the same range of machines as AMETHYST, but in addition it integrates sensor data from torque, temperature and pressure monitoring equipment. Thus, in addition to linking to one source, it integrates information from a variety of data sources.

Since the system has been designed for a specific operational environment there is no dependence on a particular commercial monitoring/database system. This allows full integration of the software with other software systems and the full CIM environment, allowing data about machines to be available at little cost.

Since there is no dependence on the intermediate database package, the system can be interactive, providing analysis as the data is collected, or even implemented as on-line in-process monitoring.

The link with specific machine information allows the system to be flexible in its response to sensor data. Baseline levels for sensor have been developed in terms of accurate performance. The system is equally capable of monitoring old machines with poor performance behaviour, performing within appropriate limits, and new machines working near maximum capacity.

The most significant aspect of integration is the extent to which the system is assimilated into General Motors' operations policy. This facilitates successful integration into the manufacturing environment but potentially limits the extent to which other enterprises can imitate this. Without the scale of the company, and the overriding CIM strategy that this provides, benefits would be at a lower level and integration would be restricted to supporting generic "commonality" between enterprises.

Design

The systems described above do not depend on applications occurring within the automotive industry. However, problems specific to the industry have delayed work in the design field.

As an engineering discipline, design requires the collaboration of a wide range of experts from an increasing range of associated fields beyond mechanical engineering – electronics, computing, fluid mechanics and so on. These problems are highlighted in the design field, where representation of design knowledge, for instance, will be inadequate unless expertise from related domains can be integrated successfully. Each domain, however, requires markedly different knowledge and reasoning processes.

In addition, and in marked contrast with electronic engineering and related domains, final evaluation of a design is highly dependent on the live performance of a complete system, in this case, a car. This is not to suggest that simultaneous engineering and design for manufacture cannot be enhanced through the use of expert systems, but that the potential to guarantee advantages is significantly reduced.

Design is a more difficult and complex application area for expert system technologies. The requirement to reduce lead-times from design to product makes it a critical strategic issue within the competitive European market. Traditional design anticipates a long lead-time, with designers from different disciplines contributing in sequence to a design, for testing and manufacture. Modern approaches emphasize the need to integrate all aspects of design, including design for manufacture, at the earliest opportunity. This aim is two-fold: to allow valid design to proceed at the maximum speed, and to ensure that design errors are identified before any additional design has been carried out. As an adjunct such systems should also speed redesign when specifications change or materials/production facilities are improved.

Clearly, expert systems are not being proposed as a replacement for design teams, and their role within the design process is usually that of the expert assistant, supporting an expert in design rather than allowing less qualified engineers to design systems. Three systems are reviewed below, each of which supports aspects of the design process but which integrates to a differing extent with the overall design function. The three systems also illustrate varying levels of design support: design standardization (the Lucas Engineering DFA system), integrated knowledge based analysis (the Kabaya Industry Company Oil Hydraulic Circuit Simulator) and integrated design/modelling (Chrysler's Coolsys).

Lucas Engineering and Systems: DFA

This design aid, begun as an expert system project in 1987 and now commercially available, is based on the "design for assembly" approach developed with Hull University (UK), initially as a paper-based design method. The analysis is based on consideration of the functionality of the system and the extent to which various parts contribute directly to this functionality. Its aim is therefore to critique designs in terms of the number of parts, handling, feeding and fitting. Average savings of 40% on part count have been achieved on a range of objects designed, from brake callipers at Lucas to computer "mice" at DEC in the USA. It is suggested that this translates into an overall saving of 10% of production costs.

This system, as currently presented, attacks the lowest level of design – detailed design checking. It runs as a stand-alone system on a PC, independently of any other computing system. This implies that all information about a prospective design must be entered directly into the system through an interactive question/answer system that is reportedly pedantic. However, the design method has been accepted as standard practice at Lucas Engineering and all designs are submitted to the system and redesigned according to the system's recommendations, if necessary.

The system currently resides as the last feature in the design process, and, although it provides some integration with design for manufacture, is limited by its independence of the rest of the design process. More sophisticated systems can either critique the task at a higher level (as in a Nissan system) or integrate properly with earlier stages of design, for example the Oil Hydraulic Circuit Simulator discussed below.

Oil Hydraulic Circuit Simulator

Kayaba Industry's Oil Hydraulic Circuit Simulator (OHCS) has been developed to integrate work at all four stages of system design within the company (Motoda 1990). Of the four stages – circuit design, component selection, static and dynamic analysis and inspection of drawings – the first and last are typically assigned to senior designers. Since the design process was traditionally sequential, problems arose when designs failed to meet the specification at the last stage, requiring redesign with considerable wasted design activity and lengthy design cycles.

In contrast with the Lucas DFA, OHCS is an intelligent CAD system. The designer works directly in a CAD environment, constructing a system through a graphic editor linked to an object oriented database. This allows the underlying expert system to interpret the drawings, automatically generating an analytic flow model.

Further static and dynamic analysis is calculated using linear approximations for interactions between variables, and employing AI search techniques to limit analysis to combinations of values that are feasible, thus avoiding combinatorial explosion. This allows design critiquing, traditionally the final stage, to proceed interactively with design, leading to fast critique and design cycles.

This system has been deployed since 1988, cutting designer level work by 50%. It is now intended to complement this system with further expert systems to consider detailed layout design and generation of quality assurance sheets to match the specification.

Coolsys

Coolsys (Friel et al. 1989) is a cooling system design tool produced by the Knowledge Based Systems Laboratory at Texas A&M University for Chrysler Motors Corporation. In comparison with the OHCS system, it raises design support to include more complex integration between design tools. In addition, it embodies integration with previous design activity, based on situational design. A system requirement was that it should include FORTRAN coded airflow and heatflow models that were already in use for design analysis at Chrysler. The current system generates design specifications for engine box cooling systems, given descriptions of components such as engine air conditioning systems and transmission. These specifications can be analysed in a variety of test conditions, with varying speed and ambient temperature, for example.

The inherent model of design assumes that design, and redesign, is continued interactively to optimize system performance. Therefore, the system must track changes in performance details during redesign, especially where changes produce improvements in one feature and decline in performance of another. The design model therefore requires a memory for previous iterations and previous model designs. Thus, the system "learns" the behaviour of each vehicle as development progresses, and alters components to match requirements.

Although initial conversations with the expert suggested that there was a valid sequence for design development, later analysis showed that the designers rapidly ignored the prescribed method whenever it appeared to be unfruitful. The system also includes a manual mode (excluding the expert system), which is often used for quick design changes and consideration of designs that are outside the system's generative capability.

The system has been operational since 1987 and is used for all vehicles other than trucks. Design specifications can be produced in minutes, rather than several days. Multiple designs are produced, which allows many more options to be considered than before. The system is now maintained and expanded by Chrysler.

Integration as a Pointer for the Future

The six systems described here illustrate a wide range in terms of scale of performance and scope of coverage. Benefits are achieved in each case, although there are major differences in considering the extent to which the expert system forms an integral part of the production environment.

The need for integration has been highlighted at several levels and from several viewpoints. These are:

- Functional integration:
  - between experts
  - between analysis methods
  - between sources of information
- System integration:
  - with data
  - with other software/models
  - AIM architecture
- Human–system interface:
  - minimizing human data input
  - assisting human expert performance
  - supporting human problem solving
  - supporting human critique of system performance
- Human integration:
  - between users and experts
  - between experts themselves

In the long term, there is also the potential to include expert systems at a meta-level of analysis compared with current activity. Gordon Wills (1986) offers the following as potential objectives for future systems:

- Identifying flexible manufacturing opportunities
- Specification of new materials
- Design and critique for families of new machinery

9 | Neural Networks in Business: A New Paradigm in Artificial Intelligence

David Browne and Ara Yeghiazarian

Introduction

Evidence is mounting that neural networks can provide cost-effective improvements in a wide (and growing) number of business applications. Specific examples are given later, but areas such as handwriting recognition, machine control, marketing database analysis, forecasting and image processing have all shown cost-effective use of neural networks. One estimate suggests that the market for neural network products will grow from $140m in 1991 to $1 billion in 1995, suggesting an explosion of interest. (Stewart 1991)

Given the recent commercialization of neural networks and the growing number of applications, evidence of their business benefits is unresolved. The hearsay evidence suggests that the benefits are large, but as with the introduction of any new technology such claims should be seen as goals – the temptation to assume that neural networks will automatically generate large profits and/or cost savings may doom implementations and cause disappointment.

In view of the recent move of neural networks from research environments to commercial implementations, it is likely that the technology will be new to most readers. A brief description is given below, and further detail can be obtained from the references.

What Are Neural Networks?

Artificial neural net models have been studied for many years in the hope of achieving human-like performance in the fields of speech and image recognition, early developments being traced back to the work of McCullough and Pitts in the early 1940s. By the early 1960s, active efforts in neural networks and learning were concentrated within relatively few research teams, mainly in the USA, the two most active groups being those of Professor Frank Rosenblatt at Cornell University and Professor Bernard Widrow at Stanford University. After several publications in the early 1970s questioned the value of this research, there was a substantial reduction in funding and little evidence of technical activity exists between that time and the mid-1980s. Academic interest was resurrected around this time, which in turn generated interest and support for the development of experimental and commercial networks.

A neural network is modelled on what is currently understood of the microstructure of the human brain, that is, a collection of nerve cells, or neurons, each of which is connected to as many as 10,000 others (see Fig. 9.1).

Scientists using advanced technology have tried to mimic the brain's own data processing. Just as humans apply knowledge gained from past experience to new problems or situations, a neural network takes previously solved examples to build a system of "neurons" that makes new decisions, classifications and forecasts.

A typical neural network has three or more layers of neurons, each of which is "connected" to the neurons in the next layer as shown in Fig. 9.2. These connections have weights that are applied to values passed from one neuron to the next. Input values in the first layer are weighed and passed to the second layer. Neurons in the second layer "fire", or produce outputs, which are based upon the sum of weighed values passed to them. The second layer passes values to the output

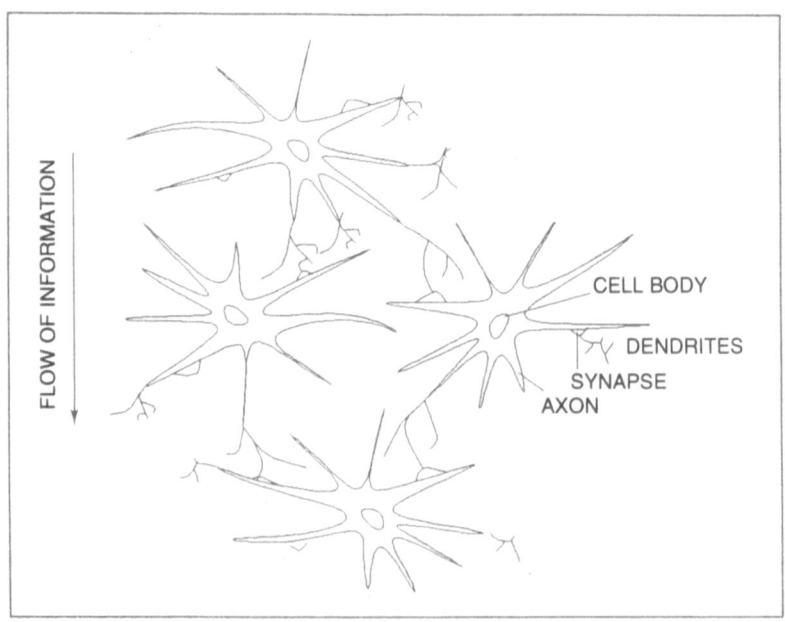

Fig. 9.1. Biological neuron.

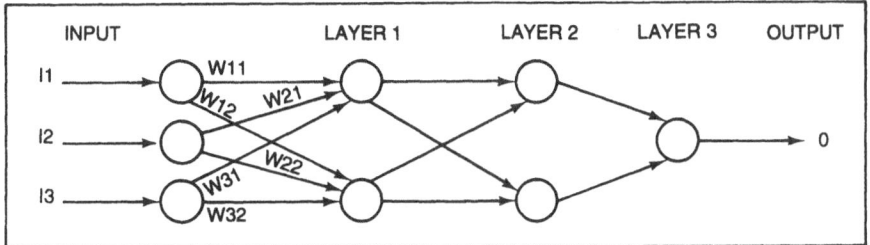

Fig. 9.2. Three-layer artificial neural network.

layer in the same manner, and the output layer produces the desired results (predictions or classifications).

The network "learns" by adjusting the interconnection weights. The answers the network produces are repeatedly compared with the correct answers, and the connecting weights are adjusted slightly, using one of several competing algorithms, to reduce the difference between the network's output and the desired output (Fig. 9.3).

Eventually, if the problem can be learned, a stable set of weights adaptively evolves and will produce good answers for all the sample decisions or predictions. The real power of neural networks is evident when the trained network is able to produce good results for data that the network has never seen before.

To train the network it is necessary to have a set of data containing sample input facts or parameters with corresponding results or answers. The data set used to train can be obtained using historical data in which the outcomes are known or by creating sample problems and solutions with the help of experts. Once the training process is completed the network should be able to classify or predict from new inputs.

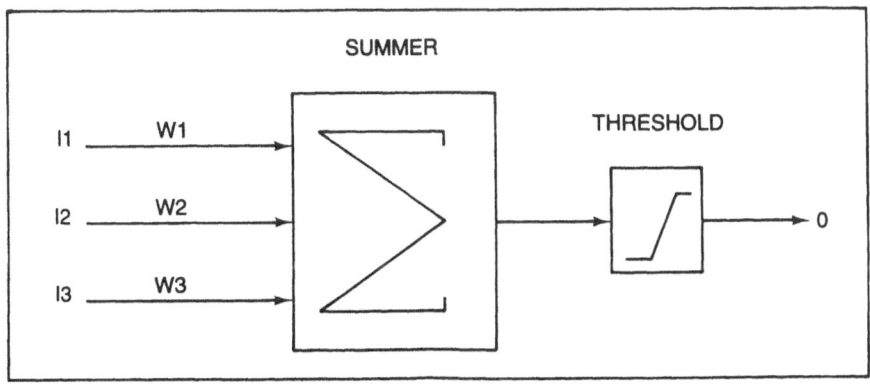

Fig. 9.3. Perceptron neuron.

The Role of Neural Networks in Business

In discussing the role of neural networks in business, it is useful to examine the following main issues:

- What can neural networks offer over expert systems and traditional statistical methods?
- How can the use of neural networks impact directly on the performance of a business?

Neural Networks versus Expert Systems

As identified in Chapter 6, expert systems grew out of the attempts of computer scientists to mimic the thinking and experience of experts, as typified by the Winograd and Flores (1986) definition:

> *Artificial intelligence is an attempt to build a full account of human cognition into a formal system (a computer program).*

Artificial neural networks have been constructed not to mimic the metaphysical thought processes, but to mimic the physical make-up of the brain itself. This leads to an important distinction between neural networks and expert systems: expert systems require someone to program the logical process; neural networks are shown many examples and "learn" the "rules" themselves. This distinction has several important implications for the comparison of neural networks and expert systems.

As discussed elsewhere in Chapters 7 and 8, many expert system projects have failed to reach implementation. There are several reasons for this. Expert systems require domain experts, who can rarely devote their complete attention to the problem and may have difficulties articulating their knowledge for the knowledge engineer. In common with traditional systems development, expert systems can have long development times, and large systems can be difficult to develop and maintain. In contrast, neural networks do not need domain experts or knowledge engineers. Furthermore, development of a neural network model requires little, if any, programming, allowing short development times. The gains are greater for larger problems.

Expert systems have some advantages over neural networks. In particular, expert systems do not just provide an answer to a problem, but will usually allow an explanation of how the answer was derived, which can be used to train those lacking in expertise. Neural networks, in contrast, may provide a good solution but give little or no intelligible reasoning. Expert systems is an older technology, and consequently there are both more experienced practitioners and a wider range of tools, including numerous shells. Less technical personnel or tools are available for neural networks, but this deficiency is fast disappearing.

Expert systems also have the advantage of being usable on standard computer hardware. Given the large number of input examples required for a neural network to be trained, standard hardware is usually too slow. This problem can be overcome at little expense by utilizing specialized hardware available from neural network software providers, and is therefore not a major issue. Neural networks are currently run on workstations or PCs with add-in coprocessing boards. The speed improvement over standard hardware can be by a factor of one hundred. For all but the smallest networks, best performance comes from the use of accelerator-assisted or specialized parallel chip boards.

There are many problems for which expert systems are preferable, such as in cases where explanation is required, where there are few examples, or where the problem has a clear underlying rule/logic (such as the VAT system described in Chapter 7).

In other cases, neural networks are preferable, such as where development time must be short, or where there are many training examples of relatively unstructured knowledge.

In certain circumstances, both techniques may be utilized together, by allowing the neural network to derive rules which are then incorporated into an expert system, for example in credit scoring.

Neural Networks and Traditional Data Analysis

There are many examples where the use of statistical methods has transformed business areas in the past 25 years: market research, asset pricing, forecasting and risk analysis, for example. The common thread in all of these is that exploitable patterns can be found in the data, allowing better targeting, risk assessment and/or forecasting.

Although sophisticated, statistical technology has mainly concentrated on linear mathematical functions which give tractable solutions. Evidence is growing that neural networks may be better able to identify exploitable patterns, giving tighter targeting and/or better forecasting.

What Is the Investment?

Neural networks can be applied in business using several different approaches:

1. *Turnkey applications.* Very few turnkey developments are currently marketed. One such is an Optical Character Recognition (OCR)

engine developed by Nestor Inc. (USA), which has been licensed to various companies for incorporation into OCR packages. A similar development for handwriting recognition on pen computers is also available. Other turnkey products are likely to arise in the near future.

2. *Neural network development tools.* Commercial packages such as Neuroshell, Brainmaker and Neural Works Professional allow the construction of small to medium-sized networks. Some of these packages can be used with an accelerator board to reduce the enormous training times that arise with neural networks, the reduction factor being of the order of one hundred.

3. *Custom design.* Research and consulting companies have developed their own neural network software/hardware combinations to provide services to clients. Although expensive, these services obviously allow users to benefit from a wealth of experience.

Examples of Commercial Neural Network Implementations

Neural network applications are starting to enter the commercial arena and more researchers have started to use them to solve "real problems".

1. *Financial applications.* There has been considerable use of neural networks in various financial applications, in part because of the ready availability of large data sets. Neural networks have successfully been used to produce score cards for credit applications. By analysing past loan applications and defaults, companies have been able to develop improved score cards and thus reduce losses, reduce costs and increase market share by improving pricing (Makram-Ebeid and Burel 1992; Stewart 1991).

Many financial institutions have investigated the use of neural networks to forecast stock prices, bond prices and exchange rates in an attempt to improve forecasts and increase profits in a highly competitive market. Claims of successes have been made but commercial secrecy has limited independent validation (Stein 1991; Windsor and Harker 1990)

2. *Energy forecasting.* Energy suppliers have large volumes of consumption data available and a need to forecast for very short periods ahead. Neural networks have been able to provide improvements over more usual statistical models in this application.

3. *Marketing.* Database marketing grew enormously in the 1980s in a drive by companies to improve targeting and hence profitability.

Neural networks have proven to be adept at improving segmentation compared with older methods such as multiple discriminant analysis, thus reducing costs and improving hit rates (Dragstedt 1991; Severwright 1992; Stewart 1991).

4. *Vision.* Examples of developments in this area include British Telecom research on a videophone service, which incorporates neural networks in order to improve transmission (Hawkes 1990) and Philips' research into reducing wastage in printed circuit based products by using neural networks to ensure correct chip placement (Makram-Ebeid and Burel 1992).

5. *Optical character recognition.* Improvements in OCR technology have been obtained by incorporating neural network technology to enable better learning, and hence improvements in the scanned documentation (Natraj 1990; Omatu et al. 1990).

6. *Industrial.* Many large companies worldwide are researching the possible application of neural networks in industry. For example, the Korean government's $100m project for intelligent computer products envisages the implementation of neural networks and related technologies in such prosaic consumer items as washing machines, refrigerators and gas boilers (Lee 1992; VerDuin 1990).

The Prospects for Neural Networks

Neural networks have excited enormous interest over the past few years and are now being applied in many varied areas. Huge investments are being made in research and development to incorporate neural network technology, often allied with other new developments such as fuzzy logic, genetic algorithms, machine learning and expert systems, not only into business applications but also as a component of consumer articles.

Commercial pressures for improved products and services will see wider implementation of neural network technology, causing rapid obsolescence of older products and methods.

IV | HYBRID MANAGERS

Editorial Overview

Hybrid management may be either a description of the problem or of its solution. As the cultural divide has widened between strategic and technical management, particularly in the UK, there have been attempts to build a bridge through the development of hybrid managers, with a foot in each camp, placed on the shoulders of those who have gone before.

Stewart Judd (Chapter 10) has investigated hybrid management on behalf of British senior management, and has been active in proposing solutions involving companies, educational institutions and support from Government. This has required an understanding of the need, a definition of standards, and the establishment of new qualifications structures and institutions.

Ann Leeming (Chapter 11) is director of an award-winning course which adds insights from IT to an established management development programme. From a technical background herself, she is a strong advocate of the primacy of business considerations, and expresses optimism about the future of hybrid management courses.

Christine Warner (Chapter 12) directs a course in the management of information systems design, which seeks to add a business context to the development of experienced IT professionals. Her chapter offers illuminating insights from experience of the growing integration of IT technologies and business functions, and accounts of transformations of company cultures.

Stuart Fitz-Gerald (Chapter 13) considers the problem of developing hybrid managers through undergraduate courses, based on his experience as course director in business information technology. A new hybrid culture must be built using ingredients from business, quantitative methods and IT.

The debate on hybrid management has been complicated by the recession, which has destabilised the IT profession, and left a legacy of uncertainty. What is clear is that industrial recovery will depend on a new amalgam of management skills, which must include intelligent use of new technology. Organizational structures and cultures will not continue unchanged, and management and business education should play a leading role. This will in turn require innovative approaches which transcend conventional subject boundaries: success comes when the workplace is also a learning environment.

10 | Hybrid Managers in Information Technology

Stewart Judd

Introduction and Background

What has caused business to seek a new approach to managing information technology (IT) and integrating it into the business structure? There is a good maxim: "If it isn't broken, don't fix it!".

There is plenty of evidence to suggest that in many cases the considerable sums of money being invested in IT are not producing the results they ought, and because poor management is perceived to be a major cause, action is needed. There is a danger, however, of resorting to labels to define an objective. The British seem to have a compulsion to label things that are fashionable, but soon tire and move on to something else. Such is the case, I believe, with "hybrid management". What we are seeking is a way of improving the effectiveness of investment in IT. There is no unique solution, but I shall consider aspects of the interaction between the needs of business to exploit the latest developments in IT for a variety of applications, and the IT and other skills necessary to implement the associated business strategy successfully. What I have to offer, however, is only one interpretation of the problems involved and how they may be solved. The views are my own and do not reflect CBI policy.

My own background is in electronics engineering research and development, followed by business development management, which explains the particular bias from which I have approached the management of IT. Although many elements are common to managing any technology properly, IT is different in the sense that it interacts with all business activities, but not in the same way. There is a maxim from electronics engineering, however, attributed to Bill Hewlett, one of the founders of Hewlett-Packard, which I think is very telling: "If you can't measure it, you can't manage it". We must try to quantify the problems we face, otherwise we shall never be in control of the situation.

CBI IT Skills Agency

My involvement with the CBI IT Skills Agency (ITSA) brought me in contact with the concept of "hybrid managers". ITSA was created in 1987, following the reports of the Butcher Committee, to investigate the causes of shortages of skilled IT staff and make recommendations to business and government aimed at solving the problem. Because of the rapid pace of developments in IT it was agreed that a Working Group should be set up, under the direction of Brian Oakley, chairman of Logica Research, to study the impact of changes in the technology on future demand for professional IT staff. The main points to emerge from the study were:

- Far fewer lower-skilled staff would be required in future.
- Demand for telecommunications and networking skills would increase rapidly.
- A growing need for "business function analysts", staff with almost equal knowledge and experience of IT and fields of applications.

The latter arose because users had become disenchanted with the design, installation and operations service provided by traditional IT departments, and because developments in the technology, particularly desktop computers and proprietary applications software, provided a potential opportunity for users to become independent. Without specifying in detail what such "business function analysts" should be capable of doing – they were referred to as "51 percenters" because they would possess almost equal knowledge and experience of IT and of their functional specialism – the ITSA Working Group commented that:

> special attention would have to be paid to the education, training and career development of these key personnel, without whom the Working Group sees no prospect of maintaining growth in new IT applications.

The Working Group did say that they thought these individuals should acquire their IT expertise during, or following, qualification in their chosen discipline, rather than the reverse. The IT expertise should include information systems engineering, architectures, software, peripherals and communications, and may lead to the need for extended courses to cover the additional syllabus. The Working Group published its report in February 1989.

IT Industry Lead Body

At about the same time, late in 1987, the Manpower Services Commission (MSC) called a meeting of representatives from various groups with an interest in IT skills and training to discuss the need for an Industry Lead Body in Information Technology to define a set of competence standards to form the basis of National Vocational Qualifications (NVQs) in IT. Most Lead Bodies were sector-specific but IT was considered such a generic technology that it demanded special treatment. After considerable debate, the need for an IT Lead Body was agreed. Under the chairmanship of Barney Gibbens, former chairman of the SEMA Group, the Lead Body has overseen the development of a set of IT competence standards for what are called "IT practitioners", funded by the MSC/Training Agency, and based on the British Computer Society's Industry Structure model and a functional analysis of the IT services industry. On the subject of competence standards for the application of IT to sectors where the technology is not a mainstream activity, the IT Lead Body decided to publish a set of guidelines for other ILBs to define the IT elements relevant to the industry sector. For example, IT aspects of graphic design would be defined by the Lead Body for the printing industry using the ITILB guidelines.

The "Practitioner" standards, as they are called, specify the areas of competence that employees should be able to demonstrate in the workplace, and the guiding principle has been to ensure that they meet the practical needs of employers. To date, they have been designed to cover the main functional areas in IT services that are most populated at NVQ levels I to IV. The NVQ levels have been interpreted as:

Level I: Carrying out mainly routine functions under continuous supervision, and/or as a basis for future development.

Level II: Carrying out functions that require some personal responsibility and a good grasp of basic technology and methods; still regularly supervised.

Level III: Frequently defining work for Level II and supervising its execution. Some responsibility for customer liaison and training.

Level IV: Usually designing or establishing requirements to be undertaken at lower Levels. Either some managerial responsibility or high level of technical competence and supervisory responsibility.

There is also a NVQ Level V which approximates to some parts of a professional engineering qualification and is defined as:

> Competence which involves the application of a significant range
> of fundamental principles and complex techniques across a wide

and unpredictable variety of contexts. Very substantial personal autonomy and often significant responsibility for the work of others and for the allocation of substantial resources, feature strongly, as does personal accountability for diagnosis, design, planning, execution and evaluation.

The basic building blocks of the standards are Elements of Competence, which are then grouped together into Units to form a consistent module. Each Element has a set of performance criteria, which specify how the competence should be demonstrated to an assessor. The Units are expressed in generic terms – that is, they express the functional requirements in terms of good practice, without specifying the hardware, software, methodology and so on. Each user of the standards has to tailor them to the particular needs of the business. As part of the development process, the standards have been piloted in a number of companies, by using them to conduct training needs analysis, to create job descriptions and for performance appraisal. Valuable feedback has been obtained, and has been used to modify the elements where necessary.

Units of the competence standards developed by the Lead Body are now being combined to form the basis for a set of qualifications and the specification of assessment methods and criteria. Underpinning knowledge, understanding and additional non-technical skills will also be required. The standards, and the qualifications derived from them, are unlikely, however, to correspond with current educational qualifications. Vocationally oriented courses may, however, provide much of the underpinning knowledge mentioned previously.

IT Investment

There is growing demand from senior managers for methods to evaluate the results of investment in IT, particularly for justifying the commitment of large sums to change an organization's infrastructure and/or methods of working. Reports of substantial time and cost overruns and failure to provide the service needed have been many and frequent, which has led many senior managers to become sceptical about improvements in business performance claimed by information technologists for new IT systems. In a recent CBI survey of investment in IT, one-third of respondents admitted that they did not carry out a formal analysis of the results. It was in response to this sort of situation that the ITSA Working Group identified the need for "hybrid managers" to link strategic business aspirations and the design, development and installation of IT systems which would help to realize them.

From my experience as an electronics engineering manager, I should note the close parallels with product development programmes. Frequently, senior managers have to take on trust what they are told by managers about progress, cost to completion and so on, particularly since many are only trained as accountants. The difference is that IT development programmes can affect all functions of the business.

Definitions

First, the definition of "management of technology":

Linking engineering, scientific and management disciplines to plan, develop and implement technological capabilities to shape and realize the strategic and operational objectives of an organization.

The BCS definition of an information system is:

The application of computing and communications technology to meet a defined need. The purpose of such systems is to collect, process, store, transfer, disseminate and display information.

In my terms, a hybrid manager is responsible for:

- Defining and determining the information needs of the business function in which he/she is specialized, for example accounting, personnel, marketing, engineering, IT services.
- Integrating IT into the function strategy.
- Assessing and evaluating IT performance within the business function.

Scope

All organizations in industrial societies such as the UK depend on information to work effectively, and this dependence is growing, in organizations as diverse as the Inland Revenue and Tesco. Information has become, therefore, a key asset comparable in value to other physical assets, if not more so in some business sectors. Thus, when we consider the scope of information management we have to consider a matrix of interdependent functions, which may include:

- Finance
- Engineering/design
- IT services
- Marketing
- Personnel

- Production

- Transport

Within the organization, therefore, there is a role for an information strategist, at a very senior level, to coordinate the needs of the various functions, and in particular to identify the linkages which any information management system must provide. This is the key role I identify for "hybrid management".

Where are these managers to come from and what should be their responsibilities?

Given acceptance and implementation of the concept of "hybrid functional managers", I suggest that the position of Director of Business IT Strategy, or whatever the post is called, could be filled by promotion from any of the specialist functions. The additional question arises as to whether such a post should include responsibility for IT services. Not necessarily, although there may be good reasons for doing so, not least because the individual may be the ideal choice to combine both responsibilities. An important consideration, however, will be the decision whether to provide all, or some, IT services from within the organization or by "outsourcing" to specialist firms. In the latter case, the most critical tasks are defining the terms of the contract and managing the interface between the two organizations.

Education and Training

There are two distinct requirements for staff educated and trained in the application of IT to business. The ITILB has called these IT Practitioners and Structured End Users. The balance of disciplines is completely different for each category. The competence standards for a series of NVQs for IT Practitioners have been developed and the BCS Industry Structure Model covers the development of professional staff to full chartered status. The IT competence standards for NVQs for End Users are being integrated into sector-based qualifications. Higher education can provide the underpinning knowledge and much of the understanding for these vocational qualifications which are designed for delivery and assessment in the workplace.

Conclusions

Many senior managers have not understood the way in which their businesses have grown to become dependent on IT. Many also feel they have been misled by information technologists more concerned with playing with the latest developments in technology than with the profitability of the company. The concept of information as a valuable resource is lost on most, although there are exceptions such as in the pharmaceutical industry, where intellectual property is managed very effectively. In much of British industry, senior executives are qualified in accountancy, but there are few examples with technical qualifications. Consequently, there is a serious communications barrier between technologists and those responsible for running the business. In today's rapidly changing, highly competitive business environment, the education and training of business managers raises several complex issues, not least the degree to which they should learn to cope with technology. Developments in technology are increasing so rapidly, however, that even specialists find it difficult to keep abreast of change. Consequently, it is not practical for one person to have competence in IT and all other aspects of a business. There are two solutions to this problem: either build up an effective in-house team of departmentally-based specialists who are also competent in IT, or "outsource" to one of the companies that specialize in providing IT services. Hybrid Manager is a label that could be applied to company-based staff but "Department" IT Strategy Manager is probably more appropriate. The Director of Business IT Strategy would co-ordinate the departmental requirements and be responsible for corporate IT strategy.

11 Information Technology Adds Value to Management Education

Ann Leeming

Organizations have long been aware of the need for improved management training, not only because of increasing investment in information technology (IT) and concerns about its effectiveness, but also through the realization that IT is an essential weapon in the battle for competitive edge. This points to gaps in our system of postgraduate education and the failure to

> orientate training content to the management perspective . . . to conduct rigorous assessment of IT training and education needs (Coopers and Lybrand 1988).

This chapter discusses the concepts underpinning a new programme provided by City University Business School within its portfolio of specialist MBA programmes. The venture has proved very successful, not only at attracting potential managers of the right calibre but also at gaining support from the industry. The programme is an MBA in Information Technology and Management; it was launched in 1989 as a full-time programme, though some students take it part-time over two years.

The use of the term "IT" intended here has two components: one is the infrastructure, the other is the information systems. The former is the set of hardware, operating software and networks that provides the platform on which the latter component, information systems, can operate to deliver their service.

It is the quality and cost of this service which now deeply concerns management. To achieve the present levels of service has cost UK plc a huge investment in resources. The recession has sharpened management's awareness that the rate of use of these resources has become unacceptable and out of control.

A further concern is the uneven quality of software installed and produced. This arises from design methods and from age, as a result of the number of enhancements and extensions to which software has been subjected and the amount of maintenance it has undergone. The causes of this state of affairs can be listed as the rapid growth of the technology, the constant advances of the methods used for developing software, the turbulent business environment and the very variable competency base of all participants. Technical specialists need to make continuing efforts to keep up to date with their profession. Developments in design techniques, programming languages and data management tools happen constantly. The need for specialist technical education at the graduate and postgraduate level is recognized and the supply is growing.

Users have become much more knowledgable with the growth in the number and variety of IT available to them. It must be acknowledged that ease of use is not often as simple as it might be. Users are aware of the link between business success and information management, and of the dependency of the business on IT. User expectations continue to be variable; managing expectations remains part of the business of developing information systems.

Managers, who in the past have had to accept what they could get from the IT department, now understand better their role in the specification of their information requirements. However, understanding the need to be involved, and being able to be involved in the production of information systems that meet the three generic benefits (Silk 1990) of effectiveness, efficiency and bringing strategic advantage, are two different situations. It is the group of managers who are not, and do not want to be, sited within an IT department that must now respond to the challenge of ensuring that their organization is capable of acquiring a portfolio of information systems that support their business goals.

A Vision for Management Education

To help in the production of a managerial force that will foster such competencies, the author and colleagues developed a new management programme. This aims to provide managers with an understanding of IT, integrated with a study of its role in supporting the goals of the organization.

The objectives are to develop in the student the following knowledge and skills:

- The ability to work in multidisciplinary teams.

- An understanding of the power, capacity and status of IT. This latter understanding is crucial to obtain the benefits appropriate to the current skills of the IT and user groups in the workforce.

- The ability to harness IT for the competitive advantage of their own organization.

- Understanding of the role of and ability to implement strategic information systems.
- Ability to implement change in management thinking at all levels.

The first graduates from the programme have gone into industry able to understand and exploit IT in many environments. In spite of the recession, they were employed rapidly, many achieving their career ambitions. One insisted:

as an IT professional I need this course if I am to reach the Board.

Dr McCullough (1991) commented that:

the course has given me the concepts to communicate with systems specialists . . . and the skills to use IT productively.

A major benefit for the graduates is that they join an international graduate network at the post-experience level, a network of business associates and friends that will serve them throughout their professional life. The technologies they learnt about are being put to use; new business ventures as well as friendships are being explored though the medium of telecommunications.

Half the contact hours in the programme are studied with MBA students from all the specialisms, concentrating on business and general management skills. Thus, students mix with others of different disciplines and learn to communicate in mutually comprehensible language.

The other half of the programme concentrates on ITM specialist and elective courses. Innovative courses study specific aspects of managing using IT and of the interface between the IT department and the business. A business project provides the opportunity to integrate learning by working on an IT and management problem in industry.

Not all applicants have a background in IT. Course applicants come with a wide range of experience, from intense IT experience to very little. All have an interest in and an understanding of IT, which has convinced them that a mix of IT and business skills is vital for the future. The mix of backgrounds is deliberate; it provides students with the opportunity to understand the language, culture and expectations of others, and fosters the development of interpersonal skills essential for good management. Colin Coulson-Thomas (1991) commented:

the students are able to see IT in the context of the business, they can integrate all aspects of the programme.

The mix of nationalities is approximately 75% from Europe and 25% from the rest of the world. There are frequently more than 25 nationalities on the course.

Assessment of Impact

Robert Martin (1991) has described the impact of employing such a graduate as providing help in:

> *identifying the policy issues to increase the value of IT to the company.*

A burgeoning understanding of the importance of IT in business across all MBA students has been transformed by the advent of the new programme. Collaboration with industry in this new area has grown with mutual benefit, and stimulation of research, providing new directions and goals, is occurring.

Conclusion

The programme has added value to management education by integrating a study of the critical success factors in the exploitation of IT into the management function. Organizations are thereby enabled to use IT effectively, their business goals are broadened and new businesses are created.

12 | Is a "Hybrid Manager" Enough?

Christine Warner

Introduction

The BCS recommended the "hybrid manager" concept in 1990 (British Computer Society 1990) as a way of overcoming the shortage of managers who could combine business and technical skills. This chapter discusses our experiences of the MSc in Information Systems Design, which predates the "hybrid manager" debate. From this course experience and published directions for organizations, it is argued that a hybrid manager alone cannot succeed, and to reap the benefit of technological change an organization will need to be restructured. "Hybrid managers" will have an important role in this organizational restructuring as their abilities include:

- Communication skills with various levels including Boards.
- Effecting strategy decisions through knowledge of technical capabilities.

Evolution

The Masters course in Information Systems Design and Management (MID), supported by the SERC under its Integrated Graduate Development Scheme, was started before the current BCS drive towards establishing the recognition of the vital role of the "hybrid manager" in an organization. However, the course arose from the perception that such skills were a crucial ingredient in bridging the traditional divide between business functions on the one hand and the new information-based technologies on the other.

I do not intend to debate the meaning of "hybrid" here, as this has been well debated elsewhere. The BCS Task Group define the term "hybrids" as describing:

> *people at various levels in an organization with strong technical skills and adequate business knowledge, or vice versa . . . hybrids are people with technical skills able to work in user areas doing a line or functional job, but adept at developing and supplementing Information Technology (IT) application ideas (British Computer Society 1990).*

Delegates on MID start with experience of computer systems, either as managers or as IS professionals, coming from various backgrounds and different sectors, including local authorities, IT Information Systems providers, retail and consultancies. Some 200 have now graduated successfully, combining part-time study with their full-time employment in their sponsoring organizations. Delegates who have attended MID believe that it has contributed to the provision of hybrid managers. To quote a graduate from British Telecom, when talking about what people had gained from the course he described the course as:

> *grounding their skills in an information and business-centred cross-disciplinary culture. Graduates have invariably gone on to enrich their companies with widened viewpoints, and embarked on the road as hybrids.*

Three important competencies for people working in organizations are:

1. *Culture*. For people to communicate effectively they need a deep level of understanding of culture differences within an organization: "Learning to interact with others who have different backgrounds and perspectives to your own" (Skyrme and Earl 1990). It is more than just a common vocabulary: it is an ability to work effectively in multidiscipline teams.

2. *Handling change*. Earl has identified one of the management characteristics of a hybrid as that of "handling and managing change" (Earl 1989). At Kingston we believe that a more proactive position is required – that of agent of change: people with the vision to anticipate and exploit change rather than merely to respond to it, who combine their management and technical skills with their understanding of the political, social and economic factors.

Such personnel are well prepared to manage the exploitation of "information" within their organizations, although, as individuals, they often meet resistance. Lindsay (1990) explores this further.

3. *Technology*. A dichotomy exists: detailed technical knowledge becomes obsolete and yet awareness alone does not give enough understanding to guide decision making. The enduring competence required is an understanding of the information resource: technology

then serves to provide facilitating tools which will change with time. Clearly, the effective strategic, tactical and operational use of information within an organization is of paramount importance: "Technical knowledge is important for appreciating strategic IS opportunities for the business, and for assessing how to implement them" (Skyrme and Earl 1990).

Just consider the impact of electronic data interchange (EDI) in shaping retail strategies.

A hybrid manager is an individual whose skills enable a unique contribution to be made to a changing environment. At the British Computer Society's conference "Developing Hybrid Managers", Dr Robb Wilmot's paper clearly makes the case that:

> one manager cannot make the difference: the entire organization, its structure, processes, job definitions and people, its systems all have to be redesigned synchronously (Wilmot 1990).

Threats and Challenges Ahead

There is no shortage of literature identifying the opportunity for organizational and technological change. The only certainty is that technological change will be continuous:

> The fact that companies have failed to gain full value from their past IT investment reflects past inflexibility in the structure of business and management, together with the rigidity and intimidating cost of then available technological solutions. Both rigidities are fast collapsing (Price Waterhouse 1991).

The Management in the 90s Research Programme undertaken by the Sloan School of Management at the Massachusetts Institute of Technology between June 1984 and November 1989 (MIT90) (Morton 1991) had the stated aim:

> To develop a better understanding of the managerial issues of the 1990s and how to deal most effectively with them, particularly as these issues revolve around the anticipated advances in Information Technology.

The programme examined a very extensive range of issues, in a research partnership between MIT and commerce, industry and government. ICL was one of the industry partners, and issues that are generally relevant to ICL and its customers have been summarized in ICL (1990).

Issues for changing organizations and individuals within them include technological change, the handling of change and organizational culture.

Technological Change

MIT90 (Morton 1991) suggests five stages of information technology exploitation:

- Localized exploitation
- Internal integration

  These two changes usually result in departmental reorganization. However, the following ways of exploiting IT require fundamental changes in business practices. Enhanced capability comes with major organizational restructuring.

- Business-process redesign

  At this level new ways of doing business are explored.

- Network redesign

  Opportunity is provided for redesigning the balance between organizations, for example, creating better links with customers and suppliers.

- Scope redefinition

A company may move into new areas of business.

The progression outlined above and the movement into the areas involving significant changes in business practices is substantiated by MID projects which are carried out in delegates' places of work.

One project (Masters 1989) was the business analysis for the production of an integrated plant and circuits information system for electricity utilities. At the start of the work the introduction of IT had greatly assisted the engineering task but much vital information was still held in a manual format, particularly circuit related data on maps and diagrams. Most engineering systems were:

> *independent applications fulfilling a single task and not interworking with any other systems. There is certainly no integration between plant and circuit data and engineers are obliged to refer to multiple information sources in the course of their work.*

Three years elapsed between the commencement of the analysis and the product launch in 1989, and:

> *in that time significant changes had occurred in the market place which have a direct impact on the success of the product (Masters 1989).*

Privatization had caused a major shift in emphasis; the immediate issues were with management of the Board's assets. In the concluding review further enhancements were proposed to assist in the new directions for the Boards. Two were identified:

- Asset management. "A major aspect of Plant and Circuits is its ability to record all the Board's assets" (Masters 1989).
- Customer cross-referencing. "Customer details are spread around a number of systems . . . and there is no way of finding out everything about a single customer. . . . An extension to the Plant and Circuits, to link a property to an existing customer is being developed [which will help provide] a single, centralised customer database" (Masters 1989).

A current project looks at inventory (asset) management and especially at the:

> task of creating and maintaining a database that reflects the real world status of machines which are under contractual cover.

I include this example project as it demonstrates "business network redesign" and the possibility of new forms of links between organizations. The author of the project states in a working document:

> the challenge is to develop an inventory control method that encourages the customer to control their fixed assets, and pass on the changes to us. I would argue that . . . the database in use by the customer is our own, so that changes are not reported as such, they merely implement the changes on what appears to be a local database.

These serve as an example of students' projects; other projects also indicate that the graduates of this MSc course, within their organizations, are taking on real challenges in proposing strategic IS opportunities.

Handling Change

The use of IT in departmental situations has shown that success results only when departmental management actively supports and is committed to the success of the undertaking. As the scope of IT increases, similar commitment is needed of the organization as a whole (Macdonald 1992). But can it be done? Wilmot (1990) emphasizes that:

> the organization has to understand that it is not programme-of-the-year stuff, but a major commitment to change in the way of doing business that is inevitable, that the enormous sunk cost in today's organization has to be written off, and that without pain there is no gain.

Not only is it essential to have a redesigned and re-engineered organization but:

> possibly more critical is the resulting organisation's ability to continuously change, or learn-acquiring experience and knowledge and putting it to competitive use (Wilmot 1990).

It is not just a case of keeping up with technological change, but also of identifying human aspects related to those changes. Pens are not merely replaced by terminals. Each change in technology changes an individual's way of working. Technology not only changes the attitude of the individual to new ways of working but also, possibly more importantly, also changes relationships with his (or her) fellow workers both inside the company and outside. Group working poses a challenge to the way people communicate in both small and large groups. Team working can extend across internal and external boundaries. The challenge for information systems in the 1990s is:

> to create the networked organization – where multi-functional teams are literally global, production resources are globally integrated, and customers and suppliers interface globally and locally, all tied together in networks with cost performance far surpassing anything we typically have in our plans today (Wilmot 1990).

The beginning of such integration was demonstrated by the MSc projects above. The management challenges will be to handle information networks with multiple alliances and collaborations, teams working 24 hours a day collaborating through a network and the understanding of people-to-people communication through IT supported networks:

> The organization is information (Wilmot 1990).

The MSc in Information Systems has been addressing and continues to focus on the vital role of information as the key to organizational success:

> Using the power of IT to liberate and empower the individual at the same time as integrating him into the global enterprise is a massive cultural challenge, as is electronic trading between corporations that in essence never sleep (Wilmot 1990).

Organizational Culture

The MIT90 findings have raised leadership issues, particularly supporting the role of agent of change:

> It is no longer acceptable for leadership to be preoccupied with maintaining the status quo. Their first priority is to predict requirements for change and the second to plan and implement it (ICL 1990).

As individual managers they don't have the power; the extent of change will depend on the scope for change within an organization, which in turn depends on the organizational culture: the learned basic assumptions of an organization. Changing culture is a slow process:

> The very nature of culture is to preserve the past, to prevent the hotshot hybrid manager . . . from succeeding and changing the status

quo. Culture is there to stop us investing in and creating the future, but leadership is what starts when consensus finishes.

Hybrids are a force for changing the business. They can make things happen. They can conceive of brilliant new ways to do things, can sell the idea, and implement it, recognizing the sociological difficulty of interfacing with the corporate establishment, and the need to involve and mobilise large numbers of people to get fast and high pay off (Wilmot 1990).

Graduates of this course have demonstrated their ability to contribute in all of these ways, but only in a changing and receptive organization can the full benefit be gained.

Education in the 1990s

The MSc in Information Systems Design and Management at Kingston has recognized not only the importance of developing individual skills as a hybrid manager but that those skills must be integrated with the organization. The taught part of the course is applied through reports and course work in the delegates' places of work. Customers are both organizations who sponsor delegates and contribute to the continuous change and direction of the course and those individual delegates who participate directly. Education cannot escape change:

If management education is to be of real use to companies in the future it will (like many of those companies) have to undergo radical restructuring. It will have to move away from the "one shot" approach towards what might be called "continuous learning". Shorter courses for experienced managers will become the key to the school's usefulness and profitability. (Economist 1991)

The above was said of MBA courses but it is my belief that it is true for all courses that claim to provide postgraduate education relevant to delegates with business experience. Continuous learning implies the opportunity to select a programme of study, from a single short course to a full programme leading to a postgraduate qualification. Programmes will need to be flexible and responsive to change, enabling customers (whether individuals or companies) to tailor their learning, taking into account previous background and current aspirations. It involves education and companies working together to allow individuals' outdated skills to be refreshed and new expertise learned. Tighter partnership will be essential to ensure both business relevance and academic rigour in the provision of education for the changing organizations of the 1990s. This is the continuing strategy for the MSc in Information Systems at Kingston.

13 Undergraduate Hybrids

Stuart J. Fitz-Gerald

It is clear that industry wants hybrids. Furthermore, it knows what it wants hybrids to do. What is not clear is where they will come from. As educators, we have an important role to play: indeed, we have a perfect opportunity to focus the debate. Since the early 1980s, polytechnics, universities and colleges of higher education have been searching for an appropriate formula to produce students who exhibit the qualities alluded to in earlier chapters. A large number of courses have been introduced, and Kingston University has been particularly active in this field.

After a number of false starts, it was recognized that a "bolt on" solution was inappropriate. Tampering with established courses such as business studies, accounting and finance, and computer science, which already possessed a well-defined market, was clearly second best. Instead, a purpose-built solution was pursued, as discussed by Skok and Fitz-Gerald (1989). This approach has resulted in undergraduate courses in the following subjects:

- Business information technology
- Information systems design

Both brands pursue a triad of principal themes:

- Business operations and functions
- Decision analysis and support
- Information technology

and include periods of industrial placement. These structures have allowed the development of a number of exciting new approaches which take advantage of the hybrid nature of the courses and also utilize the sandwich element. Firstly, the sandwich structure has allowed the final year to be treated very much as a "post-experience" year, giving ample opportunity for students and managers to benefit from joint seminars and collaboration. Secondly, substantial group projects have been introduced, where final year students have acted as independent consultants to a number of large organizations. Their hybrid skills have been used to tackle a variety of "real" problems within the participating organizations. The resulting reports have been professionally executed and presented to the companies, who have found the solutions offered both innovative and constructive. This new dimension to the courses has reinforced the belief and support of organizations in our efforts to produce hybrids at the undergraduate level.

The roots of these courses lie respectively in business studies and computer studies, and are an important addition to the typical portfolio of courses on offer within the polytechnics. A typical example set is shown below:

- Undergraduate:
  - Business studies
  - Accounting and finance
  - Business information technology
  - Information systems design
  - Computer studies
  - Computer science

- Postgraduate:
  - MBA
  - Certificate in management
  - MSc in management studies
  - MSc in business IT
  - MSc in information systems design
  - MSc in computer science

The outcome of these experiments has given considerable satisfaction to employers and students. Employers found that the products of these courses were quickly able to act very productively in the organization, adapting to a variety of computing environments and using their business training in tandem, and willing to share their skills with other members of the organization. Students have encountered a satisfying learning experience and found that their potential for ultimate permanent employment was significantly enhanced, particularly as "standard bearers" for business information technology. Substantial "ripple effects" were also generated, causing traditional business studies and accounting courses to re-evaluate their own delivery of IT. This, coupled with a rapidly developing computing infrastructure, has resulted in the generation of an appropriate IT culture among both staff and students, enabling them to adapt quickly to a constantly changing IT environment.

It should be pointed out that participating staff have been drawn from a variety of disciplines. Their various psychological "roots" have not proved a major constraint, while students have responded admirably to the many challenges laid before them. The story at the undergraduate level is therefore an encouraging one.

A Change of Attitudes

The original definition of a hybrid used by the British Computer Society (Palmer and Otley 1990) failed to grasp the enormous gulf in attitudes between undergraduate students and those who had already gained some industrial experience. A desire to learn and explore alien ideas, drawn from business and technology, is a necessary condition for becoming a hybrid.

The existing attitudes of middle management and the conventional training structures that they adopt do not encourage the necessary inquisitiveness to become a hybrid. Until this changes we will not be able to produce hybrids in sufficient numbers to meet demand.

Isaac Newton believed that he saw further because he stood on the shoulders of giants. If industry is to harness IT effectively, the giants of both business and computer science must be studied and understood to produce real hybrids. Until industry recognizes that understanding of, and not just a nodding acquaintance with, the triad of business, decision making and IT is essential for the real production of hybrids, hybrid managers will remain a rare late-20th century curiosity.

V | KNOWLEDGE BASED TRAINING SYSTEMS

Editorial Overview

It was once assumed that training systems could be developed more easily, and with more limited resources, than systems intended for mainstream business use. Expert systems could be made into tutoring systems to teach the expert knowledge represented in the system. Such assumptions have proved naive and flawed, although illuminating research has been conducted in the process, drawing together education, training, psychology and knowledge based systems. Our contributors work with affordable systems, and with real business and professional users, rather than in the research laboratory.

Jonathan Briggs, Chris Tompsett and Nick Oates (Chapter 14) describe work in the emerging field of intelligent hypermedia, where they have been developing training systems for pharmacists. Representing expert knowledge and making it available for interactive exploration has proved successful in pilot trials, and raises major questions for business applications. How much do we know about our users, and how much do we want to allow them to learn? Should exploration and learning be tightly structured, or free and unconstrained, and what are the implications for interfaces and system design?

Sheenagh Wreyford (Chapter 15) reports on the development and use of ATR-trainer, a training expert system tool, and its evaluation as a training tool in comparison with conventional computer based training methods. As with similar earlier honest evaluations of innovative technology, it provides some chastening conclusions and questions concerning the operation and culture of organizations.

Robert Taylor (Chapter 16) and his management consultancy colleagues have sought to develop a methodology for the development of knowledge based systems, offering greater reliability for systems developed by the growing community of knowledge based software engineers. Focusing on the application category of knowledge based training systems, and ATR trainer in particular, he returns to issues raised earlier by Skok (Chapter 3).

Knowledge based systems, and information systems in general, should not be considered simply as products for sale and exploitation, but as outcomes of processes of interactive development. Managers may gain from experience of using such tools to probe their areas of uncertainty and incomplete information, offering a form of qualitative decision support to complement the battery of quantitative tools and techniques. Success depends on an admission of fallibility, that in the real world managers cannot always be "right first time", and must be able to learn from experience.

14 | Towards Knowledge Based Hypermedia

Jonathan H. Briggs, Chris Tompsett and Nick Oates

Introduction

This chapter outlines the development of hypermedia systems for training and job support. It proposes the application of techniques from knowledge based systems to support their effective development. The central focus concerns a project for the UK Department of Health to construct a computer based learning package for updating community pharmacists, and results of an evaluation are included. The chapter concludes with a discussion of further possible applications of these techniques in the production of hypermedia.

Hypertext and Exploratory Learning

Hypertext provides a new way for information to be organized using computers. Instead of the formal structure imposed by most flat file or relational databases, hypertext allows informal links to be established between data items. Reading a hypertext becomes similar to browsing a reference book or encyclopedia – it's up to the reader to decide on their own route through the material. With the addition of pictures, graphics, sound and moving video, hypertext becomes hypermedia.

Trainers and educators have welcomed the arrival of hypertext and hypermedia, represented by a rush of products, including HyperCard, Toolbook, Guide and Plus. No longer is the trainer constrained to the limited resources available within a few textbooks and a handful of films, but is now offered an almost unlimited resource centre open to each student. Linking the concept of hypertext to the storage technologies of CD offers a learning resource of unparalleled richness.

Both technical and non-technical subjects can now access source materials that lie at the heart of the study of these subjects. The critical question is whether these resources can become a genuine exploratory learning environment or whether they will remain as underused as the typical reference library or archive of art and photography.

The Hyperspace Maze

The most efficient users of information resources today are those who already know what knowledge is available from the resource. They understand how related knowledge is conceptually organized and how the resource is logically structured. The logical structuring determines the physical arrangement of the information, and all that hypertext/media offers is a richer mapping of the logical structuring of the information.

In training we are faced with the problem that those who will use the resources may not have a clearly defined structure of how the information is conceptually related or of how it is organized. Although exploratory learning is not the only educational application of hypermedia it is the most exciting, and this approach implies that the exploration is of new knowledge rather than a re-examination of what is already known. From this point of view the hypersystem is a hyperspace maze of information. The rooms of the maze are nodes at which information is located and the doors leading to further rooms represent allowed links between the rooms.

Learning in this maze can only take place if the student is able to navigate the maze efficiently, but major problems arise when a student is presented with a new large hypermedia system. The progress of the student from node to node is made as a series of decisions based on the information that is available at a node and the links that have been created by the author.

The dangers facing all users of large hypermedia systems arise from the very freedom that is allowed to them. There is nothing to prevent the associations that link two adjacent nodes being used to traverse an incoherent collection of information nuggets. With a large hypermedia system you can progress from Beethoven to piano to ivory to elephant to India to tea to coffee houses and so on, and end up totally lost, possessing some knowledge but having gained nothing from the hypermedia system. Too much information has been ignored and too much has become irrelevant for the associations between pieces of information to support either learning or insight.

Problems of Construction

Although the hypermedia concept provides an ideal model for the way in which we wish our own knowledge to be recorded, this ideal is based on *post hoc* considerations. If we are asked to describe why we leap from one idea to the next we quite happily provide the connecting link (as with the early views of semantic nets (Quillian 1968)). If asked to specify in advance what direct links there should be from one piece of knowledge to any other possible pieces of knowledge, we realize the lack of methodology that exists for the generation of large hypermedia systems. Without a coherent methodology, many existing interactive systems could claim to be hypermedia systems. The most restrictive forms of computer based training contain the same ingredients (nodes and links) even if the links are non-democratic (you do not choose which link to follow). Hypermedia is still an ideal but not yet an identifiable approach to information structuring.

Authors face similar problems in constructing hypermedia systems as users do in making use of them. Above a certain size, the author loses track of which parts have been completed and which elements remain to be extended. Structuring is advocated before writing, but this presupposes that the material does not already exist – in most cases we will want to make use of existing textual resources, augmented by new material. As hyperdocuments grow the combinatorial complexity of providing links increases dramatically. The authoring problem is the problem of creating large documents with sufficient openness but sufficient structure to guide the authoring of the system itself.

This problem is symptomatic of the current total lack of principles and support for the writing of hypermedia systems. When it is answered, the author (and teams of authors) will be able to create systems within an editorial structure that manages the addition of nodes, automates the provision of links and provides structures and boundaries to the authoring process.

Creating Links

The intelligent creation of links is the most difficult process required of the author. At this stage it is worth categorizing links into three types:

- Global
- Generated
- Hand-crafted

Global links provide direct access between nodes irrespective of the information content or structure of the nodes. An example of such a link would be a "find next occurrence of this word" link, based strictly on the existence of the word in a piece of text and bearing no relationship to the meaning of the word and context of its use.

Generated links are created by the system, are more restrictive in their action, and presume that the author has made decisions about the purpose and function of a node. A simple example would be the use of keywords to describe the approximate content of a node. Although this is similar to the previous type, these links provide semantic associations rather than syntactic ones. The authoring decision in this case is the selection of the set of keywords. Such a decision makes implicit assumptions about the purpose of recording the information.

The third type, hand-crafted, are the individual, non-systematic links created by the author. Such links may encompass the most interesting experiences in using hypermedia systems but are the most difficult to plan coherently, and fail to map consistently onto the document as a whole.

Our interest is in the application of knowledge based techniques to the authoring problem and the benefits that this approach offers to the guiding and assistance of students in browsing the resulting system. Of particular interest is constructing systems based on existing teaching and learning resources. Large hypertexts, if they are to meet the needs of a wide variety of learners, must also be easy to update and maintain.

Linking Automatically

The work of the authors has focused on trying to assist the process of constructing links by using techniques from knowledge based systems, and attempting to form the links automatically from text using an intermediate representation. Associated with each card or text chunk is a collection of formal statements. These are coded in a high level formalism such as that provided by the language PROLOG. These statements describe the "knowledge" contained in a card and together constitute a "concept network".

The concept network provides an underlying knowledge based framework to support browsing. Hierarchical structuring of the concept network provides the higher level organization of the knowledge, and each concept can be related – linked – to more general concepts in a deterministic fashion.

These links provide a conceptual structure that allows each of the documents or images in the system to be accessed in a consistent manner, using generated links. Further global links are provided to mimic the global access methods that are typically used – dictionaries, glossaries etc. Hand-crafted links are only present as serendipitous, self-contained experiences, which are not expected to be generalizable in their character.

The problem for new students browsing the network is still, however, the vast range of information available if browsing is unconstrained. Four approaches are possible with this knowledge based
structure to systematically restrict the nodes that are accessible and
the material that is presented. The use of focusing techniques related
to information that is available (as above) is one such method.
Two further techniques, bottom-up and top-down restrictions on the
hierarchical structure, limiting browsing to sections of the network, are
both simple to achieve and consistent with natural teaching strategies.
A fourth strategy, which we have termed "slicing", was founded on
user modelling concepts but is applicable in knowledge base terms
alone. The knowledge base was designed to represent many facets
of the knowledge concerned, from economic aspects to operating
instructions. For various "users" areas of the knowledge base were
defined to be irrelevant and these aspects of the knowledge were
"closed off" (with soft boundaries that could be broken if the user
"forced" the system to open them).

Each technique provides a coherent approach to limiting the size
and scope of the nodes, and hence the information that is initially
accessible. The knowledge based structure then allows for systematic
relaxation of any of these restrictions as the student explores the
knowledge.

Case Study: Computer Aided Learning
for Pharmacists

For the past two years, the authors have been funded by a Department of Health project to design a training system for community
pharmacists. The learners in this particular system are the practising
pharmacists, who have already undergone many years of professional
study, and the system is aimed at updating their skills and knowledge
while providing the opportunity for revision of core information.

Design for a Hypertext Learning Environment

The authors proposed a model for the system that went beyond the
"diagnostic expert system" envisaged by the funders, making use of
the knowledge based augmentation already described. A system that
could only review a set of presenting symptoms and recommend a
treatment might be of use to pharmacy customers, but would be

of limited interest to pharmacists. Pharmacists need to be aware of the complex relationships between similar sets of symptoms and similar sets of products and drugs, and, in recommending a product, must feel secure both in their selection of one treatment and their rejection of others. A straightforward expert systems approach supports the correct selection in a particular case but is weak in supporting the more general knowledge required to reject other treatments. Indeed, training systems built in this way convey most of their "knowledge" in text presented after a decision has been reached.

The system we proposed supports exploration of the problem space (and thus learning) in many different ways. By volunteering partial details for a patient, a restricted view of the domain can be explored: for example, with all material on elderly patients filtered out. The system supports comparison – of different types of medication, for example – and the study of alternatives. It combines the diagnostic capabilities of the expert system with additional features to support the decision making of the pharmacist, by functioning as a reference manual, as a refresher course on basic material, and by allowing "what if" questions to be raised. By changing one detail about the duration of a symptom, for example, the user can see what additional (or changed) information would be provided.

The system design attempts to enhance the simple hypertext model (Conklin 1987) with the addition of knowledge based guidance rules. From the learner's point of view, cards or pages of information are presented, concerning drugs, symptoms, diseases or advice about general therapy. The cards are presented to the reader one at a time. From any card, the user can browse to related or associated cards. These "links" are selected from a menu, and it is this feature that gives the system its multidimensional "hypertext" character. The reader can retrace his or her steps to allow previous cards to be reviewed and alternative links to be explored.

The knowledge contained on each card has been elicited from pharmacy experts and/or adapted from appropriate textbooks. Associated with each card is a formal summary of the knowledge it contains (Fig. 14.1). It is important to note that the text that appears on the screen, is "as described by the pharmacist". It uses appropriate technical language and has been phrased as far as possible in the same form as it would appear in a book or indeed in a more conventional computer based learning program.

The system generates a link between two cards by reasoning about these descriptions. A set of general rules is used to define different types of links, and additional special links can be crafted by describing the relationships between the appropriate cards.

Links are of the general form:

link from any card about a condition (e.g. asthma) to cards about the
symptoms of that condition (e.g. shortness of breath, wheeze etc.).

```
Croup

This usually occurs in infants, with a peak incidence of 18 months to 3
years.  The cough has a harsh barking quality.  It develops a day or so
after the onset of cold-like symptoms.  It is often associated with
difficulty in breathing, and an inspiratory stridor (noise in throat on
breathing in).  GP referral is necessary.

CARD 7 ABOUT CROUP

introduces croup.
presumes symptoms includes inspiratory stridor.
typically patient restrictions includes
         age of patient is young child.
if disease is croup then
         nature of cough is harsh and barking.
typically associated symptoms includes
         difficulty in breathing.
typically nature of cough is inspiratory stridor.
advice includes GP referral.

KNOWLEDGE for Card 7
```

Fig. 14.1. A LINCTUS PB card with its associated knowledge base.

Knowledge Based Diagnosis

A second knowledge based component has been introduced into the
prototype system with the inclusion of a "current patient" card. Additional links into the network of information cards can be generated
automatically once a patient has been described, thus providing a
"conversational diagnosis" facility. The patient card is initially blank.
The reader uses a "volunteer information" command, and associated
menus, to build a description of a particular individual case using a set
of predefined terms. This was selected as a mode of input in preference
to typing because it allows the easy entry of complex medical terms
without these having to be checked for spelling and synonyms.

At any time the system can browse from this information into the
web of cards. The information contained in the patient card is then
used to restrict the valid links that can be followed. For example,
the pharmacist could describe a patient with the following signs and
symptoms:

Age: elderly
Presenting symptom: cough
Nature of cough: productive
Colour of sputum: clear/white

The system would now provide the reader with links from the patient card to cards that describe the recommended action for an elderly patient with a productive cough. At the same time the cards relating specifically to children or unproductive (dry) cough will be made unavailable to the browser, as the system constructs hierarchies of the major concepts, distinguishing between subset and partitioning classifications. Links to the wider set of cards is possible if the user issues a "free browse" instruction to the system. This diagnostic behaviour is achieved by including additional rules within the system. Examples are shown in Fig. 14.2.

The authors selected this style of "diagnosis" for several reasons. It is common for the pharmacist to be confronted with only a partial description of a patient; customers are often asking for advice on behalf of someone else. This means that the conventional question and answer dialogue favoured by most expert systems would be inappropriate because often some of the information is not available. With the LINCTUS PB prototype, as many or as few details can be entered as required. The order in which facts are added is also arbitrary, reflecting once again the reality of the existing pharmacist/customer relationship. The design adopted, however, does prioritize the items in the questioning menus to cause "more important" information to be placed near the top. In the absence of further volunteered information, the pharmacist would be encouraged to ask for this information first.

The explicit exclusion/inclusion model described has been designed to reflect the way in which our experts wish trained pharmacists to work. When provided with a symptom or observation (for example, blood in the sputum) pharmacists should not rush to any single conclusion but should include in their possible recommendations all the conditions/advice for which this could be appropriate. The system behaves in a similar fashion, excluding cards that are inappropriate to the described symptoms and prioritizing the included cards to highlight critical material.

```
if duration of cough is recurrent
  then include advice is GP Referral

if nature of sputum is frothy
  then include possible diagnosis is Heart Failure and
  exclude possible diagnosis is bronchitis and
  exclude possible diagnosis is pneumonia.

if age is elderly
  then include what you need to know and
  exclude possible diagnosis is croup and
  exclude possible diagnosis is childhood wheezy bronchitis
```

Fig. 14.2. Diagnostic rules to include/exclude links.

The Current System

LINCTUS PB has been prototyped using PROLOG. This has allowed a clear separation between the knowledge rules and processing engine. To allow large amounts of text to be viewed without holding the text in memory, the system accesses appropriate cards directly from disk. Sufficient speed is achieved by indexing the text and holding the index in memory. The knowledge statements for each piece of text are stored in the same text file. A PROLOG program loads and parses these to create the database from which the links can be deduced. A separate file of general rules (directly coded in PROLOG) is used to generate these links. These links can be "pre-compiled" before the system is used. To allow the prototype to be small enough to fit on the target hardware it is then possible to remove the knowledge used to generate them. The diagnostic rules, however, remain in the final distributed software because these are required to manipulate the patients presented.

The first small prototype was constructed and evaluated with ten pharmacists. Their initial reactions and requests for changes were incorporated into a revised system. The major change at this stage was a revision of the language used in the text, which they considered too simple.

The second prototype contains over 250 cards and 120 include/exclude diagnostic rules. The information encoded supports up to 11,000 potential links, which are reduced and sequenced at any particular instance by further knowledge based rules. It covers the treatment of most major upper respiratory tract symptoms/conditions such as coughs, colds, hay fever, and so on.

The system does not recommend particular products or preparations, but identifies appropriate drugs that these products should contain. This was a decision taken by our experts and the steering group for the project. Inclusion of a few selected products would have been open to criticism from those pharmaceutical companies whose products had not been selected. Inclusion of all products would have resulted in a system that became rapidly out of date. In addition, it was felt that, though such information was valuable to particular pharmacies, it should be a professional decision for the pharmacists concerned on the basis of the material that was provided in the system, i.e. the therapeutic content and not the promotional literature provided by the drug companies. Automatic linking of diagnosis to products could reduce the attention paid by pharmacists to the content of the "over the counter" preparations that they sell. This particular feature distinguishes the system from a more routine decision support tool.

Text Based Materials

The system is supported by written case studies and other learning materials. It is important to put this sort of software in an educational context. Learning is not equivalent to looking up information. It is vital to indicate to the learner the patterns in the knowledge; the similarities between conditions, for example, or the exceptions to particular rules. These are highlighted by offering case studies that bring out these differences and similarities. This reflects the common approach to post-qualification training in the pharmacy field, which is through presentation and discussion of case studies.

Evaluation

In general, reactions to the materials have been varied but favourable. The results are striking both in terms of the response to the materials and the variation in the trial group. The group is evenly split between computer literate and non-computer literate users. This is reflected in patterns of usage, with computer-literate users taking advantage of home computers and using longer sessions with the materials, while others use the system in the workplace as the opportunity arises, alternating use of the computer between labelling and training. In the latter case, pressure of work varies from pharmacy to pharmacy, and influences the length of sessions used to study the materials. The open structure of the materials seems to accommodate this variation successfully, with "intelligent" browsing being an appropriate access vehicle both for short (10 minute) and longer (1 hour or more) sessions.

Access to the material through the diagnosis model or through the general browser and index has also allowed different patterns of study to emerge. Some of the trial group have principally used the diagnostic model to support controlled exploration of the material, linked to the study materials in a coherent training programme. Others have preferred the more open access directly available through the browser and index mechanisms. In effect, these users take more active participation in exploring the materials themselves, using their own knowledge to cut off non-relevant information. Perhaps the clearest statement that can be made, on the basis of the size of the trialling group considered so far, is that the materials offer a single resource that users have been able to adapt to their own style of learning. It might appear that where users are not happy to make use of the materials in any of the ways considered, then these people are already taking advantage of existing "traditional course" provision.

Further Applications

The model that has been described could be applied to many different domains. Firstly, it provides a paradigm for any hypertext learning system that is to be based on existing textual materials. In reality this will only prove useful if it makes sense to link together material that has a degree of organizable content matching that of the pharmacy area. The chosen domain contains well-defined categories of information: drugs, products, symptoms, patient characteristics and so on. This identifies, in an abstract sense, the associativity and dependency between concepts, and provides a clear focus or purpose for the browsing in that the browser will usually be attempting to locate appropriate information to reflect a particular case.

The nature of the learning supported (which we currently term "information based learning") is not, however, that supported by conventional computer based training. Where a clearly defined and homogeneous group of learners can be identified, the flexibility inherent in the system could be considered to be a limitation. This system is of most benefit where the learner is assumed to be in control of their own learning – typically, where their own needs are distinct from others either through design (being given open tasks to perform) or through opportunity (having a specific and unpredictable need for new information and the development of relevant new concepts).

A comparable application under discussion is in the field of management education. New entrants to a company require access to a range of information concerning the personnel, practices and procedures particular to the organization. Comprehensive training programmes for new staff provide too much factual information too quickly for learning to take place. Information based learning on the model proposed allows the pertinent information to be acquired according to need, ensuring early application of the information and concepts. Issues in project management, for example, can be presented through the proposed model in a format that allows comparison of perhaps non-compatible viewpoints, with the advantages and limitations of each being resolved as a particular scenario (a "case") is described.

In parallel to this project, a series of studies is also being conducted into the application of this approach to student learning at Kingston University. Funded through the Academic Development Fund of the university, the authors are currently developing pilot materials in the fields of programming languages, building construction, art history and music appreciation. Studies are also under way to design a version of the software to support multimedia presentation of materials.

Acknowledgements

The work described has been funded by the UK Department of Health, and managed jointly by the College of Pharmacy Practice and the National Council for Educational Technology. Expertise for the project has been provided by Dr Alison Blenkinsopp and Dr John Purvis of Bradford University.

15 | An Intelligent Computer Based Training System: Evaluation and Development

Sheenagh Wreyford

Introduction

ATR trainer, a courseware authoring tool developed at Kingston University, was the subject of a research project to evaluate its effectiveness compared with conventional computer based training (CBT). A nationwide field study, with a matched-subjects design, was conducted by Royal Insurance. The objective of the courseware was to teach trainees to underwrite and rate proposals for private car insurance.

Results of the study showed no significant differences between the teaching effectiveness of the two types of system. Trainees in the CBT group demonstrated positive attitudes to the courseware, while the attitudes of those using the ATR trainer courseware were essentially negative. Further developments made to the ATR trainer system in the light of these findings are reported, with a discussion of how the technology might provide improved training systems.

ATR Trainer

ATR trainer was developed by Advanced Training Research at Kingston University (French 1987, 1990). Based on expert system technology, it takes the form of a "shell" into which the courseware author inserts only the knowledge to be taught. Knowledge is entered as if–then rules with associated presentation material, and all decisions about how to teach the material are made by the system itself.

A Learning Environment

In ATR trainer, a knowledge base can be used in two modes (see Fig. 15.1). Firstly, it can be used as a conventional expert system, to

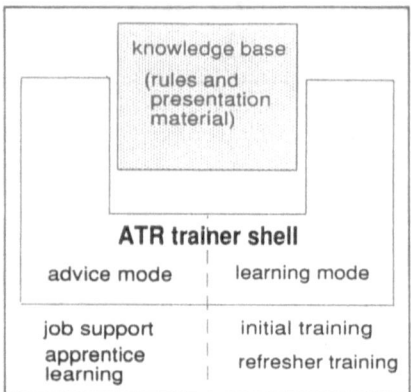

Fig. 15.1. Dual mode of operation in ATR trainer.

provide advice with full explanation and "what if" facilities. This can supplement other forms of training, or perform a job-support role, a recognized value of expert systems. It is the second mode of use, a training mode, which makes ATR trainer unique and innovative; it provides a learning environment that gives the trainee access to knowledge contained within the knowledge base which would normally only be revealed to the user in expert system mode in a piecemeal fashion, if explanations were demanded. From the trainee's perspective, the courseware is divided into a network of related topics, each topic consisting of a number of pages of information (see Fig. 15.2).

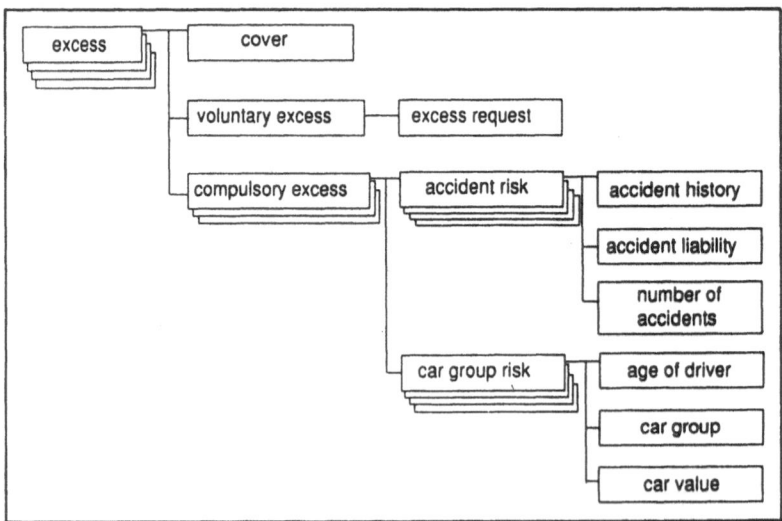

Fig. 15.2. A network of related topics.

Topics are the conceptual entities in the knowledge base, whose relationships are determined by the logic of the rules. The trainee is free to browse at will between related topics along the pathways determined by the logical structure of the knowledge base. The trainee has control over progress through the material to be learnt; and can retrace chosen pathways in order to review material.

Illustrative Examples and Tests

Once sufficient information on a topic has been seen, the trainee can view illustrative examples or undergo tests on that topic. Appropriate examples and tests are generated automatically by the system as they are requested.

Trainee Modelling

ATR trainer maintains a model of each trainee, which records the individual's progress on a particular piece of courseware and fulfils the following purposes:

- To guide the trainee's progress through the courseware.
- To allow ATR trainer to decide when the trainee is ready for illustrative examples or tests.
- To monitor the trainee's performance on tests.
- To allow the trainee to suspend and resume a training session whenever convenient.

The model forms the basis of a report to the trainer on the trainee's progress and performance. ATR trainer courseware provides a learning environment which offers flexibility of use to the trainee, while monitoring the trainee's progress for the benefit of both the trainee and the trainer.

The Evaluation Study

ATR trainer was evaluated in a project carried out with Royal Insurance (UK) Ltd between October 1988 and March 1990, funded by the Training Agency under the Artificial Intelligence Applications to Learning

Programme (Phase II). A full report of the study has been published by the Training Agency (Department of Employment 1991).

Objectives of the Study

The study proposed to evaluate the effectiveness of ATR trainer used in training mode, by comparing it with an equivalent conventional CBT course. The incorporation of trainee-modelling in ATR trainer provides a flexible learner-centred approach, allowing the system to respond to individual needs and learning styles. The study concerned the effect that the use of a trainee model might have on the speed and accuracy of learning, and its retention over time.

The teaching objective selected was the training of new entrants to Royal Insurance to underwrite and rate proposal forms received from prospective clients requiring private car insurance. Trainees need to learn to assess the acceptability of proposals, and to prepare quotations, if appropriate.

Evaluation Methodology

The evaluation study was carried out by Royal Insurance at twelve branches located throughout the country.

Design

The study was a matched subjects design. Trainees were matched according to three criteria: their education level, their length of time with the company, and post-test scores on CBT induction courses. Of each matched pair, one trainee studied the ATR trainer courseware, and the other studied the CBT courseware. The CBT courseware, prepared by Royal Insurance, was a modification of existing modules using the SAM IV authoring tool. To guarantee the equivalence of the two pieces of courseware, a content specification was compiled which described the training objectives, and the scope and range of the material to be included. The presentation styles of the two pieces of courseware were dissimilar, in that the ATR trainer courseware was purely text based, whereas the CBT contained animated graphics.

Procedure

Each trainee was allocated a maximum of 10 hours, in study sessions lasting 1 hour, over a 4–6 week period, to complete the courseware, and a further 1-hour revision session reading the Motor Rating Manual not more than 5 working days before the first post-test. This was intended to minimize the effects of some trainees having completed the training early in the 6-week period, who might otherwise have forgotten some of the material. The first post-test was conducted at the end of the training period, and the second a further 6 weeks later. For both tests, trainees were required to underwrite twenty examples of proposal forms.

Measures

Trainees were marked on their ability to allocate proposal forms appropriately to three categories (acceptable, referable and unacceptable), and on the accuracy of the quotations prepared for acceptable proposals. A total of 19 statistical tests were carried out on the data from the first post-test, to examine:

- Differences between the two groups on the accuracy of answers to various parts of the first post-test, on speed of learning and on retention of material.
- Correlations within the two groups between overall scores and other measures (e.g. amount of note-taking during training).

The measure of trainees' retention of material was the difference between their overall scores on the first and second post-tests. Two statistical tests were carried out on this measure; one considered trainees who had gained some experience of car insurance underwriting since the first post-test, and the other those who with no such interim experience. Trainees' attitudes to the courseware were measured by their responses to a 7-point scale questionnaire completed after the training. They were also invited to justify their ratings. The questions were designed to elicit attitudes on ease of use and enjoyment of the courseware.

Results

Analysis of the data was carried out by Royal Insurance.

Quantitative Data

The average overall score for rating the twenty proposal forms in the first post-test was 40% for the ATR trainer group and 38.5% for the CBT group. There was no significant difference between these scores; none of the statistical tests carried out showed any significant differences between the two groups, except for the measure of hours spent studying the courseware. The ATR trainer group took significantly longer to complete the courseware (an average of 9.68 hours) than the CBT group (an average of 7.59 hours).

Qualitative Data

On all twelve measures of attitudes to the courseware, ratings indicated that the CBT courseware evoked more favourable attitudes than the ATR trainer courseware. The two groups expressed almost opposite views to the question "How enjoyable did you find the course?". The ATR trainer group on the whole did not enjoy the course, with comments such as "annoying", "confusing" and "frustrating". Two responses of "interesting" and "quite enjoyable" were tempered with comments about the software problems encountered. The CBT group, however, mostly indicated that the course was enjoyable. Only one respondent in this group described it as "long and boring".

Opinions on the colour schemes and graphics were varied in both groups, but with the balance in favour of the CBT courseware. Both groups complained of screens being too bright and garish, and giving them headaches. However, attitudes to the presence (CBT group) or absence (ATR trainer group) of graphics were diverse in both groups.

Points were felt to be made more clearly in the CBT group. Comments from the ATR trainer group suggest that individual points were clear, but that the confusing nature of the system meant that the context was lost. Twice as many trainees in the ATR trainer group found problems using the courseware, and this group had considerably more technical and procedural problems. A common criticism of the ATR trainer system was that it was "like a maze", "difficult to find way around" and "jumped about a lot". Technical problems were encountered with the ATR trainer system, and these contributed to the negative experiences of this group: "problems with the system", "errors and problems with the system meant loss of motivation and frustration", "a good course apart from memory load being exceeded".

Conclusions Drawn from the Evaluation

There was no difference in the accuracy or retention of learning between trainees using the ATR trainer system and those using the conventional CBT system. The only identifiable difference is the speed of learning. Trainees using the ATR trainer system needed to spend more time studying than those who used the CBT system. Although both systems were equally effective in providing training, trainees show positive attitudes to using CBT courseware, while the attitudes of those using the ATR trainer courseware are essentially negative.

These findings presented a paradox: the trainees using the ATR trainer system learnt as well as the other group, despite the fact that they had problems with the system and did not like using it. This raises the issue as to whether the inadequacies of ATR trainer could be alleviated so that the system could show significant improvements in effectiveness over conventional CBT.

Speeds of Learning

The measure of speed of learning was the number of hourly sessions that the individual trainee used, out of the 10 hours that were available. This measure does not indicate how much of those hours were actually spent learning. There were technical problems with the ATR trainer system, which meant that learning time within the allotted hour was lost. Several trainees in this group reported that they did not complete the courseware.

The question of time available for learning is an important issue. The ATR trainer courseware, unlike the CBT, is not constructed in 1-hour modules. The nature of the system allows for flexibility of use:

- The courseware may be suspended and resumed at any point.
- No fixed duration of study is required.
- The trainee is free to review as much material as necessary, as often as necessary.

The trainee is also free to view as many illustrative examples and undertake as many tests as she feels necessary; and works at the pace required for a full understanding of the material. There were some criticisms in the CBT course that points were "explained too quickly" and that it is "a problem remembering something which flashes up on a screen for only a few seconds". It is expected that learning times will vary using a flexible system of the nature of ATR trainer; time constraints place an artificial barrier on learning.

The Effectiveness of Technology Based Training Systems in General

On eleven measures of trainees' test performances there was no significant difference between the two types of courseware. Neither group can be said to have performed particularly well (40% and 38.5% mean overall scores). The results should not, however, throw into question the validity of technology based training. The luxury of hindsight suggests that the teaching objectives for this study were somewhat ambitious. It was perhaps unreasonable to expect that 10 hours training would produce trainees able to deal with the full range of insurance proposals. Some of the proposals given in the tests were representative of the types handled by the most experienced branch personnel; for some of the forms, it was difficult to get experts within the company to agree on the correct response. It is unlikely that even the expert underwriters would have scored a perfect 100%. To serve as a comparison, the details of an unofficial, non-statistical study are interesting. One branch training officer used the post-test on five trainees whose training had been "on the job". The extent of their training had varied, but all had included 6 weeks' experience in Motor Services. The average score was 48.8%. In the light of this information, scores of 40%, achieved with only 10 hours distance learning, seem more remarkable.

Developments to ATR Trainer in the Light of the Evaluation

How much better might the trainees have performed on the ATR trainer system if they had found it an easier and more enjoyable system to use? This full-scale evaluation provided feedback from users to indicate the course of future development of the user interface. Concerns of the trainees have since been addressed by ATR, by implementing certain improvements or by specifying the course that future research might take.

The major criticism of the ATR trainer system is its confusing nature. There are two factors that may contribute to this sense of confusion: the need to understand how the system operates, and the need to be able to locate oneself in the learning material.

Familiarization with Learning Environment

The richness of the learning environment brings with it a penalty for the trainee in the form of the need to learn how the environment works. The alternative would require the learner only to press the return key or select an option from a menu, inducing passivity. There will always be a trade-off between how easy a teaching system is to use, and how stimulating it can be as a learning environment.

There are four command options in ATR trainer that the trainee needs to grasp in order to browse the learning material: two for moving between topics (browse and go-back) and two for moving within topics (next and previous) (see Fig. 15.3).

Printed instructions were supplied, but not all trainees received them. Some trainees were confused initially, or did not know how to gain access to the material they wanted. Printed instructions are no substitute for guided hands-on experience of the system; there is a case for a built-in tutorial on the use of the learning environment. Until trainees are clear about the hierarchical relationship between topics, and the function of each command option, selecting an option might produce unexpected results. The tutorial need be no longer than 20 minutes; it could form a key part of the training courseware. An alternative is to provide instructions to the trainee as part of the courseware package; this can be stored as an item in the glossary, which the student can access at any point.

Orientation in the Learning Material

Browsing environments of the hypertext type are generally well received. Users enjoy the freedom to select the material they want to investigate, but this style of free-range environment has its drawbacks. The experience can be equated with being set down in an unknown city without a map, without any clear idea of what points of interest you ought to be looking out for. The traveller is likely to lose both his sense of direction and his sense of purpose. The problem of locating oneself within the courseware presents one of the major drawbacks of all browsing environments. The user can become lost or disorientated.

There are two ways in which this problem can be addressed. Firstly, the difficulty of orientation within the car insurance courseware might have been exacerbated by the sheer volume of material. The ATR trainer system was constructed as a single knowledge base of approximately 250 rules and 20 database files, covering all the underwriting and rating knowledge. One desirable facility in ATR trainer would be the ability to partition knowledge bases into subject areas of manageable proportions. Although the trainee's pathway through the material is constrained by the structure of the knowledge, pathways in a knowledge base of the size of the car insurance courseware can grow to a considerable length, with numerous choice points along the way. Knowledge bases need to be partitioned in order to restrict depth and breadth of browsing.

Learning material is structured according to the concepts in the knowledge base (see Fig. 15.2), presented as topics to the learner. The material presented for each topic consists of the rules about it that are represented in the knowledge base; rules appear to the learner as pages (or screens) of text and graphics, with a page for each rule.

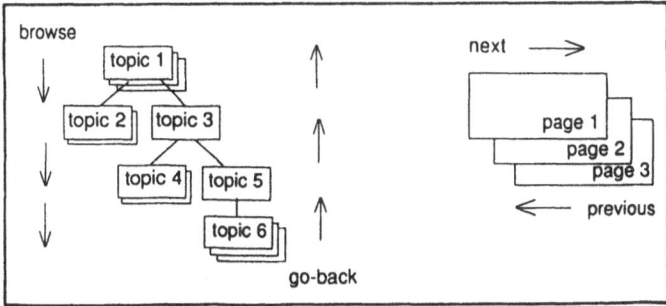

Fig. 15.3. Command options for browsing material.

This segments the knowledge into many small components, each of which has to be "visited" by the learner. This disadvantage has been addressed by allowing the teaching material to be more loosely linked to the knowledge base structure and provided in larger chunks of knowledge. Learning material is still attached to the topic, but the courseware author is able to decide how to present the topic (how much information, how many pages, etc.), and whether to override the knowledge base structure by collapsing topics within topics. The latter facility ensures that the learner is not required to traverse the system to glean what may be a trivial item of information, but essential to the operation of the expert system. The topic map provided to the learner thus becomes a simplified version of the concept structure that is the knowledge base. This is discussed by Gregory and French (in press). Further developments to ATR trainer could allow the courseware author to take complete control of the structure of the topic map.

In the evaluated version of ATR trainer, navigation was simply by moving through the tree structure, requiring learners to retrace their steps in order to recap material. In the current version, the learner may more easily revisit topics to recap material. ATR trainer builds a glossary of topics as they are visited, which the learner is able to access, choosing either to temporarily reference a topic already viewed, or to go back to a topic in order to follow a different pathway.

This improvement addresses the problems of navigation and dis-orientation, a recognized handicap of all browsing environments. ATR trainer incorporates a facility to help the trainee to check his whereabouts: a menu option which, when selected, displays the title of the topic that is currently being looked at, and the topic to which the current topic is related. This facility is of limited usefulness, and the provision of a graphical representation, or map, of the knowledge structure is a more obvious solution. Since ATR trainer knows the structure of each knowledge base, this could easily be produced automatically for each piece of courseware. The nature of the representation remains to be resolved; a printed representation would be a starting point, and in the most recent version of ATR trainer this can be incorporated in the glossary, where the learner can refer to it at will. The ideal form would be a screen display of the map, which could be used by the learner to navigate around the topics, and from which the learner could access a topic simply by clicking on it. This would be feasible in any future Windows implementation of the system.

Use of Graphics

Attitudes of trainees to the use of graphics were ambivalent, but the role of relevant visual material in learning is indisputable. At the time of the study, ATR trainer did not have facilities to incorporate graphics into its displays; this was recognized as a limitation of the software.

All learning material, including tests and worked examples, can now be presented in graphical form.

Summary

The primary objective of the study was to evaluate the effectiveness of a system which incorporated trainee modelling. The results indicate that, on the measures taken, the ATR trainer system is as effective as conventional CBT. With continued enhancements to the system, ATR trainer should become a considerably more effective training system.

ATR trainer does present other advantages. The development of courseware is considerably faster than for conventional CBT. Approximately 1 hour's training material can be prepared within 35 hours of development time (Gregory 1990); it can then be used both for initial training and as an advice and support tool for on-the-job training. These advantages could be significant in the choice between technologies.

16 | Modality of Knowledge Based Training Systems: A KADS Approach

Robert M. Taylor

Introduction

What is difficult about managing and developing knowledge based training systems (KBTS)?

When this question was put to an industrial audience, the following answers, prioritised according to the ensuing discussion, were given:

- Identifying KBTS opportunities
- Managing the development process
- Obtaining management support and funding
- Knowledge elicitation
- Knowledge acquisition from other sources than by elicitation
- Knowledge representation
- Combining the knowledge of more than one expert

Following some discussion, a further point was added, because it was felt to be a matter of special difficulty in the development of KBTS as opposed to other knowledge based systems (KBS):

- The analysis of human–computer interaction (HCI) and the design of the user interface (UIF) for the training mode of operation, where a richer, more adaptive communication is required in the case of KBTS than for most KBS.

This chapter explores how far KADS (a methodology for KBS development) and in particular its modality theory, satisfies these needs of KBTS developers.

Requirements for KBTS

As a starting point, it is helpful to consider what a KBTS consists of, and to reflect on what might be entailed in developing one.

Figure 16.1 is an outline diagram of the architecture of a KBTS, showing some of the major components. This provides clues about what would be needed to develop such a system:

- A framework for capturing and modelling knowledge. This could be used to model the subject matter to be trained, the skill of training itself and the trainee's knowledge.

- An advanced user interface to manage the interaction with the trainee according to the subject to be trained, the training strategy and the state of the trainee's knowledge.

The major difference in comparison with KBS is that two kinds of knowledge are involved. The problem solving and domain knowledge is found in KBS, but the inclusion of the training strategy knowledge

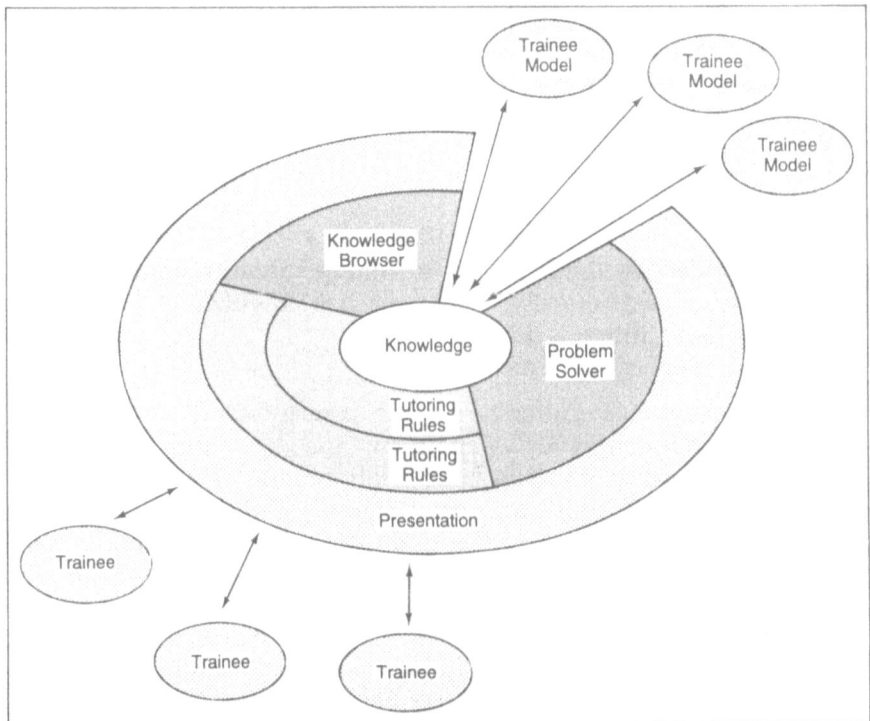

Fig. 16.1. Outline KBTS architecture for ATR trainer. Source: Kingston University Advanced Training Research.

only appears in the case of KBTS. KADS, which has been developed to assist in the development of KBS, is also applicable to KBTS, and includes an approach to HCI analysis and UIF design, known as modality theory, that may be of special relevance in the case of KBTS, where the management of the interaction is a more complex problem.

The KADS Methodology

KADS (Hesketh 1989; Hickman 1989; Wielinga 1989) is the name of what is probably the best-known methodology for KBS development currently available. KADS supports KBS development by providing a number of models that address the difficulties in the process. These include modelling frameworks for the analysis of the organization in which the KBS is to function, the task to be performed, the expertise to be used in the KBS, the system design, the intended users of the system and the user–system communication.

KADS describes the activities involved in KBS development (Barthlemy et al. 1987; Killin et al. 1989) and details the milestone states of deliverable products to be produced. KADS is structurally similar to conventional software development methodologies, but is adapted to the particular concerns that present themselves in knowledge engineering.

The Model of Expertise

KADS provides an implementation-independent notation for the documentation of the analysis of expertise (Breuker et al. 1987). It is a four-layered structure (Fig. 16.2).

The four layers of the model are:

1. The *domain layer* contains domain concepts and structures that show the relationships between them, and facts and rules in the domain. The most commonly used relations are "is–a" (e.g. cat is–a mammal), "part–of" (hub-cap part–of wheel) and "causes" (pressure causes pain). For example, in the credit card fraud detection domain, concepts include types of cardholder, transaction and merchant, and the rules express inferences that can be made about them.

2. The *inference layer* includes an inference structure that defines the problem solving behaviour. In the credit card fraud identification domain the inference structure describes the assessment of the likelihood of fraud. The inference structure for assessment in this domain is shown in Fig. 16.3.

3. The *task layer* describes the ordering of execution of inferences.

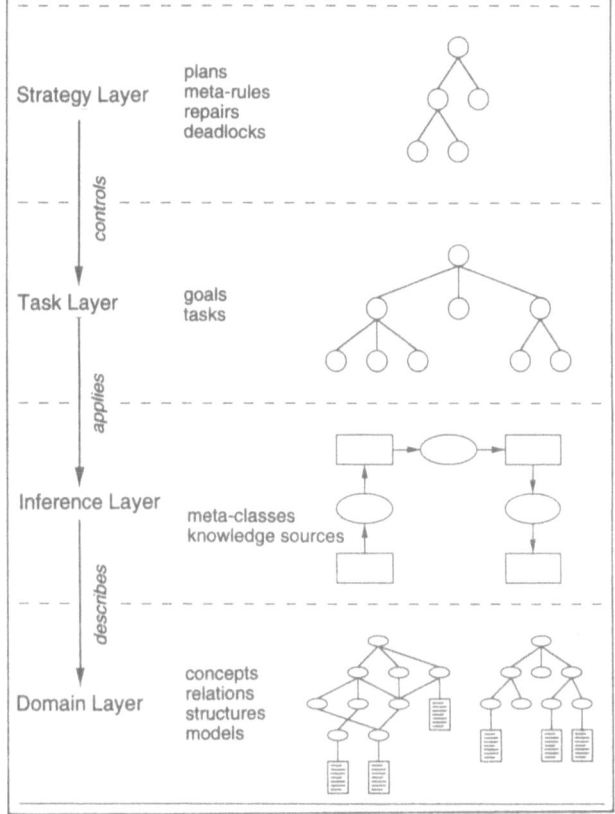

Fig. 16.2. The four-layer model of expertise.

In the case of assessment, there are two basic task structures: either starting with data and comparing that to the model (starting on the left-hand side of the assessment model); or starting with the model and matching this to the data (starting on the right-hand side of the model). Allowing variability in task structures is one way of achieving flexible interaction in KBTS.

4. The *strategy layer* describes control, which means selection of task structure and modality and deciding on the general approach to the problem solving and interaction. For instance, the strategy might be to start with the case data, but, if this does not work, turning to the model-driven approach.

Interpretation Models

KADS provides a library of inference structures that can be used as interpretation models. That is to say that they can be used to assist

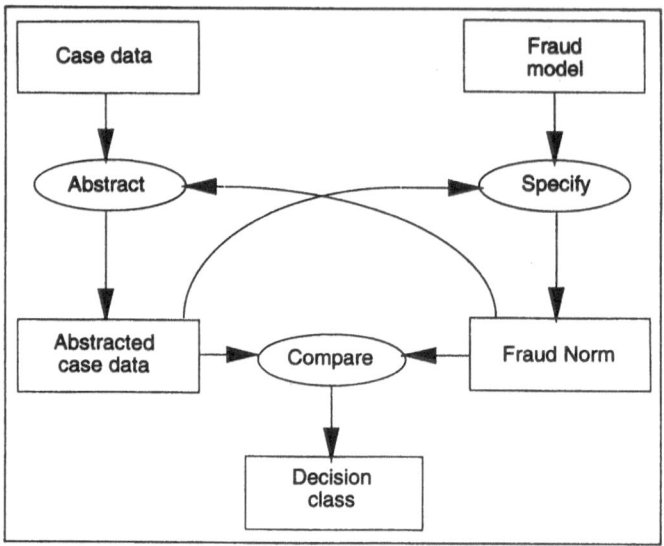

Fig. 16.3. The assessment inference structure.

in the interpretation of elicited protocol. The models are generic: for example, the credit card fraud identification model is an instance of the assessment generic task. The assessment model is equally applicable to other assessment tasks in other domains. The KADS interpretation model library includes: design, diagnosis, monitoring, prediction and configuration interpretation models.

Design in KADS

KADS has a three-step design process (Davoodi 1987). Neither the process nor the design description language are covered here, although Fig. 16.4 shows a summary.

Other Models

The organizational and agent (user) models are not covered here, mainly because they are the subject of ongoing work in the continuing development of KADS. The organizational model is concerned with the selection of problems (and opportunities) in the organization that are suitable for KBS (or KBTS) solutions. Since the task and communication models are concerned with modality, they are not discussed in this section. The next section covers modality theory.

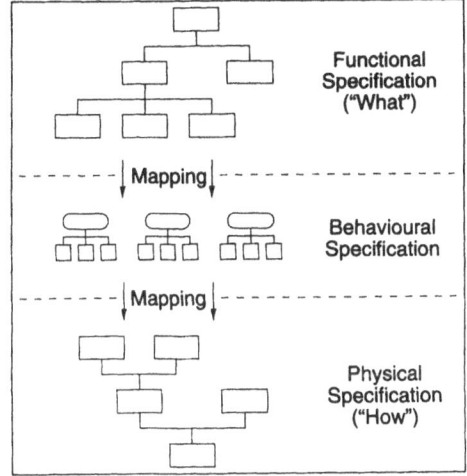

Fig. 16.4. KBS design in KADS.

The Management Cycle and Spiral Model

The development process in KADS is controlled by an iterative management activity cycle consisting of four basic stages (each of which consists of a number of activities) (Taylor 1989):

- Review progress
- Assess risk
- Plan
- Monitor development work

This framework is inspired by the spiral lifecycle model (LCM) of Boehm (1986, 1988) and also by the work of Iivari (1987). A spiral representation of the LCM is also sometimes used in KADS. Project management consists of iterations of the same stages, though the activities may be different in subsequent iterations, and the models under development are updated in each cycle (Fig. 16.5).

Modality

The modality of a KBS is its mode of interaction with the user and other systems. It is evident that different task types (diagnosis and monitoring, for example) may have different modalities. KBTS need to adapt their modality, as they adapt their training strategy, to suit the needs of the trainee.

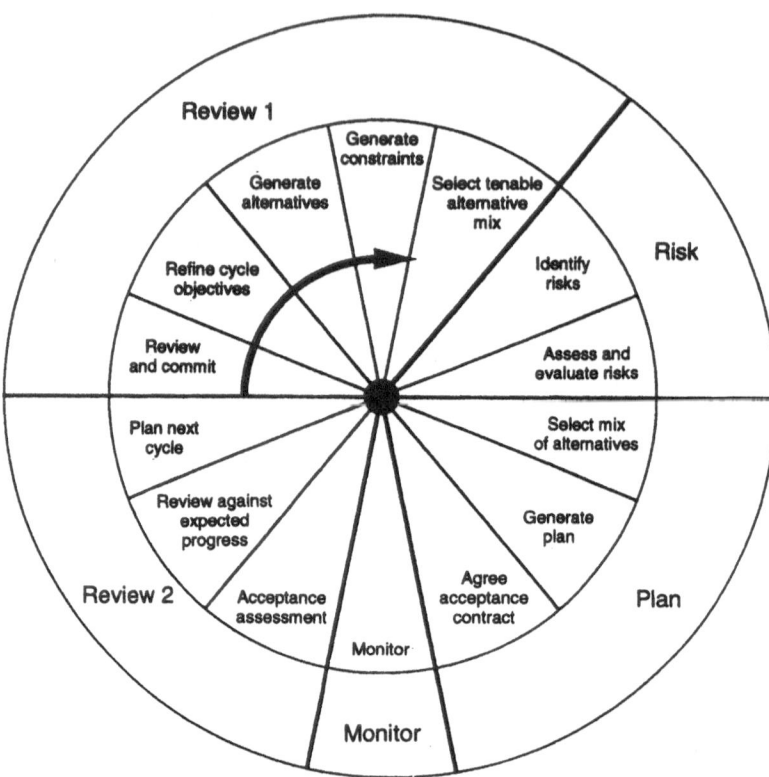

Fig. 16.5. The project management activity cycle (Bright 1991).

The Modality Matrix

Modality analysis is best presented by the modality matrix (de Greef 1988) (Fig. 16.6). The matrix is divided into two columns and three rows. The left-hand column concerns the problem solving element of the KBS/KBTS (i.e. the subject area to be trained). The right-hand column concerns the assignment of tasks to particular agents (computer or human). Box 3 corresponds to the KADS four-layer model of expertise. The bottom row is largely to do with design issues and is not discussed in this paper.

Modality Analysis Activities

The models and activities in modality analysis are as follows.

1. *Box 1*. Complete a hierarchical task decomposition of the task to be trained to a point at which subtasks can be assigned to a single agent. Many different task allocations may be possible. Capturing them would be a means of providing flexible interaction (see Fig. 16.7).

	Problem Solving Domain	Cooperation
Task level	1 Task Model	2 Task Distributions
Semantic level	3 Model of Expertise	4 Model of Cooperation
Communication level	5 Transparency	6 Interaction

Fig. 16.6. The modality matrix.

2. *Box 2*. Augment the box 1 decomposition by mapping the flow of data (a, b, c, d and e in Fig. 16.8) between different tasks. Where there is a flow of data between tasks owned by different agents, show the interface (a line cutting the data flow in Fig. 16.8).

3. *Box 4*. At each interface show which agent (user or system) will initiate the exchange of data by putting a dot on their side of the interface. This shows what is called the initiative (Fig. 16.9).

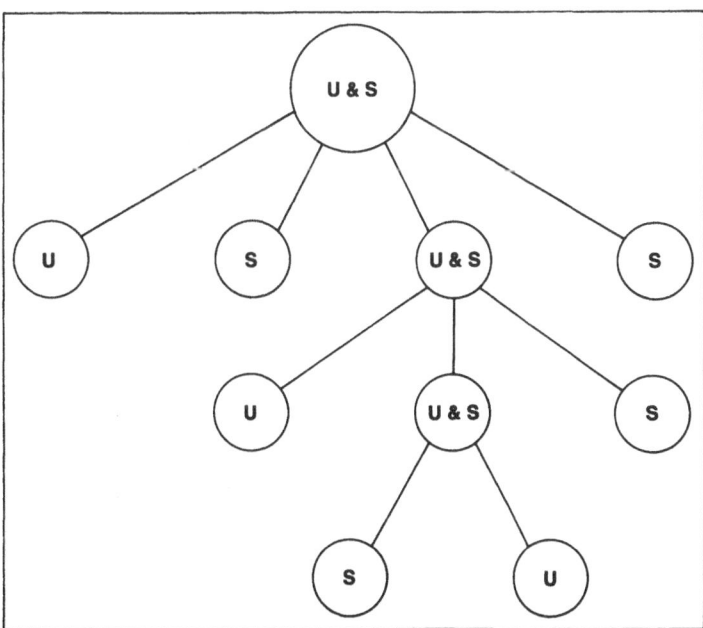

Fig. 16.7. Task model: U, user; S, system.

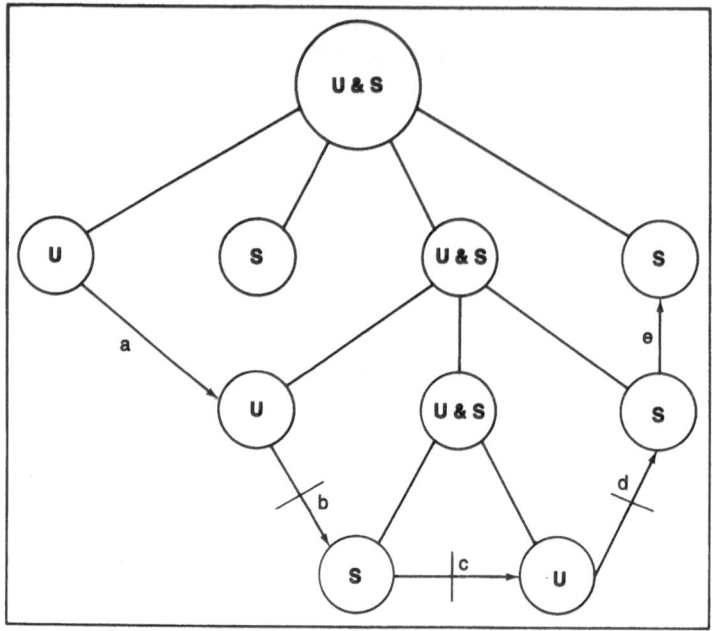

Fig. 16.8. Box 2: U, user; S, system.

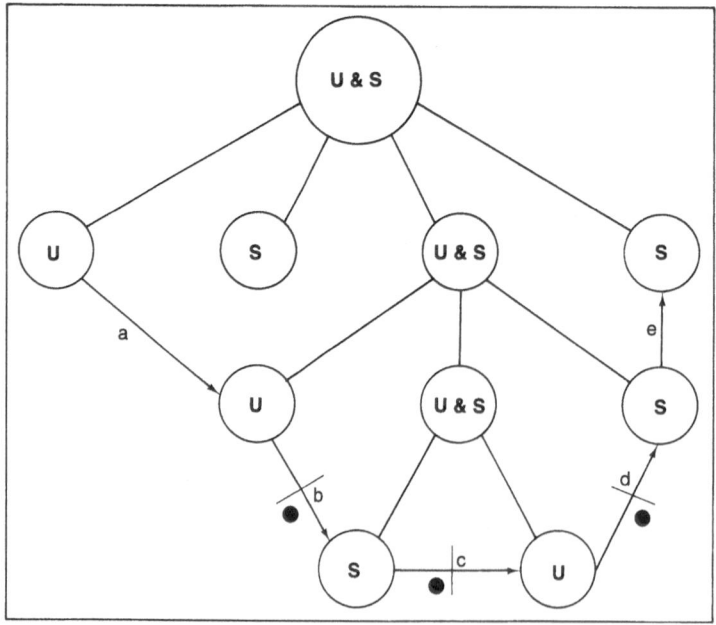

Fig. 16.9. Cooperation model.

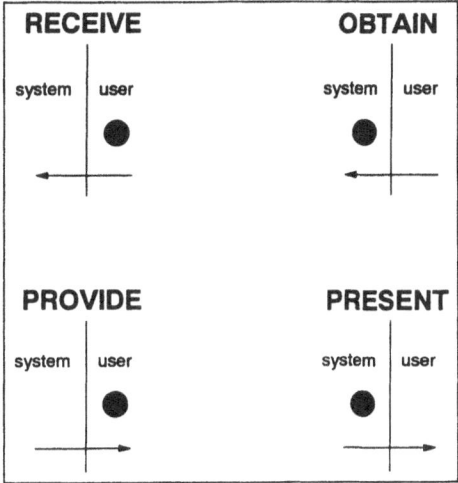

Fig. 16.10. Initiatives.

There are four different types of initiative (Fig. 16.10). A further degree of flexibility can be built into systems by specifying alternative initiatives at each interface.

Alternative modalities can be noted in a table such as the one shown in Fig. 16.11.

The Communication Manager

In order to encapsulate such flexibility into a KBS/KBTS, an outline architecture for the strategic control (a design for the strategy layer of the expertise model) has been proposed. It is called the communication manager (COMA) (Fig. 16.12).

COMA uses the modalities to control the problem solving and the user–system (trainee–trainer) interaction. It monitors performance for problems. If it can diagnose the problem easily, a local fix (remedy) is employed and the modality does not change. For example, if it is the trainee's initiative to select a topic, and he does not respond, after 2 minutes the system might diagnose a problem and prompt. If the problem is more severe, an alternative modality is negotiated or selected (the system might take over).

Modality Conclusions

The modality framework is a very promising simple solution to the problem of HCI analysis and UIF (communication) design for KBTS.

Ingredient	Modality 1		Modality 2	
	owner	initiative	owner	initiative
a	–	–	–	–
b	user	system	–	–
c	system	system	system	system
d	user	user	user	system
e	–	–	–	–
...	...	...	...	...

Fig. 16.11. Modalities.

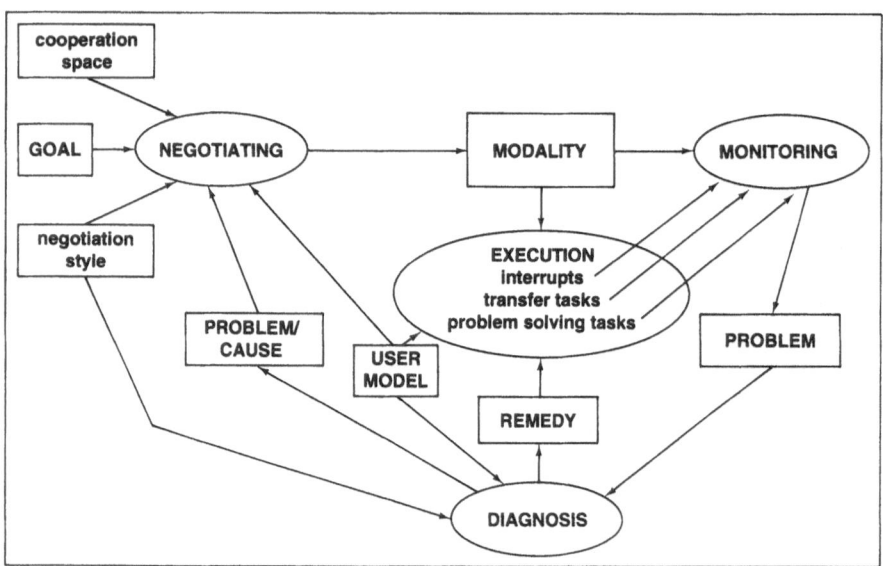

Fig. 16.12. The communication manager.

In its full exposition, modality accounts for a range of HCI problems, from the simplest single-user, single-task systems, to systems with dynamically changing training strategies adapting to trainees with differing needs.

Conclusions

In response to the initial question, "What is difficult about managing and developing knowledge based training systems?", a number of issues were raised. So what is the verdict?

- *Knowledge elicitation and acquisition from other sources.* Little has been said about this topic in this chapter (although the following sources are available: Breuker and Wielinga 1988; Hayball 1987; Wielinga and Breuker 1984). However, the use of interpretation models has been proven to be of value in interview planning, protocol analysis and knowledge analysis in many systems developments.

- *Knowledge representation and combining the knowledge of more than one expert.* The four-layer model provides a rich framework for the intermediate, machine-independent representation of knowledge. It can be used as a repository for combining knowledge from more than one source, and presented back to experts for validation and acceptance.

- *Managing the development process.* The management cycle integrates project management and control with the development process.

- *Human–computer interaction.* KADS modality theory provides an approach to the analysis and design of KBTS with adaptive communication strategies, though the practical difficulty of actually doing this should not be underestimated.

- *Identifying KBTS opportunities and obtaining management support and funding.* These are the real problems of KBTS development. Further work on the models and new models for organizational analysis may help. Having a structured methodology itself increases management's confidence in the KBS/KBTS development enterprise. However, there can be no substitute for the judgement of experienced project managers.

- *KADS KBTS architecture.* It is now possible to interpret the initial KBTS architecture in terms of KADS models (Fig. 16.13).

Summary

The KADS methodology, and in particular its modality theory, goes a long way towards meeting the needs of KBTS developers. The major

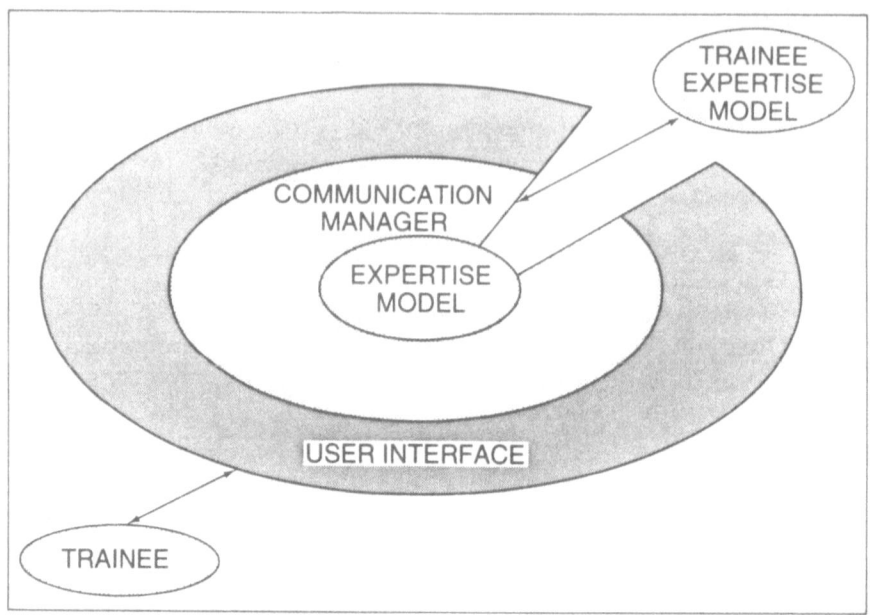

Fig. 16.13. KADS KBTS architecture.

issues now, however, are those of management of the technology as a business weapon, and are less easily addressed by methodologies.

Acknowledgements

This chapter reflects work from a research project partially funded by the ESPRIT Programme of the Commission of the European Communities (project number 1098), in which the partners were: the University of Amsterdam, K.B.S.C. Ltd (later the Knowledge-Based Systems Centre of Touche Ross Management Consultants), STC Technology Ltd, SD-SCICON Ltd, Cap Sogeti Innovation (later Cap Sesa Innovation) and NTE NeuTech GmbH.

The original work on modality of de Greef et al. (1988) is particularly acknowledged.

This chapter is part of a research project partially funded by the ESPRIT Programme of the Commission of the European Communities (project number 5248). The partners in this project are Gap Gemini Innovation, Cap Gemini Logic, Netherlands Energy Research Foundation ECN, ENTEL SA, Lloyd's Register, IBM France, Swedish Institute of Computer Science, Siemens AG, Touche Ross MC, the University of Amsterdam and the Free University of Brussels.

The results of project number 1098 are often known now as "KADS-I". Project number 5248, which is ongoing, is called "KADS-II". This chapter reflects KADS-I with some modifications to the LCM from new work carried out under project number 5248. Any errors are entirely the author's. The author would like to acknowledge the work of all KADS project collaborators, and David Porter for providing the diagrams.

VI | HUMAN CENTRED SYSTEMS

Editorial Overview

The topic of human centred systems has moved, over a few years, from the fringes to the centre of concern in business information technology. Advances in technology mean little or nothing unless they empower human users in purposeful activity; thus, human users need to be involved in the process of development from the earliest stages. We are gaining an appreciation of the respective abilities of humans and computers, and as the price of computers falls, human values and human dimensions of systems become paramount.

Professor Karamjit Gill (Chapter 17) provides an account of human centred systems research in Europe, tracing the rich traditions in Britain, Germany and Scandinavia, the roots of which go back many centuries. Whereas the history of western technology has involved the progressive division of labour and strengthening of the management function, computer technology offers the prospect of reuniting hand and brain, manufacturing and design. He raises fundamental questions that go beyond conventional debates in business and technology, and that have stimulated innovation.

Kevin Harris (Chapter 18) works in the community and voluntary sector, where IT is becoming of central importance, and issues of management and use are being addressed for the first time. He identifies aspects of the community and voluntary sector from which business and industry should learn, including approaches to networking and cooperation, which offer a crucial counterbalance to the conventional rhetoric of competitive advantage.

David Hopson (Chapter 19) is a specialist IT consultant in the community and voluntary sector. His chapter reinforces Molyneux's earlier arguments for the enduring role of programming (Chapter 1), albeit in a revised form. Hopson's account of "power users" and the growing area of desktop publishing and shareware offers considerable food for thought to those in the business and academic sectors. Given the widespread availability of compatible technology, what impediments remain to mutually beneficial communication and exchange?

The debate is no longer restricted to the narrow sphere of commercial management, as the spread of commodity technology has illuminated commonalities of problems, and scope for sharing and collaborating in solutions. Striving for competitive advantage for the individual or single organization may be too limited and short-termist, and a broader cultural perspective is required. This in turn has implications for education and management development.

17 | Human Centred Systems: Foundational Concepts and Traditions

Karamjit Gill

The Human Centred Tradition

Human centredness is a new technological tradition which places human need, skill, creativity and potentiality at the centre of the activities of technological systems. It is an emancipatory tradition, which is rooted in the diversity of European cultural, scientific and philosophical traditions. Human centredness is not anti-technology or anti-science, but a tradition that transcends narrow mechanistic notions of science and technology (i.e. statistical control, objectivity, quantification), and crosses the boundaries of academic and working life disciplines.

The tradition originated in Britain in the 1970s as an alternative to the Taylorist approach to production and industrial rationalization, resulting from rapid advances in microelectronics. Since the 1970s, it has influenced the development of culturally-oriented traditions in Europe, for example "humanization of work and technology" in Germany and "democracy in participation" in Scandinavia. These developments are now providing the creation of a new European tradition of anthropocentric systems, which emphasises the social and cultural shaping of manufacturing culture.

The Scientific and Intellectual Challenge

One of the most important barriers that human centredness had to cross in the 1970s was the mechanistic view of science, which regarded forces of production, and in particular science and technology, as ideologically neutral. It was considered that the development of these forces was inherently positive and progressive. It was science that, through Galileo and Darwin's revolutions, liberated humanity from the bondage of superstition. What was needed, it was argued, was to invest adequately, to plan for science and to provide a rational framework for its widespread application in the elimination of disease, poverty and toil. Science thus appeared as critical knowledge for human progress.

However, by the early 1970s, as Cooley (1989a,b) points out, there was a gradual realization that science has embodied within it many of the assumptions of the society that has given rise to it. This led to the growing questioning of the neutrality of science and technology, as well as to the questioning of the nature of scientific process itself, beyond the scientific use/abuse model.

The 19th century's concern with energy gave rise to the consideration of the machine as essentially an extension of arms and hand. With the dawn of cybernetics, information replaced energy as the centre of emerging technology. Interest in the notion of control and transformation of information provided the impetus for investigation into issues such as the human ability to know, limitations of human information processing, how we deal with uncertainty and how we use feedback of our own action to regulate these actions. With cybernetics, the process of the separation of the machine from the human had started, but the machine was still a model of human labour.

The advent of the computer completed the process of the separation of the machine from the human. Previous collaboration between the human and the machine was now transferred to the collaboration between the machine and knowledge extracted from the human. This led to machine centred production and control. Simon's *Sciences of the Artificial* in the 1960s allowed for the separation of subjective from objective knowledge and provided a basis for the design of computer artefacts as machines. Computer science was defined in terms of artificial languages of logic, mathematics and statistics. The computer was seen to simulate the human mind. The processes of the human mind could only be conceived by an understanding of the processes of human behaviour and language. Human behaviour and language, therefore, could only be defined in terms of their functionality as closed systems. Just as complex computer systems are decomposed into functional units, so was human behaviour and communication. The process of design itself was therefore reduced to a problem of declarative logic.

This process of viewing human behaviour and human communication resulted in the design of artefacts as mechanistic tools which marginalized human subjective knowledge, and hence excluded experiential knowledge of human practice and skills from the design process and the use of the tool. In the 1970s this view was challenged by researchers such as Dreyfus and Weizenbaum. Recently, European researchers such as Bodker (1989), Ehn (1988) and Laessoe and Rasmussen (1989) have provided an alternative vision of participatory design to set against Simon's rationalistic approach. The point of departure of this approach is an emphasis on human involvement and dialogue throughout the design process. Design becomes a process for anticipation of possible breakdowns for the user in future use situations. The design focus is now on the human use of computer artefacts rather than conventional detached reflection.

There has also been questioning of mechanistic ideals of science and technology. Norbert Wiener's book *The Human Use of Human Beings*, which first appeared in 1950, inspired many critics. By 1965, Hubert Dreyfus was comparing artificial intelligence (AI) to medieval alchemy. His critique of AI developed and culminated in the book *What Computers Can't Do* in 1972. Also in 1972, Joseph Weizenbaum produced his paper, "On the impact of the computer on society", with the challenging subtitle "How does one insult a machine?". By 1976 these concerns had found fuller expression in his book *Computer Power and Human Reason*, which had the subtitle *From Judgement to Calculation* and highlighted the dangers surrounding an uncritical acceptance of computerization. During the same period, Rosenbrock had been working on the use of computers in systems design, and his "Computer aided control systems design" appeared in 1974, to be followed in 1976 by his seminal paper "The future of control". In 1979, Cooley's book *Architect or Bee?*, later revised as *Architect or Bee? The Human Price of Technology* (1987), generated a proactive international debate on human centred systems. In 1986, *Artificial Intelligence for Society* (Gill 1986) became a focus for extending the human centred debate to the social domain.

The third development was among industrial workers and trade unions, questioning what was made and how it was being made. Fertile discussions took place amongst the Fiat workers in Italy, those at LIP in France, Algotsnord in Sweden, and, perhaps the most renowned, the Lucas Workers Plan for Socially Useful Production. Although the Plan is probably best known for the range of products described in it, of equal importance to the Lucas Workers was the notion it embodied of systems that enhance human skill and ability: hence, the coining of the term "human centredness" by Mike Cooley.

The Challenge of the Rule

The challenge of the rule comes from the philosophy of design, which accepted the separation of the hand from the brain, skill from practice, objective knowledge from the subjective. Sixteenth century Europe witnessed the appearance of a new word, "design", to describe the occupational activity of "designing". This proved to be a momentous event – the beginning of the separation of hand and brain, of manual and intellectual work, and of the conceptual part of work from the labour processes. It signified a historic trend that "designing" was to be separated from "doing". This trend began with the separation of the designing (by architects) and the construction (by builders) of great churches in Europe (e.g. Italian churches).

Cooley (1987) gives an insight into "the challenge of the rule", and into the "separation of hand and brain". The separation of manual from intellectual work provided the basis for further subdivisions of work, both intellectual and manual: the beginning of "Taylorism". The process of subdivision found theoretical expression in the writings of early economists such as Adam Smith. The growing factory system thrived on it. Some 19th century writers warned about the human consequences:

> To subdivide a man is to assassinate him. The subdivision of labour is the assassination of a people (Urquart 1978).

Rules for Design

The first person to succeed in rendering visible the rules underlying various craft skills in any significant way was the great Filipo Brunelleschi, architect of the Duomo in Florence. As early as 1413, Brunelleschi had developed a systematic technique for constructing representations of buildings using true perspectives (Saalman 1980). This systematic approach was further refined by Leonardo, and by the end of the 15th century, architects such as Mathias Roriczer of Regensburg were publishing generalized methods for various aspects of cathedral construction.

The consequence of the emergence of the rule and objectivity was that not only the conceptual part of the work of craftsmen (masons) was being taken away from them, but the academic hegemony over theoretical knowledge resulted in the denigration of the skill of practitioners which was the embodiment of the fusion of intellectual and design skills.

Mitter (1986) points out that the concept of universal rule is rooted in the deep-seated empiricist epistemology of the west, according to which knowledge can be formulated in the form of rules, and transferred without taking into account cultural diversity. The importance of specific cultural experience is often forgotten or ignored, partly because, after great advances made in physical sciences during the 19th century, the notion of pure "objectivity" came to take firm hold on intellectual imagination. A persistent and persuasive assertion of the social sciences in the 19th century was that scientific objectivity transcended cultural variety, and this view of "scientific reductionism" was powerfully enforced by Social Darwinists. This doctrine of "cultural homogeneity" of human society and "universality" of human knowledge even now forms a great deal of scientific thinking. It is, however, crucial to recognize that while there are common and universal traits that humans share, there is a great deal that is culturally specific. The cultural factor cannot be discarded in the domain that deals with human knowledge, skill and experience.

Implications of the Rule

The pervasiveness of the "rule" is reflected even in the designing of technological systems for human use. It permeates, for example, research into knowledge based systems, natural language processing and human–computer interface design. In the case of knowledge based design, important questions of contexts and background are ignored. Human knowledge that cannot be explicated in the form of rules is abandoned. This ignoring of the "tacit" dimension of knowledge leads to the design of technological systems that map only part of the reality. This discrepancy between reality and technological systems results in vulnerability and brittleness of systems. Where such systems are integrated into human organizations, human judgement becomes subordinated to systems, which, ultimately, leads to technology-led human disasters such as Three Mile Island, Chernobyl and Bhopal.

The "rule" model of systems design tends to find solutions to the "discrepancy" problem (between the technological system and the reality) through the design of internally consistent and highly synchronized systems that aim to eliminate human subjectivity and redundancy. Thus, both design process and use become and remain prisoner of the straitjacket of consistency, thus removing crucial elements of human–machine collaboration. For example, as pointed out by Gill (1988), in the design of expert systems, knowledge acquisition is considered to be the "quantification" of expertise. The construction of expert systems means reducing human expertise into syntax recognisable by the computer. This imposes constraints upon the user in the sense that both dialogue and decision making process are expressed in terms of machine-understandable rules. The computer becomes the dominant medium of communication, and both expert and user become distanced from their own knowledge and skills.

Implication of Separation of Hand and Brain

The separation of hand and brain has led now to the separation of "knowledge" from "knowing" and theory from practice. This separation is most complete in the design of IT systems (Weizenbaum 1976). An example of this is the case of a designer of an afterburner igniter, who calculated the dimensions on the CAD screen, and generated the numerical control tapes, which deskilled workers on the shop floor used to produce an igniter ten times larger than it should have been.

The alarming part of this story is that the designer, when confronted with this object, saw nothing wrong with it.

The whole area of knowledge based systems and intelligent information systems separates theory from practice, and, as in the case of the igniter designer, assumes that practice is subsumed within explicit knowledge (Cooley 1987).

The implication that the computer defines the whole of "real" knowledge is a powerful device for distancing ordinary people from effective decision making, and it could be monstrously counterproductive.

Human Centred Concepts

The Metaphor of Sun and Corona

This was coined by Howard Rosenbrock (1988) and is used to explain the idea of human–machine symbiosis. As objective knowledge is used in practice, it is seen as adding to the tacit dimension of human knowledge. Similarly, as tacit knowledge is practised, it becomes accessible and explicable and thus adds to the objective part of the knowledge. In other words, both objective and tacit knowledge increase through practice. This means that tacit knowledge will always exist so long as the objective knowledge exists; in other words, tacit knowledge can never be fully explicated. The sun metaphor signifies objective knowledge, and the corona metaphor signifies tacit knowledge. Just as the sun cannot exist without its corona, so objective knowledge cannot exist without its complementary tacit knowledge.

Tacit Knowledge

The concept of "tacit knowledge" was coined by Polanyi in his book *The Tacit Dimension* (1967), where in essence he described it as that which we cannot express, but which we know. In terms of experts in the workplace, tacit knowledge can be described as entailing:

- Personal knowledge: that which we gain from our personal life experiences, e.g. family culture, school, friends, such as social values, beliefs and so on.

- Experiential knowledge: that which is specifically context based, in the workplace, e.g. work colleagues, group culture, organizational culture and so on.

Tacit knowledge may be expressed in the form of concepts, metaphors, examples, stories and other non-formalistic expressions.

Rule-Following

The concept of a rule lies in the way a rule is used, i.e. a rule is meaningful only when it is applied in practice, because it is only the practice that gives reality to the rule. In this sense the rule becomes "rule-following", that is, it becomes embedded in the tacit dimension of knowledge gained through practice. Since the application of a rule cannot itself be determined through a rule, practice cannot be defined by rules alone.

Scientific Knowledge

Scientific knowledge includes objective knowledge consisting of causal and quantitative relationships between various measurable properties of a system. The validity of this knowledge remains constant over different contexts, except that the context may not allow its full application. Once extracted from expertise and expressed explicitly as objective knowledge, this scientific knowledge bears little mark of the human conditions of its production. It is transmitted to non-experts as definite, in a way that strongly implies a division of labour, where experts create knowledge and others comply with it.

The Nature of Science and Technology

The human centred tradition regards science and technology as part of culture. Just as different cultures produce different languages, different music and different literature, so any particular society should develop appropriate forms of technology to meet its varying cultural and historical requirements and its long-term aspirations. Science and technology on the one hand and social development on the other are in fact closely intertwined: they do not develop in isolation from each other.

Theory of Action

A theory of action is a person's set of norms, strategies and assumptions about the (causal) relations between the strategies and the norms under various conditions. Outsiders wishing to establish this set have to do so empirically by observing the person in action, since individuals may espouse a different set without being aware of it.

Theory in Use

Theory in use is largely tacit; it derives from (and belongs to) the person's personal knowledge. This knowledge consists of facts, beliefs and assumptions, whether science-based or not. Much of this is connected to the setting in which it was acquired, i.e. it has psychological, or social, or political, or economic or affective connotations. It is definitely connected to purpose; otherwise it is meaningless. Some of this knowledge is acquired by means of all five senses and becomes embodied in a literal sense, particularly activities we are good at.

Dialogue

The significance of dialogue in human centred systems lies in the exchange of knowledge, experience and practices among participants during the design process itself. There are different perspectives on the concept of dialogue. In one of the perspectives, three levels are identified: communication, which is the transfer of objective knowledge; interlocution, or goal-oriented communication, which includes a value set; and dialogue, which in a way is about the sharing of souls. At the pragmatic level it is about cross-cultural understanding, sharing of values, minimizing of misunderstandings and accepting conflicts. The concept of empathy is fundamental to both interlocution and dialogue. Another perspective on dialogue is in the idea of language games. Language games are the expression of the practices and expertise of users and designers. Dialogue here is about the understanding of each other's language games.

In current systems design, the concept of dialogue is used in the context of human–computer interaction. From the perspective of human centredness, human–computer interaction can not go beyond the level of communication, i.e. it can never involve dialogue.

Paradigm Shift: From Mechanism to Human Centredness

The Need for a New Paradigm

As Europe approaches the 21st century, we find that established paradigms of science and technology such as the Newtonian–Cartesian "mechanistic paradigm" and the Tayloristic "management science paradigm" are being challenged as to their relevance to the design of new technological systems. These challenges arise out of the narrowness of these paradigms, which limit humans' capability to shape work, technology and environment consistent with the requirements and aspirations of the industrial cultures and social systems of 21st century Europe. In the world market of "competitive displacement", there is serious concern about the management science paradigm developing a high quality, flexible and adaptable manufacturing base without questioning the production structures that merely attempt to replace human work and skills. Alternative production systems, which aim at combining unique human abilities and skill with the high performance of machines, are gaining attention.

The mechanistic paradigm views the human mind as a symbol processing machine, thus leading to the assumption on the part of cognitive psychologists that it is possible to explain human behaviour, or at least produce human behaviour, through designing intelligent machines. This computer metaphor is used to propagate the idea that:

> *humans making mistakes and being unreliable can be replaced by superior machine systems (Brodner 1990a,b).*

The greatest potential of this rationalization is seen to lie in designing the automated office. Although the automation of complex information processing tasks such as drafting, planning, inventory control and scheduling may have reduced costs, the rationalization does not seem to have made any fundamental improvement to the office working situation.

There is no doubt that the mechanistic paradigm has been so successful in its paradigmatic technological applications that it became the ideal prototype for nearly all scientific thinking. The post-war period has seen the acceptance of the Tayloristic paradigm of the division of work and the division of time for modelling industrial and management systems. The division of academic disciplines, as well as the boundaries of professions, are the products of this paradigm. Now, as we move into the area of the quality revolution of high quality and small batch production requiring a highly skilled, flexible and adaptable workforce, there is a need for a new paradigm that recognizes the environmental and social concerns of the world of working life, and builds on the strengths of human knowledge, experience, skill, creativity and ingenuity. There is increasing recognition that:

> *The success of a production process depends on the degree to which the knowledge and skill of the human is used when working with technological systems rather than on the degree to which human work has been displaced by machine artefacts. It is necessary to realize that human work is the primary and most important force of production rather than merely a source of disturbances and a cause of costs and consequently that a sensible design and technology must provide humans with appropriate tasks and sufficient scope for action (Rauner et al. 1988).*

Paradigm Crisis in Work and Technology

We consider three perspectives that reflect different assumptions of human and machine relationships. The technique oriented approach, according to Nurminen (1988), places machines or technically mediated communication before human beings and direct personal communication.

The sociotechnical approach seeks a point of equilibrium between the machine and the human. The concept was developed by the London Tavistock Institute of Human Relations in the 1950s. In this approach, the technical and social systems of an organization are considered more or less on equal terms. Initially its area of interest was industrial work: how the technical system, usually a manufacturing or production system, could be designed in such a way as to be socially acceptable and to correspond to human needs. The conceptual development of sociotechnical design has gone through many stages. Its modern principles include the following job properties (Hellman 1989):

- Variety and challenge
- Continuous learning
- Discretion and autonomy
- Recognition and support
- Meaningful social contribution
- Desirable future

During the 1960s and 1970s, sociotechnical ideas became attractive to management in an attempt to increase productivity and reduce turnover without any additional costs. The experiments of Volvo Kalmar in the 1970s and of Volvo Uddevalla in the 1980s are well known examples of work satisfaction and health and safety aspects of technical functionality and quality of products.

One of the most valuable principles of the sociotechnical approach is the centrality of participation. The human is perceived as a member of a group, an active and a responsible member doing "a good day's work". An informal communication network is considered just as important as the official one. There is, at least, some scope for end-user collaboration and democratic participation of the workforce. However, the approach has several conceptual limitations. The organization is treated as two separate systems, technical and social, in a state of equilibrium of some kind. This means that the technical system is, by and large, taken for granted, and the equilibrium is achieved through making the social relations adaptable to existing technical devices, or via management dominated decisions. Thus, the scope for radical changes in human–organization relations was rather limited from the very beginning.

The human centred approach places human beings in direct personal communication before machines or technically mediated communication. The shaping concept of the human centred approach is described (Corbett et al. 1991) as a perspective that intends to cross the borders between technical and social sciences as well as between theoretical and practical knowledge through an action-based dialogue.

Human Centred Research Traditions

Three main human centred traditions, which provide the central focus for the European research on human centred systems in Europe, are the British tradition of "human–machine symbiosis", the Scandinavia tradition of "collective resource", and the German tradition of "humanization of technology".

The British Tradition of Human Centredness

In the 1970s Rosenbrock became concerned with the increasing automation of CAD systems based on Taylor's "Scientific Management", with its goal of eliminating skill and responsibility in the worker (Rosenbrock 1989). Whereas the algorithmic approach to CAD design aimed at continual reduction in the need for human skill, his aim was to foster skill and cooperate with it. The rapid change in technology in the 1970s offered scope for experimenting with alternative routes of development to Taylorist approaches. In 1979 Rosenbrock received a research fellowship from the Science and Engineering Research Council.

Rosenbrock's concept of alternative technological development rests on two basic ideas. The first of these he calls the "Lushi Hill effect", which basically signifies that there are many ways to reach the peak of Lushi Hill, and one cannot say which is the best, i.e. there is no one best way. The second idea encapsulates the dynamic development of productivity. According to this idea, the strategy of rationalization and investment based on the further reduction of skilled workers is bound, in the long run, to prove economically inferior to the strategy designed to use the skill and potential of skilled workers.

The term "human centred" in the UMIST project concerns autonomy and the use of skill. The basis of the project was a recognition that Taylorism had been (or rather, is) about minimizing autonomy and the use of skill on the part of operators, and the central focus of the design activity was in these two areas. However, that left two more: interaction with others and development through learning. Interaction with others and group aspects cannot be designed into a piece of equipment; they are a matter of how that equipment is then installed and used by the purchaser.

The Lucas Plan

The rapid development of microelectronics in the 1970s gave rise to a wave of rationalization in the British aerospace industry. Workers at Lucas Aerospace put forward an action plan to use their expertise to develop socially useful products. The idea of human centredness and socially useful products was identified as follows:

- Workers have a right to play a dual role, as producers and consumers.

- Production should be compatible with social needs, and should be determined by use value rather than exchange value.

- The economy should be a mixture of market-oriented and socially useful.

The Lucas Plan has had a major impact on the British and international debates on alternative, socially compatible production. Highly skilled engineers, technicians and skilled workers who lost their jobs due to rationalization turned their protest into constructive ideas for socially useful products, and

> demonstrated in a practical and direct way the creative power of "ordinary people" . . . the audit of their own skills and abilities, and surveys in different factories and workshops analysing and assessing the production equipment, product ranges and skills, represented an enormous extension of consciousness (Cooley 1987).

The Lucas Plan provided the basis of a large-scale programme launched by the Greater London Council (GLC) to develop a regional technology policy for London towards socially useful and use-value-oriented product design. Under the leadership of Mike Cooley, the London Technology Network was founded. The aim was to put to community use the large-scale capacity for innovation represented by the competence, skills, experience and expertise of researchers, workers, professionals and community groups. Human centredness was reflected through the design of technological systems aimed at shaping the future of London and meeting the needs, requirements and interests of the people of London. The belief behind the London Technology Network was that collaboration between producers and users would lead to the shaping of socially compatible technology.

The British ideas and initiatives created a great deal of interest in Scandinavia and in West Germany among both trade unionists and academics. A Scandinavian project, UTOPIA, was launched in 1980, with aims similar to those of the Lucas Plan. In West Germany, both IGM (metal workers union) and DGM (top organization of German trade unions) launched a similar discussion in the 1980s around the issue of "work and technology", with the aim of formulating a labour and technology policy geared towards a concept of "shaping", which extended the concepts underlying the German humanization of work programme. "Shaping" ideas were developed further by the Vocational Education research group at Bremen University in the mid-1980s. The Bremen group's research work on shaping, London Technology Network's work on socially compatible products, and UMIST's work on human centred CAD systems led to the creation of the ESPRIT Project, Human Centred CIM, a collaboration between British, Danish and German research groups on human centred systems design.

The Scandinavian Tradition of Human Centredness

Scandinavian tradition relates to "collective resource" and "action research". In the industrial work, this tradition is concerned with human working conditions and the cooperation of users. Laessoe and Rasmussen (1989) give an insight into the Scandinavian tradition. They point out that user-oriented working life research in Scandinavia has been largely influenced by the historical role which Scandinavian labour movements and social democratic parties have played in shaping industrial and technological policies. Active labour market policies and legislation to establish workplace democracy have helped the creation of strong worker participation in technological developments, and also countered the disadvantages of technology in working life.

The emergence of the Scandinavian tradition of user-oriented working life research goes back to the 1960s when the sociotechnical approach (developed at the Tavistock Institute in 1951) was introduced in Norway, with the aim of creating new production relations and new types of organizational design which would guarantee new forms of participation, even within national politics. The ideas did not take root in Norway but found a ready market in Sweden. While in Norway, the key words were "industrial democracy and participation", in Sweden they became "job satisfaction and productivity".

Trades unions in Sweden found a possible solution to a critical period of illegal strikes and unrest among their members as a consequence of changes in production processes. The ideas were attractive to the employers because they would allow for a stable workforce, making it easier both to plan and to improve efficiency and product quality. In Norway the pilot projects initiated by the Norwegian employers and Norwegian Federation of Trade Unions failed, while in Sweden the project on "humanization of work" and "science of work" became dominated by management.

The 1970s saw opposition to managerial domination and a revolt against traditional science, which led to a tradition of "Collective Resource" in opposition to the sociotechnical approach. In Denmark, slogans such as "Research for People" became a focus of attention, while in Norway, "Action Research" became the keyword for methodological discussions and a basis for a large number of user-oriented projects in all areas of society.

The Collective Resource Tradition

The Collective Resource tradition consciously assumes a "conflict perspective", and through cooperation with workers aims to develop user participation in the design of the organization of work and technology. While the sociotechnical approach focused on:

How do we design systems to fit people?

the Collective Resource tradition became:

How do we make it possible for people to design their own systems themselves? (Ehn 1988).

The UTOPIA Project (in Swedish, UTOPIA is an acronym for Training, Technology and Products from a Quality of Work Perspective) was launched in 1981 with aims similar to those of the Lucas plan. A team consisting of Danish and Swedish researchers, social scientists and computer scientists, collaborated closely with the Graphics Union in Sweden. The objective was the development of a demonstrator project to illustrate the compatibility of work quality such as high craft skill, democratic decision making and high health and safety requirements, with the production of high quality products. UTOPIA also included an education objective as part of the design of alternative systems. The design-by-doing method enables users to express their know-how in action, and involves both the researcher and the user as active contributors to problem understanding and problem solving. One of the central aspects of the UTOPIA project is a concern for "tools", i.e the attempt to design computer based tools for human work processes, in accordance with the human centred research tradition.

The German Tradition of Human Centredness

The German tradition of "humanization of technology and work" is influenced by the West German programme on "Humanization of Work" and the "shaping" approach. The "Humanization of Work" programme was very much influenced by the British Lucas Workers Plan.

Humanization of Work

The development of the West German programme on "Humanization of Work", discussed by Dankbaar (1987), started in 1974 with two aims: to improve working conditions in traditional industries with traditional technologies, and to research and develop new emerging technologies. One of the innovative aspects of the humanization programme has been the involvement of union representatives at all levels, ranging from agreements with the works councils to participation in scientific conferences and in the formulation of new research directions. The programme was modified in 1979 and 1982, following critical responses from management and unions, who saw the need for better integration of scientific support and applied projects. In 1984 the Ministry of Technology proposed a distinction between technology induced innovations that call for humanization measures, and innovations that are produced by goals of humanization.

Work-Oriented Shaping Approach of Human Centred Systems

The German tradition of human centred systems is emerging in the form of the work-oriented shaping approach of human centred systems (Corbett et al. 1991). The essence of this approach is:

- It must adhere to the values of the human-ecological tradition, i.e. enrichment of work quality, use values of products and ecological balance of energy processes in a broader sense.

- It must transcend the individualistic man–machine perspective of the human–machine symbiotic approach.

- It should integrate theoretical and practical knowledge into a new kind of collective skill formation and corresponding software and hardware development, based on the human-ecological tradition.

- Fundamentally, technology is always a combination of the union of the technologically possible and the socially desirable.

Human Centred CIM: ESPRIT Project 1217

The Human Centred CIM Project (1986-89) was launched:

> *to produce the World's first ever human-centred and computer integrated manufacturing system.*

It was probably also the first European project to bring together three European traditions of human centredness – British, Scandinavian and German – to develop a framework for future research into human centred systems, as well as to establish a basis for technological developments from the human centred perspective. The project began in 1986, with the Danish partner concerned with computer aided design (CAD) work, the British partner concentrating on computer aided manufacturing (CAM) developments, and the German partners on computer aided planning (CAP) work. The project was based on the premise that a computer integrated manufacturing (CIM) system under the direct control of a person will be more efficient, more economical, more robust and more flexible than a comparable unmanned system.

By May 1989 the results of the project consisted of three principal human centred prototype products at three demonstration sites. The British prototype, "human centred lathe controller", is at BICC and Rolls Royce. The German prototype, "shop floor monitoring and control workstation" is at the BITZ demonstration site based on the campus of Bremen University. The Danish Sketch Pad module is being further developed at the Technical University of Denmark.

Lessons from the ESPRIT Project: Some Challenges

A period of rapid change in technology offers scope for experimenting with alternative routes for development. Once the new technique has become established, it becomes much more difficult to examine alternatives: the entrance fee for the alternative is the cost of matching the performance of the dominant technology, which rapidly becomes so high that options that were available become closed off.

Bureaucratic management fails to take advantage of the skill and initiative of the workforce, because the Taylorist view is of the production system, including its people, as a machine, existing only to fulfil the purpose of its originator.

Attitudes embedded in the scientific and technological culture make it hard to acknowledge and accept human purpose, and the skill which represents a purpose accomplished in work. To the engineer and technological worker, a system which relies upon the existence of human skill, and particularly manual skill, will appear defective and incomplete. Only knowledge that is explicit and definable is accepted: knowledge that can be embodied in textbooks, transmitted to a new generation, and used as a basis for further advance.

The dream of the workerless factory may never be achieved, because scientists are unable to incorporate human purpose into machines. Rosenbrock states that:

> No machine which we can build, and no computer system, can have the purpose of "keeping the production working". . . . Machines do not care whether they work or not, and we do not know how to incorporate the purpose which would make them care. So machines will work well until something occurs which was not envisaged in their design (Rosenbrock 1989).

The design process is not generally deterministic. The choice of alternatives during the process is guided by the principle of the "elimination of misfit". The norm is only known when it is infringed. In other words, the process is driven by the designer's discontent. What is needed is the generation of discontent, not only with designs that are technically unsatisfactory, but also with those that do not satisfy the social criteria.

To achieve a fruitful collaboration between social scientists and technologists, it is necessary for both disciplines to respect each other's point of view. For the technologists, the problem is to include in the decision making process of design a social dimension, which is usually ignored. This also means the inclusion of consideration about whether the users will be subordinated to the technical means of the final system or will be able to use it as a tool to achieve their role as a creative part of the production process. Here, Japanese experience may be a valuable guide to show that an organization which values, obtains and uses the initiative and ability of all those who work in it will be more effective, more flexible and more successful, other things being equal. For the social scientists, on the other hand, converse problems arise. Generalities have to be made specific, and this has to be done in the face of very demanding constraints. The first constraint is time, i.e. how to achieve goals of production and marketing of products in the face of rapidly developing technology. Other constraints arise from economics and the limits of technical feasibility.

Conclusion

Human centredness is increasingly being recognised as the alternative 21st century paradigm to the "mechanistic paradigm" that has dominated technological developments. Human centredness has its origins in European industrial cultures, and its roots in the cultural diversities of European nations. This centrality of diversity allows for the emergence of diverse concepts of human centredness that are culturally and socially shaped.

18 | Information Technology in the Community and Voluntary Sector

Kevin Harris

Introduction

Information technology (IT) is crucial in supporting the voluntary sector's fundamental role in economic and social development. IT is a necessary and integral aspect of various kinds of community and voluntary support – training, welfare, counselling, advice – in a wide range of fields, from education to planning, from arts to small business development, from health promotion to crime prevention. In the community and voluntary sector, the processes whereby it carries out its activities are a very important part of those activities; the means and the ends are closely interrelated. IT, as a tool for certain processes, can have a significant impact oṅ how voluntary agencies work and what they achieve.

The work of voluntary agencies is increasingly information-intensive. This reflects a general social trend, but can also be attributed to government policies that place greater reliance on market forces and principles in the area of social policy, and a more general trend of decentralizing public responsibility for economic development and human services to the local level. These national policy changes place strong financial pressures on the community and voluntary sector, and a growing emphasis on public--private sector partnerships, necessitating higher levels of efficiency, flexibility, and competitiveness. Information requirements have risen and become more complex, in terms of contract bids, financial accounting, consumer research, report writing, public relations and advertising, and so on.

IT in this context is not necessarily less powerful or less appropriate than elsewhere; it is as worthy of investment and the ways in which it is used as likely to be instructive and worthy of emulation as in other sectors. As complex, flexible computer based networks become commonplace and new relations develop between organizations newly exchanging information, practices and policies of the voluntary sector may provide examples widely applicable beyond that sector, because community and voluntary agencies have always survived and thrived on an ethos of co-operation, networking, sharing and innovation.

This chapter is based on the report of the IT and Communities Working Party (Community Development Foundation 1992), established in 1990 by the Community Development Foundation. The report concludes that the voluntary sector is well placed to use IT in the 1990s; that more thorough exploitation of the technology could enhance the degree to which the sector's expertise is applied to address economic and social needs; and that appropriate structures for collaboration and development merit investment and stimulation.

The Context

Certain current factors are important for an understanding of communication and IT in this sector:

- The development of microcomputers is no longer as uncertain as before, in that a number of hardware industry standards have become established and equipment is now relatively less expensive.

- The convergence of computer and telecommunications technologies (in "telematics") has become clearer.

- Many arguments on the relevance and application of IT have been won.

- Government exhortations to adopt the technology in the 1970s and 1980s were based on the message that IT is crucial for commercial survival and competitive advantage; benefits to community and voluntary organizations have not been set out, hence social benefits to be gained from investment in IT for the voluntary sector remain unproven.

- The social policy context for IT in communities is characterized by rapid change, increasing pressures on limited resources, and new relationships with organizations in other sectors. Recognition of the role of the voluntary sector has increased, and there is demand for agencies to provide services. New kinds of information and new skills in information handling are called for, as in the role of organizations which contract for service delivery.

Networking

Networking takes place when people establish and maintain contact to support one another in their activities and to exchange information.

It may be more or less formal: it may depend upon conferences or meetings of formally constituted organizations, or it may take place informally, as people make visits to each others' agencies, speak on the telephone or in the street, or send messages and electronic documents to each other. The importance of networking among development agencies and communities is well established. However, networks can be difficult to sustain, for example where poverty, unemployment or lack of time are factors. They tend to depend upon reciprocity: if reciprocity is perceived as being unequal, people withdraw. (Chanan and Vos 1990). The community and voluntary sector may depend upon networks by default, in the absence of appropriate support structures. Networking has not succeeded in providing the levels and quality of support needed for advice and training in IT.

It has been suggested that electronic networking matches perfectly the characteristics of community and voluntary organizations:

- It supports the informal non-hierarchical exchange of information.

- It helps lateral communication and decentralized co-operation.

- It cuts out unnecessary forms of bureaucratic "dead wood" (Polman 1990).

This potential is being realized, and among agencies working internationally, the use of telematics is established. Electronic mail and bulletin board systems have been shown to be effective for campaigning organizations, but among organizations that depend more on ideas and processes than news and facts for their work, the advantages remain unclear; the need for a critical mass of users means that adoption will continue to be gradual. It has also been found that:

> computer networking worked better when participants already had a
> history of interacting through conventional methods (Rubinyi 1989).

Telematics may stimulate a form of networking based on information dissemination and sharing; where the networking lacks objectives the applicability of the technology may remain unproven. The benefits of networking are difficult to assess, and many organizations will want to extend traditional human networks with electronic networks in an experimental and developmental way.

Horizontal Communication

"Horizontal" communication is seen in conjunction with the notion of "vertical" communication, described by Halloran (1983):

> the flow of information and the direction of most communication is
> from the top downwards. Invariably the vertical prevails over the

horizontal. It is important to consider the implications of communication being so often a matter of the few talking to the many, directly or indirectly, about the perceived needs or problems of the many, from the unquestioned standpoint of the few.

Vertical communication has dominated in our society, in terms of both volume and influence; for example, through the traditional broadcasting and newspaper industries. Telematics has strong potential to reduce this domination.

The logic of the technologies is fundamental. The technology of printing has proven enormously powerful because (for those able to invest in it) it allows the transmission of a message from one to many. Radio and television have similar power, the power of mass media, whereas telephony works according to a different, more interactive, logic. The former are vertical and formal systems; telephony is interactive and informal. Much of the potential of telematics lies in the integration of the two, in enabling formal and informal communication, information production and sharing, and so on. The notion of "horizontal versus vertical" is a simplification: the technology will give rise to greater and greater fluidity in information transfer and availability.

Vertical communication carries messages from centre to periphery, from desk to field, from haves to have-nots, and these inequities can be reinforced and perpetuated by the vertical systems themselves. It follows that the promotion of horizontal communication is in the interests of empowerment and participative democracy. The notion of horizontal communication implies a potential shift in the origin of much of the information that people receive. It has been suggested that we need information models which:

> *assume human beings to be capable of initiating actions rather than merely serving as reactive targets of persuasion (Donohew and Springer 1980).*

The potential of telematics, which in theory enables efficient, inexpensive horizontal communication at local level, has been heralded widely. That potential has not yet been demonstrated clearly, as a result of three particular factors:

- Many groups lack the confidence with computers to be ready to go beyond word processing and databases.

- There are concerns about uncommitted and potential costs associated with on-line communications.

- There is a dearth of case study material from which agencies can identify models of use appropriate to their practices. Valuable experience should be provided by such initiatives as the Welsh Information Network, the Manchester Host and the Greenspace Networking Resources Project.

Information Sharing

Availability of information relates to power. Organizations concerned with the empowerment of disadvantaged people tend to be active in making information available. This issue is related to "information as a right of citizenship", "freedom of information" and so on. An ethic of information sharing does exist within the sector, but often this may be weighted more to giving than to receiving, with little interest in on-line searching of databases. The interest is in organizing and making available their own information, not in searching out more information and new sources.

The potential for IT to promote information sharing arises in three areas. The first of these concerns the exchange of information in machine readable form on disk, by cable links between computers, or on-line using telematics. In spite of occasional but realistic scares about viruses, disk-swapping in particular is widely practised, being inexpensive and relatively straightforward. Each method of sharing machine readable data remains troubled with occasional technical difficulties: incompatibility of disks or of disk formats, or the peculiarities of communications software, for example. These should not obscure the enormous potential for sharing and exchanging reusable information. Improvements in compatibility within the IT industry and enhanced skills within the community and voluntary sector would result in a small technical improvement, which could lead to significantly increased levels of information sharing.

The second area where IT can promote information sharing is the use of fax. The technology is generally felt to be user friendly, and it is convenient for the transfer of relatively time-sensitive intelligence, but the potential for information sharing is limited by the fact that the information is not received in machine readable form.

The third area of IT application is information design, the presentation of information. The advent of relatively inexpensive desktop publishing systems has enabled many organizations to improve the quality of the material that they produce, giving rise to increased confidence in the message that the organization is trying to deliver, and in the value of sharing it.

Information as a Commodity

The three principles outlined above suggest a distinctive culture of communication, including other factors associated with information handling, such as the importance of informally published and semi-published documents, diversity of sources, and so on.

At the same time, IT is deeply implicated in various social trends, in particular with regard to the treatment of information as a commodity that can be bought and sold: a function of the power of the technology to enable people to collect, store and retrieve large quantities of data quickly and efficiently; to transfer it rapidly; and to repackage it in new ways tailored to specific requirements. This technical power has been combined with political and economic pressures to charge for services of all kinds:

> *Current pressures within many organizations, both public and private, have led to the setting up of budget control centres. These tend to work against the concept of data as a shared resource since each budget centre optimises its own resources. As a result, duplication of effort increases. The national or corporate good and the additional benefits that come from combining data sets, tend to get squeezed out (Dale 1991).*

Problems such as these confront organizations in the private and statutory sectors: they represent a more serious challenge to the community and voluntary sector's culture of communication. As Moore and Steele point out:

> *Any shift towards the market-oriented provision of information will deprive some groups in the community of access (Moore and Steele 1991).*

Political and commercial pressures have generated a culture in which information is regarded as a commodity, and it is legitimate to make a charge for it. This is entirely consistent within the private sector; however, the dominant "currency" in the community and voluntary sector is not cash, but time and energy. People help each other and share knowledge, and thus they create and invest in an alliance.

There is a clash between these two information cultures: one where information attracts a price (and therefore is not available to everyone who may need it), and one where it is exchanged, given in contribution to building an alliance.

The discomfort that many organizations feel over this issue is compounded by the issue of information resale, i.e. the operation of brokers who are able to use the technology to make money from repackaging information. This raises questions about ownership of information and threatens to lead to a culture in which less information is disseminated freely. Ownership of information, or of the channels by which it is made available, can limit its flow, leading to various inequalities, including those between geographical regions.

There have always been costs and charges for printed information. The new information market-place, based on the availability of machine readable data and telecommunications, has given rise to an awareness of the costs associated with information; the situation appears to be irreversible. The continuing tendency to charge for information services threatens to exclude many people and groups from the new market-place, including non-users of the technology.

IT allows for the establishment of mechanisms whereby community groups can be paid for the information they produce or the services that they offer. Some groups, while obliged to pay for information that previously they might have obtained without charge, now have opportunities to raise income from their research and other work. Questions arise:

- How does this new raised income compare with their new expenditure on information?

- Are there important audiences whose access to the information is denied because of cost?

These issues are developing quickly: they are complex and have significant implications, indicating a conflict between the provision of information for profit and its use as a public good. Processes and implications must be examined so that regulatory mechanisms can be established.

IT and Community and Voluntary Organizations

The Survey Literature

A number of general points emerge from a consideration of the survey literature. Successful adoption of IT is mostly associated with the larger and/or better-resourced organizations within the sector. Less well-resourced organizations often find the time and money barriers highly problematic or insurmountable. Many people and agencies have undergone frustrating, distracting and unsatisfactory experiences in attempting to adopt IT. Nonetheless, several studies are unambiguous about the levels of satisfaction recorded and advantages reported by those who were positive enough to respond to questionnaires.

Community and voluntary organizations tend to underestimate the time, energy and costs required to establish computer systems; unrealistic expectations are commonplace, sometimes leading to wider organizational complications when the benefits of computerization are slow to emerge.

The adoption and use of IT will continue to be problematic, and its exploitation will consistently be far below potential, as long as organizations lack money, appropriate advice, and appropriate training, in order to commit the kinds of investment that the technology calls for.

Non-users of IT

The risk of wide differentiation between users and non-users of IT in the voluntary sector is highlighted by Deacon and Golding (1988), who noted that while the differentiated pattern of usage is not really surprising:

> *what is particularly striking is the difference in attitudes towards computer technology displayed by users and non-users.*

They note that groups and agencies who take the plunge into electronic information storage, desktop publishing or word processing are amply impressed by the merits of doing so (Deacon and Golding 1988).

Such attitudes contrast sharply with the indifference shown by the majority of non-users surveyed. Deacon and Golding's evidence here suggests that:

> *for most non-users, computers are seen at best as being a luxury they cannot afford, and at worst a total irrelevance.*

Ultimately, this may exacerbate existing inequalities within the voluntary sector. Failure to confront this issue amounts to collusion in the widening of the "information gap" at a crucial point. We are not suggesting that people are foolish not to adopt IT, but we point to the benefits that, users have found, accrue from using the technology, however basic or crude the machines or software happen to be.

There is a case, as Deacon and Golding point out, for increased investment and co-ordination of voluntary sector computing resources. They argue that it is necessary to go beyond established "community computing" if non-users are not to be excluded from opportunities to adopt IT. There is a need for clear, accessible demonstration of the benefits that users have found.

IT within the Organization

Many organizations in all sectors experience unexpected disruption internally with the introduction of IT. We consider some aspects of this experience for voluntary agencies.

The reasons for introducing IT into organizations are often obscure or undefined. It may be that the decision follows an assessment that the technology will enable the organization to achieve its objectives more efficiently or more effectively, or to achieve additional objectives which it has been agreed are desirable. There are often motives to do with greater control over internal operations or procedures, which have little to do with the organization's objectives. There may be an assumption that IT can help in the delivery of information or services. But these motives may be inappropriate in the first place, and the power of the technology exposes this. It is critical for organizations considering the adoption of IT to address this point, and to try to be explicit about the reasons for introducing the technology.

The adoption of new technology implies a great change in the way people think of information, the ways they use it, and the methods by which they pay for it. This change is going to take place at a much slower rate than that at which technology can develop (Maslin 1982). Organizations need to be aware that subtle changes are implicit in the technology, beyond the straightforward automation of procedures. Some organizations meet this by establishing working groups, which not only take decisions on IT purchase but also monitor the effects of its introduction, discuss implications, and explore ways of handling the changes that they initiate.

This helps to avoid another difficulty which organizations experience: the tendency to allow IT expertise to become or remain invested in one person. This leaves the organization vulnerable to that person's absence, and to the perhaps unquestioned level of their expertise; it also constitutes a barrier to the creation of a desirable learning environment.

IT may affect relationships with other organizations. On the whole, these are likely to be positive developments, promoting networking and the sharing of resources and information. However, such development takes up time which might have been dedicated to working with non-users of IT.

Awareness: Access to Information and Advice About IT

It is possible to waste a lot of time and money, and even to jeopardize the whole organization, if you get it wrong (Computanews 1991).

The quality and availability of information, advice, training, and support are critical questions for the future development of IT in the voluntary sector. Organizations may begin by wanting information concerning computers, then advice, followed by training, help and support; subsequently, they are likely to require further help with one or more of these elements. Many of the problems experienced in voluntary organizations result from the lack of information and advice, or its poor quality. The technology is an increasingly accepted part of any office environment; it is more and more accessible in terms of prices and availability in high street stores: yet inadequate advice remains the norm. It is easy for the converted and for computer dealers to talk about the tasks that could be carried out, and their potential benefits, without fully appreciating (or wishing to appreciate) the needs of an organization and its ability to perform the tasks and exploit the technology fully.

There is often inadequate appreciation by voluntary organizations of the need to get good impartial advice; together with the real difficulty of knowing who to turn to.

So on both the demand side and the supply side, there is room for improvement in the provision of information and advice. Two examples may illustrate this: these are the "leading light" and "trojan horse" syndromes.

The "leading light" is someone, paid or volunteer, who "knows about computers" and is invited into an organization to "help get the computer system right". Very often it "simply" requires a little bit of programming comparable to another piece of work that the expert or enthusiast carried out recently. It is possible that the needs and nature of the agency's work have not sufficiently been taken into account in the choice and design of the software; and it is likely that the agency is vulnerable to the departure of their consultant, because the system they are left with is unique, but not necessarily tailored to their requirements.

The "trojan horse" syndrome refers to the situation where an agency receives an unsolicited donation of equipment, inappropriate for its needs or for the way it works. It can be difficult to decline an offer from a benefactor; supporting and maintaining superseded equipment can be expensive or impossible; committing the organization to compatibility with inappropriate hardware can be extravagant and restricting; working methods can be distorted to accommodate the technology; and so on. In both examples, agencies need access to advice that is impartial, sensitive to their work, and technically knowledgeable. The "leading light" syndrome is really a version of the "trojan horse": before a service is offered to a busy agency, even by an expert volunteer, it makes sense to take advice when significant changes to work practices are implied, as is so often the case with IT. Many voluntary organizations may have little appreciation of the impact that IT can have internally; as staff are busy with their jobs, in and out of the office, they may not consider the implications of the volunteer or consultant's contribution until it is too late, and the cost and time commitment can be a shock.

Usually the need is less dramatic; for example, it may be that advice on a particular piece of software is sought. An organization considering a purchase knows it can benefit by talking to a similar agency which is using that software, but often there is no simple way of identifying such a contact.

These examples raise questions about the availability and accessibility of advice. The risks of organizations making mistakes, and considering IT half-heartedly, are high. Among the most important needs are for advice on the time required to adopt IT and incorporate it into the office environment, and advice on the full costs of computerization.

Handling the Technology: Education, Training, Awareness

The need for training and outreach work is as vital to the success of the systems as the technology itself. Without the explanatory power of trainers and educators the potential of the systems for a wide range of users is lost (Jones 1991).

All users of IT need an infrastructure to support their handling of the technology, to provide training in operation, troubleshooting and help in developing new applications. In the community and voluntary sector the development of this infrastructure is restricted by various factors such as the financial insecurity of some agencies, or the low priority of administrative work. Users are frustrated at being unable to exploit the technology. The need is generally referred to using the shorthand term "training", which can be misleading. Where organizations are mostly small, have temporary and voluntary staff with a wide range of backgrounds, work in co-operative rather than hierarchical environments, with little capital and no tradition of investment in support systems or services, it is essential to promote the complete culture of IT use. This means much more than "training": it includes "understanding", education and support. It involves an appreciation of the role of information and of the potential of information systems to help exploit it.

The recent UNET survey (Hopson 1990) showed that the level of skills within the sector remains quite low, in terms of anything more advanced than office automation. Information handling using machine readable data represents a stage of development barely recognized, let alone reached. Most people in voluntary organizations have not been exposed to IT environments with multitasking and multifile systems where data transfer is a routine and creative activity.

Information Awareness and Use

IT can be of benefit if it helps people to improve their use of information, but this requires an explicit recognition of the importance of information handling in community and voluntary organizations, and that IT may be applied only to a proportion of the information needed and used. Voluntary organizations generally have a low appreciation of the potential contribution that information could make in their work; it is accorded low status and little investment.

Often, people prefer to refer to others, through networks, rather than address their information need to a formal service or system. Many information needs will go unsatisfied as people fail to find a person to help them and are disinclined to use an information system. IT can change the nature of information transfer, and can therefore affect interpersonal communication in information seeking; telematics will add significantly to other options like telephony in promoting communication for information use. Simply promoting improved access to information is not sufficient, and could be counter-productive.

IT as a Tool

In promoting IT we risk promoting human behaviour as analogous to machine processing, at the expense of other human values and potential. It has been noted that computers are representative of values that are "basically deterministic, reductionist and mechanical". This culture inhibits consideration of concepts that are social, cultural or spiritual (Rosenberg 1974). In organizations where social, cultural or spiritual values are significant in themselves, therefore, we can hardly be surprised if the set of values associated with computers is sometimes felt to be alien, threatening or unacceptable.

The difficulties lie not with the technology itself, but with the cultural "baggage" that comes with it, which includes approaches to training and management that are rigid and hierarchical; decision making at the expense of debate; consistency at the expense of innovation and individuality, and so on. Many organizations are clearly put off by these concerns. The key problems affecting the future development of IT use in the community and voluntary sector have to do with the ways in which IT is introduced, used and supported in sympathy with the users' needs and aspirations. The problem is to ensure that the organizational culture – which may reflect egalitarian, co-operative, or spiritual values, for example – is not distorted in an attempt to match it with the culture of IT: it is the technology and its baggage which must be shaped to the needs of the organization. The technology comprises a range of tools, many of them interrelated, which can be used to accomplish tasks, often extremely efficiently and quickly. IT is not a panacea that can simply be applied and beneficial results awaited. Organizations have to work hard at using these tools, and invest time and energy, both in making sure that the tools are configured appropriately and in making sure that people can use them effectively and rewardingly.

There are two factors to which we wish to draw attention:

- The technology consists of elements that can be compounded – computers, printers, software, video, broadcasting, telecommunications, and so on. This introduces a need for new management skills. Effective application of IT might thus require "facilitators", facility managers who can help an organization arrive at the optimum combination, but there is a severe shortage, within the community and voluntary sector, of such people, and a lack of a facilitating, resourcing infrastructure.

- The technology could be far more accessible and easy to use than it is. It has been pointed out that "There are too many situations where it is taken for granted that the imperfections of the technology are made up for by the ingenuity of the users" (Baddeley and Dawes 1987).

While software becomes increasingly powerful and complex, relatively simple programs that can be used by novices are few and far between. All the impetus within the IT industry seems to be on greater power for existing users. Since, by definition, they have some experience, there is little pressure on programmers and systems designers to create for novices. While this gap is partially filled by shareware writers and consultants within the community computing movement, their impact remains limited. There is considerable dissatisfaction among community and voluntary agencies already using IT, let alone those who have been put off and remain non-users. This dissatisfaction relates to various areas such as lack of clarity in promotional literature for hardware and software, unreliability of printer technology (a point of frustration for many), incomprehensible manuals, incompatibility of disks, and so on.

The inadequacy of much IT systems design should not be accepted by users: it constrains community and voluntary agencies. There are roles here for the industry, the academic sector, and the voluntary sector to work together on developing and publicising more accessible, human centred systems. We see a particular need for attention to be paid to systems design: this concerns the tendency for systems to take action and render people passive. We need systems that are configured to encourage people to be proactive rather than reactive, which means the development of systems for two-way communication.

IT Handling Skills

You program a robot, you train a dog (or possibly a soldier), but for human beings you provide educational environments (Cooley 1987).

The acquisition of IT handling skills has to do with more than just "training"; we distinguish between "operational" and "exploitative" skills. There is an assumption that people only need training for their operational needs, but this leads to underexploitation of IT and underdevelopment of human potential. Some people will just want to learn operational skills, with only an awareness of wider potential. An emphasis on operational training can be constraining, because it denies people the kind of rich, developmental environment that they merit:

> *Training produces narrow, over-dedicated capabilities which are generally machine, system or program-specific. With the ever-increasing rate of technological change, the "knowledge" required to cope with a particular machine or system may be obsolete in a couple of years' time. The trainee is then lost, and requires further training (Cooley 1987).*

The potential of IT calls for familiarity with its "context": why it is there and what its capabilities are. The transfer of IT handling skills needs to include the following:

- Education: basic knowledge about the technology.
- Awareness: of the principles of different applications, including potential applications.
- Training: for a given task or application.

These categories should not be regarded as hard and fast: all three approaches are interrelated and should not be offered independently.

Sources of Help

> *The problem always is that you know someone, somewhere has experienced this problem/situation, but who are they and where are they? (Bell and Harris 1992).*

The development of IT use in the community and voluntary sector depends upon the competence, accessibility and availability of certain key sources of help. Such sources exist, including networks and umbrella organizations; we focus on consultants and resource centres.

Consultants, Secondees, Advisers

> *Most IT advice needs of the voluntary sector will best be met by peripatetic consultants with experience and skills in a wide range of hardware and software (Thorpe 1989).*

We include those who offer consultancy in IT to agencies within the sector, typically on a self-employed basis; those seconded from private companies to work with a given organization for a specific period, in an arrangement where their expertise is offered in exchange for the developmental experience of the voluntary sector working environment; and those who contribute advice and expertise more informally, and often without payment – many are students, have posts in the academic sector, or are retired people. We also include here those dealers and suppliers of hardware and software who offer more than the basic level of technical support.

"Good consultants have full diaries": that is to say, their services are in considerable demand. Secondments can be difficult, and are less easy to establish in the current adverse economic climate, and informal arrangements with advisers can leave organizations vulnerable to the "leading light" syndrome. The potential contribution of these sources has not been tapped; more consultants are coming into the field with something to offer: they should be encouraged and supported, and the networks that we discuss below have a role to play. There are possibilities for more flexible arrangements with private companies, whereby more limited but carefully prepared contributions of time could still make a significant difference without eating too deeply into the company's resources.

There is also expertise, time and energy within the academic sector, which the voluntary sector has been slow to exploit. There are instances of effective collaboration with academic institutions, but the combined power of staff, students and equipment in academic institutions could be marshalled more effectively to help community and voluntary agencies adopt and apply the technology. Every year, thousands of students have to carry out projects, many of which could be related to the real practical problems of agencies at work. There are opportunities to apply the time, energy and expertise they have to offer, provided it is properly supervised.

There is considerable concern over the appropriateness of available consultants, advisers, dealers and suppliers. Some agencies have had unhappy experiences, pointing to the damaging effects and unnecessary costs of working with someone who had little or no understanding of the nature of their work, and who made no attempt to find out. Stories abound of agencies whose dealers have sold them systems that are more complicated than they need. We must stress the importance for agencies of ensuring that any consultant they use is right for them, is in sympathy with their aspirations and bases his or her work on an understanding of what they do. This usually means someone who starts by asking "What do you do?" and not by saying "This is what I sell".

Community and voluntary agencies have a responsibility to ensure that any adviser they use is adequately briefed. Time has to be committed to this exercise, and the reasons for the adviser's presence should be explained to all staff.

Resource Centres

The voluntary sector has a tradition of using resource centres for community development through the sharing of resources (Taylor 1983). IT gives rise to a demand for access to equipment, for advice and information on choosing and using it, and for bureau services for those without access to it. Centres appropriately equipped and staffed could make a difference within the voluntary sector by minimizing mistakes and maximizing efficient use. Various models of resource centre for diverse purposes have been tried.

Community Computing in Newcastle

Together with the Coda Project in Nottingham, Community Computing in Newcastle (CCiN) has long been seen as a leading example of a community computing resource centre, but due to lack of funding CCiN had to close in March 1992. While we would not argue that it should be regarded as a "model" in the sense of being appropriate for close imitation, we feel that there are several lessons to be learned from an understanding of CCiN's experience:

- The importance of appropriate premises.
- The need for a careful balance of bureau services (desktop publishing, word processing, database design etc.), training and support.
- The need for a range of equipment that is compatible with that used by voluntary organizations and, ideally, familiar to users.
- The need for clear policies on cross-subsidizing work for the community and voluntary agencies, by selling services to other organizations.
- The need to balance a professional approach to serving clients with a sensitivity to the difficulties many voluntary workers may have, for example in keeping appointments during normal office hours.

A problem with traditional resource centres for community groups is that resource centre staff can find themselves distracted into helping groups in other ways (Taylor 1983).

Community Teleservice Centres

Community teleservice centres (CTSCs or "telecottages") developed in rural areas of Scandinavia in the 1980s; they are community development initiatives aimed at providing access to various kinds of IT for communities traditionally denied such access through geographical and other factors. This access is provided usually with a primary aim of promoting local economic development: additional objectives include community education, access to information services (e.g. local authority databases), training, and so on. A typical CTSC will have a range of computers and software, fax and telex facilities, on-line access, video equipment, and so on, and will be run by staff appointed from within the community served.

The CTSC movement worldwide is now quite extensive and there are a number of UK initiatives. The Highlands and Islands Development Board in Scotland has applied the Scandinavian experience with advanced telecommunications facilities. In England, a telecottage and teleworking adviser has been working with Action with Communities in Rural England (ACRE) to help promote CTSCs. Telecottages Wales/TeleFythynnod Cymru has been set up as a coordinating and support organization for CTSCs in Wales. Developments are not confined to rural areas: urban examples, such as those associated with the Manchester Host initiative, called electronic village halls (EVHs), have also begun to emerge.

There has been debate over the funding and sources of income for CTSCs, particularly their orientation towards providing fee-based services to the private sector. One report suggests that:

> The least successful Finnish telecottages ... have been those which set out to grow into commercial ventures (Oksa 1991).

A report on the development of EVHs in east Manchester, however, makes the following points:

- The Scandinavian experience indicates that long-term security can only be achieved by building a firm base of marketable services.

- The institutional structure of the EVH also seems important. The first need is to foster the fledgling EVH in an established institution, thereby being able to focus on setting up the EVH, training new staff and developing an awareness of the service in the local community, without having to create the organizational structures from scratch (Shenton et al. 1991).

This movement is at a critical point, as economic recession puts pressure on sources of funding for CTSCs and obliges them to spend time and energy selling services in the market, at the likely expense of community development. There is concern that local communities do not lose out in these cases, and find that CTSCs are using non-local expertise or cheap local labour to provide services to organizations beyond the community, such as by telecommunications from rural to urban areas. There is a need for a clear evaluation of the trends in this area, and for the development of guidelines in matching the financial strategies of CTSCs to their community development objectives.

The frequent funding problems faced by community computing resource centres draw attention to the lack of strategies from central and local government for IT support in the community and voluntary sector. There is sufficient experience to show that the contribution of such services to the work of voluntary agencies is always likely to justify systematic investment. The vulnerability of CCiN probably reflects the fact that the project remained too small to cover the field fully and win a broad enough constituency of users and supporters. There exist numerous successful, more modest local initiatives; we need more evidence of their impact in relation to their vulnerability. Perhaps the larger, better staffed and better resourced centres, covering small regions rather than local areas, will survive and have an impact (although they might run the risk of losing credibility at local level). This calls for more collaboration between several bodies, including local authorities, which can be difficult to effect. At least in the short and medium term, the development of CTSCs depends on the vision and commitment of local authorities, to provide help in preparing strategies, start-up funding, and ongoing support.

Concluding Remarks

Social and economic well-being at local and individual level is greatly affected by the effectiveness and efficiency of voluntary organizations. The potential for IT to contribute to the work of such organizations is beyond dispute. IT is worthy of strategic investment, and existing resources (equipment, data, expertise) could be better co-ordinated, through advice services, resource centres, networking, registers and switchboard services. This chapter has sought to outline the contribution of IT, to put it into context, to indicate problematic areas, and to suggest ways in which various participants – local groups, national agencies, policy makers, private companies, academic institutions, local authorities – can help to facilitate the appropriate adoption and use of this technology.

19 | The Human User Interface

David Hopson

Human Centred Voluntary Organizations

What do you get when you put a human centred technology into a human centred organization? The answer is the human user interface (HUI). Voluntary organizations are, almost by definition, human centred. This chapter looks at some of the issues that have arisen as PC level computing has been introduced into such organizations.

The voluntary sector has always demanded that any computers should be "accessible" and "user friendly". "Accessible" means that the technology should be understandable in terms of familiar practices, and presentable in plain English – no jargon. A machine which can be used for writing letters, managing a list of volunteers and producing copy for the newsletter is accessible. An IBM PC-AT 80286 compatible, running word processing and database applications is not.

"User friendly" means that the machine should be capable of delivering a consistent result with the least amount of effort and skill on the part of the user, and in an environment that is hedged about with procedures manuals, Post-its, and on-line help screens.

Very similar demands are doubtless made by most computer users in all sectors of the economy. Voluntary organizations differ from commercial, industrial and government organizations in a number of important ways:

- They do not have computer, information technology or data processing departments – users have to fend for themselves.

- Training opportunities and/or funding are often limited, and in-house support for learning and development is difficult to provide.

- Equipment is shared and used by many different people, each with individual requirements and abilities.

- People have much wider discretion to determine for themselves how they do their work – they cannot be directed to use and become familiar with computers.

These differences reflect the fact that most voluntary organizations have very small numbers of regular staff – a voluntary organization with eight staff could be described as medium-sized, and one with twenty as large. Few voluntary organizations have staff numbers in three figures.

Voluntary organizations are therefore most often comparable with small businesses, but differ again in that:

- The primary objective of the enterprise is not to produce a living for people, but to provide social goods and services.
- Time is seen to be only loosely connected with money.

This means that people working for voluntary organizations are willing to put in huge amounts of time and effort to get the best of their systems, and are relatively unwilling to buy in consultancy and development labour from elsewhere.

Hacking, Power Users and Front Ends

The upshot is that the voluntary sector has become a potent breeding ground for hackers. I use the term "hacker" in its original sense of someone who can motor round keyboard and software, rather than in the pejorative sense of someone who invades the US Defense systems using a modem. Hackers can do a bit of everything that's needed with a computer. They act with a kind of sage confidence in the face of anything new or unusual. Often, they are also living proof of the adage that "in the valley of the blind the one-eyed man is king"; although she is often a queen!

It is in the work of hackers (the people whom the computer press now dignify with the term "power users"), and in the differences between them and the people they work with, that you can begin to discern the human user interface.

What the voluntary sector hacker does is to customize and tailor systems so that "real" users, ordinary computer-disinterested people, can get from the machine what they or their organization require. The need for this role arises because all off-the-peg software applications are generic in nature. None are designed for or dedicated to a single task, so they do nothing very well. Even to write something as simple as a letter using a word processing package will require a fair amount of software setting up before it can be done well, and time after time in a consistent house style.

It is the power user, or hacker, who builds document templates, writes macros, designs menus, creates batch routines and so on. These things then sit as the real "front end" between the everyday user of the system and the technology of hardware, operating system and software.

The front end is a distillation of a power user's skill and knowledge batched up as meta-functions of the environment which is being used. Front ends are designed to do what your hacker would do if he or she were constantly available at the beck and call of anyone who sat down at a keyboard, or picked up a mouse. In brief, what can often be found in voluntary organizations are prototypical expert systems, where the domain specialism is that of knowing how to use a computer "properly" and achieve desired results.

Information Management and Dissemination

An important area of work for the voluntary sector concerns information management (including retrieval) and information dissemination. The functional, technological mechanisms for handling, manipulating and distributing machine readable data are readily available using disks and on-line systems. But the difference between having access to say a large .DBF (dBase format) file and being able to get something sustainably useful out of it is usually dependent on the skill of the local, and committed, hacker.

For the hacker, many issues are involved, from the relatively simple ones to do with operating system and file management, to the complex ones of database routines, queries and so on. In the midst of this, the likely requirements of the everyday user must remain paramount – including those of which they may have no conscious knowledge.

For example, all automated data file handling needs to embody the checks that are second nature to the hacker and ensure that existing files and structures are not corrupted. This can often be more complicated than the actual information handling processes, and may even be of greater importance to everyday users than a single information task.

In building a human user interface as a quasi expert system, the ultimate complexity arises when the question of publication comes up. Putting information systems into alien machines is a daunting prospect. Here, the knowledge elicitation process must plumb to the very depths of the expert's understanding. People do weird things with their PCs and somehow these anomalies (and/or their consequences) have to be allowed for and accommodated.

Publication also throws up another issue which has to be addressed in the voluntary sector, arising from:

- The ease with which data can in any event be copied.
- The fact that "copyability" is necessarily enhanced and embodied in human user interface software.
- The desire of the sector to make resources (and information resources in particular) available at the point of need.
- The lack of funds which those most in need often suffer from.
- The need for information authors to get an income from their work.

It is easy to discern the contradictions. The sector wants to get information out in a highly usable and mobile form, which is just what the medium (disks and on-line) and the human user interface make possible. But then a lot of people don't have enough money to pay for the information, so with the best will in the world there's going to be an awful lot of easy-to-do copying going on. The author loses out on income, and eventually may find it economically impossible to carry on "writing", and so the sector loses an information resource.

This problem is very similar to the one faced by software publishers, and is one of the reasons why the Federation Against Software Theft (FAST) has had to be set up.

Making a Feature out of a Problem: Shareware

In the building trade, it often happens when you are fitting a kitchen that a rope of pipes drops down the wall right in the middle of one of the new work tops. At this point, the builder boxes the pipes in, sticks a load of hooks on the box, and calls it a mug-tree. In the trade, this is known as "making a feature out of a problem".

One solution which the voluntary sector is trying out reflects just such a philosophy. Instead of trying to stop information being copied using technical means, and legal and moral injunctions, the act of copying is being positively encouraged and facilitated in products. This is done to try to ensure that information becomes available to everyone who can use it (of whatever degree of computer literacy), regardless of their means. The financial interests of the author are protected by adapting the shareware licence that many software writers have been using to market their programs.

Shareware information, like shareware software, is information that can be copied, "tasted" and tried before it is paid for. The standard shareware licence places a legal and moral requirement on people who use a shareware product to conform to certain conditions; the most important normally is that the user registers their use of the product, and pays a fee. It is customary, too, to say the user cannot exploit the product directly for their own commercial benefit.

A key principle at the heart of voluntary sector ethics is that service should be given without cost to those with slender resources. The idea of shareware information is consistent with this core value of the sector. The voluntary sector, unlike business and industry, is committed to maximum dissemination of the information it creates and uses. Shareware information offers improvements in the efficiency and cost-effectiveness of dissemination from the perspective of producers and users alike.

For producers, the desire to maximize the diffusion of their information has to be tempered by the need for an income to support their work. Grant aid and subsidies for information work have always been difficult to get, and are probably harder to acquire now than ever. Information producers must get a growing proportion of their income from the market. The resources of the voluntary sector as a whole are under pressure. This is a market that has strictly limited budgets for information purchasing and where price is a key issue.

For information producers, therefore, it is essential to keep costs down if the price they can realistically charge for their work is to produce sufficient surplus to support its production. Disk-based information is significantly cheaper to produce than paper-based information. Unit costs of manufacture are lower, and, moreover, less capital need be tied up in stock – disks can almost be produced to order whereas in most cases books have to be printed in minimum quantities of 500. When disk-based information is released as shareware, further cost benefits accrue. Good shareware products reproduce and distribute themselves without cost to the original supplier. The efficiency of this form of distribution is amply demonstrated by the thriving businesses of shareware software authors like Marshall Magee, Phil Katz and Vernon Buerg (all of whom have work included in UNET's Information Studio), despite the cost of their products being remarkably low.

Producers who release information as shareware can sell their product in the normal way to their primary customers. They can then hope to see a new, secondary market develop without further cost or effort on their part. Producers who are in the position of not needing to charge for their information can use the shareware mechanism for free distribution. By requesting user registration, they can then ensure that subsequent releases of their material reach the parts that they want them to reach.

Turning to the position of users, the first benefit of shareware information is that it can be legally acquired without payment at the time of acquisition. Use of the information after evaluation places a legal and moral obligation on the user to conform with the conditions of the licence that the producer has given. In line with a common practice in the voluntary sector, it is possible to envisage a shareware information licence that has a scale of charges. Low income individuals, and unfunded groups could well be allowed to "self-certify" their status and pay nothing, or a much reduced registration fee. The secondary benefit of shareware information for users is that they will not waste money on materials that are not actually useful to them. The prices they pay will also tend to be lower, so they can acquire a wider range of material.

Users benefit from the medium of disk-based information itself. Material can easily be incorporated into users' own word processors and databases, saving all the rekeying that is required when information comes on paper. "Disk-top publishing" is dynamic and interactive.

Overall, organizations which distribute their information as shareware are in effect "selling to the sector" rather than to individuals. For the voluntary sector, shareware is a mechanism that allows those who have resources to subsidise those who do not, without loss to producers and without increasing costs for the user who can afford to pay.

A legitimate anxiety about shareware information is the apparent ease with which it can be abused. In reality, the potential for abuse has far more to do with the disk medium itself than with the shareware licence. Software manufacturers are well aware of the problem. For example, a graphics program that we use in UNET is sold for nearly £400. You can make a copy of it for the price of four disks – about £3.20. An hour with the photocopier will clone the manual. Major software houses have therefore set up FAST, the Federation Against Software Theft, to combat the problem.

No licence, whether commercial or shareware, can prevent copying of disks. Technical means to prevent copying have been tried, but in most cases the constraints they impose on the actions of the legitimate end-user have proved unacceptable to the market. Unlike software authors, information producers have the option of not making their work available on disk. The financial and functional imperative of the technology is such that producers are going to have to use disk-based media for information dissemination. Where a topic is unrepresented on disk-based media, someone, somewhere will do it if the existing producers in the field do not.

The shareware licence legitimates disk copying. When copying is illegal there is a positive disincentive to owning up to it – technically at least, you can be penalized. With shareware the contrary is true: by "owning up" you probably incur some cost, but you also acquire access to the source of the material that you value (you can get more, or get an update), and have the satisfaction of a warm moral glow!

The shareware idea itself can be seen as part of the human user interface. The hacker/power user has invented a means for economic exchange with their everyday users, and has somehow to facilitate and encourage that exchange in the systems they build.

The Continuing Need for Programming

There is an area of human–computer interaction that simply cannot be built in to hardware, operating systems and software applications as "human centred technology". There is a surprisingly large amount of "programming" that must always be tailored bespoke, and can only be created in and for a given context. It is then possible to start asking for new features from software application publishers. It would be wonderful if every word processor offered a simple way of setting up a user/task login routine.

The voluntary sector will be most interested in a combination of a standard "rich text format" file specification and stand-alone printout utility. Information could travel around in machine read-able/processable form, be printed when required, and then come out in a decent, readable form. After all, ultimately most computer users, one way or another, still want to get access to their information on paper.

References

Arthur Young (1987) The Arthur Young Practical Technology Group Guide to Information Engineering. Wiley, Chichester

Avison DE and Fitzgerald G (1988) Information Systems Development Blackwell, Oxford

Backus J (1978) Can programming be liberated from the von Neumann style? A functional style and its algebra of programs. Comm ACM 21(8): 368

Baddeley S and Dawes N (1987) Information technology support for devolution: Vision and reality in Walsall housing department. Local Government Studies July/August, 14

Barthlemy S, Edin G, Toutain E, Becker S (1987) Requirements analysis in KBS development. Deliverable D3, ESPRIT project number 1098, Cap Sogeti Innovation

Bell J and Harris K (1992) The ITaC survey of adoption and use of computers in the community and voluntary sector. Community Development Foundation, London

Birkhoff G (1969) Mathematics and psychology. SIAM Review 11(4): 429

Boden MA (ed) (1989) Benefits and Risks of Knowledge-Based Systems. Council for Science and Society and Oxford University Press, Oxford

Bodker S (1989) Human activity approach to user interface. DIAMI PB-291, Aarhus University

Boehm B (1986) A spiral model of software development and enhancement. ACM Sigsoft Software Engineering Notes 3(4)

Boehm B (1988) A spiral model of software development and enhancement. IEEE Computer, May

Born G (ed) (1988) Guidelines for quality assurance of expert systems. Computing Service Association

Boynton AC, Shank ME, Zmud RW (1985) Critical success factor analysis as a methodology for MIS planning. MIS Quarterly, June

Breuker J, Wielinga B, Schreiber G, de Greef P, de Hoog R, van Someren M, Wielemaker J, Billaut J, Davoodi M, Hayward S (1987) Model-driven knowledge acquisition: interpretation models. Deliverable A1, ESPRIT project number 1098, University of Amsterdam/STC Technology Ltd

Breuker J, Wielinga B (1988) Models of expertise in knowledge acquisition. In: Guida G, Tasso C (eds) Topics in Expert System Design: Methodologies and Tools. North Holland, Amsterdam

Bright C, de Hoog R, Martil R, Taylor RM (1991) Framework life-cycle model, ESPRIT project number 5248

British Computer Society (1978) Report on user requirements for data processing. BCS, London

British Computer Society (1989) Report on undergraduate curricula for software engineering. BCS/IEE, London

British Computer Society (1990) From potential to reality: "Hybrids" – A critical force in the application of information technology in the 1990s. A Report from the British Computer Society Task Group on Hybrids. BCS, London, January

Brodner P (1990a) Towards the anthropocentric factory. In: International Workshop on Industrial Culture and Human-Centred Systems. Tokyo-Keizai University, Tokyo

Brodner P (1990b) The Shape of Future Technology: The Anthropocentric Alternative. Springer-Verlag, London

Bullinger HJ, Fahnrich KP, Kurz E (1990) Expert systems in production, VDI-Z 131.10

Butler Cox Foundation (1987a) Competitive-edge applications: Myths and reality. Management Summary Report 61. Butler Cox & Partners Ltd, London

Butler Cox Foundation (1987b) Using system development methods. Research Report 57. Butler Cox & Partners Ltd, London, June

Cash JI Jr, McFarlan FW, McKenney JL (1988) Corporate Information Systems Management: The Issues Facing Senior Executives, 2nd edn. Irwin, Homewood, IL

Cash JI Jr, McFarlan FW, McKenney JL (1989) Information technology – A new competitive weapon. Sloan Management Review, Fall

CBI (1991) The effectiveness of IT investments survey. CBI, London

Chanan G, Vos K (1990) Social change and local action: Coping with disadvantage in urban areas. European Foundation for the Improvement of Living and Working Conditions, Shankill, Co. Dublin, p 39

Chang C (1991) Managing investment in IT: A review of best practice. Presented at the Business Intelligence/Computer Weekly Managing IT Investment Conference, London

Chekaluk R, Hofziger EM (1989) Expert operator: Deploying YES/MVS II. In Schorr H, Rappoport A (eds) Innovative Applications of AI. AAAI Press, New York

Cohen J (1988) A view of the origins and development of Prolog. Comm ACM 31(1):26

Cohen J (1990) Constraint logic. Comm ACM 33(7): 52

Community Development Foundation (1992) Press enter: IT in the community and voluntary sector. CDF, London

Computanews (1991) Factsheet: Buying a computer. Available from: London Advice Services Alliance (LASA), 2nd Floor, Universal House, 88–94 Wentworth Street, London E1 7SA, UK

Conklin EJ (1987) Hypertext: An introduction and survey. IEEE Computer 20(9)

Cooley M (1987) Architect or Bee? The Human Price of Technology. Hogarth Press, London

Cooley M (1989a) Human-Centred Systems in Designing Human Centred Technology: A Cross Disciplinary Project in Computer Aided Manufacturing. Springer-Verlag, London

Cooley M (1989b) European Competitiveness in the 21st Century. FAST, EEC

Coopers and Lybrand (1988) Managers and IT Competence. London

Corbett JM, Rasmussen LB, Rauner F (1991) Crossing the Border: The Social and Engineering Design of Computer Integrated Manufacturing Systems. Springer-Verlag, London

Cottrell N, Rapley K (1991) Factors critical to the success of executive information systems in British Airways. European Journal of Information Systems, January

Coulson-Thomas C (1991) Lecture presented at the City University Business School (CUBS)

Dale P (1991) GIS: The issues. Information Technology and Public Policy 9(3): 188

Dankbaar B (1987) Social assessment of workplace technology – Some experiences with the German programme "Humanization of Work". Research Policy 16: 337

Darlington J, Field AJ, Pull H (1986) The unification of functional and logic languages. In: DeGroot D, Lindstrom G (eds) Logic Programming Functions, Relations and Equations. Prentice-Hall, Englewood Cliffs, New Jersey

Davoodi M, Bredeweg B, Schreiber G, van Someren M, Wielinga B (1987) A design methodology for KBS. Deliverable D8, ESPRIT project number 1098, STC Technology Ltd/University of Amsterdam

Deacon D, Golding P (1988) The information needs of voluntary and community groups. Centre for Mass Communications Research, University of Leicester, p 64

de Greef P, Breuker J, de Jong T (1988) Modality: an analysis of functions, user control and communication in knowledge-based systems. Deliverable D6, ESPRIT project number 1098

Demb A (1979) Computer Systems for Human Systems. Pergamon, Oxford

Denning PJ (ed) (9188) Report of the ACM Task Force on the core of computer science. ACM Press, New York

Department of Employment (1991) The effectiveness of student modelling: Learning technologies. Department of Employment/Central Office of Information Project Report OL 109. HMSO, London

Dijkstra EW (1968) Goto statement considered harmful. Comm ACM 11(3): 147

Dijkstra EW (1982) Selected Writings on Computing. A Personal Perspective. Springer-Verlag, London

Dijkstra EW (1989) On the cruelty of really teaching computing science. Comm ACM 34: 1400

Donohew L, Springer ER (1980) Information seeking versus information diffusion: An alternative paradigm. Community Development Journal 15(3): 213

Downs E, Clare P, Coe I (1988) Structured Systems Analysis and Design Method. Prentice-Hall, Englewood Cliffs, New Jersey

Dragstedt C (1991) Shopping in the year 2000. Discount Merchandiser, September

Dreyfus HL (1972) What Computers Can't Do. Harper and Row, New York

Dreyfus HL, Dreyfus S (1986) Mind Over Machines. Basil Blackwell, Oxford

Drucker PF (1988) The coming of the new organization. Harvard Business Review 66(1)

DTI (1988) Expert Systems in Britain. HMSO, London

Earl MJ (1989) Management Strategies for Information Technology. Prentice-Hall, Englewood Cliffs, New Jersey

Eason KD, Damodaran L, Stewart TFM (1974) A survey of man– computer interaction in commercial applications. Report LUTERG No. 144, Department of Human Sciences, University of Technology, Loughborough

Economist (1991) Management Education Survey. 2 March

Ehn P (1988) Work oriented design of computer artefacts. Swedish Centre for Working Life, Stockholm

Euromethod Public Procurement Group (1990) Phase 2, Deliverable 1, State of the Art Report, December

Feigenbaum EA, McCorduck P (1984) The Fifth Generation: Artificial Intelligence and Japan's Computer Challenge to the World. Pan, London

Financial Times (1992) Software at work. 19 March

Finkelstein C (1989) Introduction to Information Engineering: From Strategic Planning to Information Systems. Addison-Wesley, Wokingham

Finzi S (ed) (1988) Principles of Software Engineering Management, Addision-Wesley, Wokingham

Fisher AS (1991) CASE: Using Software Development Tools, 2nd edn. Wiley, Chichester

Fitzgerald G (1990) Achieving flexible information systems: The case for improved analysis. Journal of Information Technology 5

French PD (1987) Intelligent training. Presented at Intelligent Tutoring (Training) Systems '87, Israel. Available from: Advanced Training Research, Millennium House, 21 Eden Street, Kingston upon Thames, Surrey KT1 1BL, UK

French PD (1990) A domain-independent student model for an AI-based training system. In: Kibby M (ed) Computer Assisted Learning, Selected Proceedings from the CAL '89 Symposium, University of Surrey. Pergamon, Oxford

Friel PG, Mayer RJ, Lockledge JC, Smith GM, Schulze RC (1989) Coolsys: A cooling systems design assistant. In: Schorr H, Rappaport A (eds) Innovative Applications of AI. AAAI Press, New York

Gane C (1990) Computer-Aided Software Engineering. Prentice-Hall, Englewood Cliffs, New Jersey

Ghezzi C, Jazayeri M, Mandrioli D (1991) Fundamentals of Software Engineering. Prentice-Hall, Englewood Cliffs, New Jersey

Gilb T (1988) Software engineering. In Finzi S (ed) Principles of Software Engineering Management, Addison-Wesley, Wokingham

Gill K (ed) (1986) Artificial Intelligence for Society. Wiley, Chichester

Gill SP (1988) On two AI traditions. AI & Society 2(4)

Goguen JA (1992) The denial of error. In Floyd C, Zullighavan H, Budde R, Keil-Slavik R (eds) Software Development and Reality Construction. Springer-Verlag, London

Gregory D (1990) Affordable intelligent tutoring. In: Estes N, Heene J, Leclercq D (eds) Proceedings of the 7th International Conference on Technology and Education, Brussels. CEP Consultants Ltd, 26-28 Albany Street, Edinburgh, UK

Gregory D, French PD (in press) ATR trainer: Intelligent CBT for the rest of us? In: Seidel RJ, Chatelier PR (eds) Advanced Research Applied to Training Design. Plenum Press, New York

Halloran J (1983) Information and communication: Information is the answer, but what is the question? Journal of Information Science 7: 162

Hawkes N (1990) Computer is capable of spotting bad grammar. The Times, 24 August

Hayball C, Land L, Mulhall T, Wright I (1987) Model document, F6 Experiment. ESPRIT project number 1098, The Knowledge Based Systems Centre/STC Technology Ltd

Heany DF (1972) Education: The critical link in getting managers to use management systems. Interfaces 2(3)

Hellman R (1989) Approaches to user-centred information systems. PhD thesis, University of Turku

Hesketh P, Barrett T (1989) An introduction to the KADS methodology. Deliverable M1, ESPRIT project number 1098, STC Technology Ltd

Hewett J, Durham T (1989) CASE: The Next Steps. Ovum Ltd, London

Hickman F, Killin J, Land L, Mulhall T, Porter D, Taylor RM (1989) KADS: Analysis for knowledge-based systems. Ellis Horwood, Chichester

Hochstrasse B, Griffiths C (1990) Regaining Control of IT Investments – A Handbook for Senior Management. Imperial College Kobler Unit, London

Hopkins N (1990) Euromethod Information Notice. CCTA, London

Hopson D (1990) Voluntary sector computing and IT development: A report based on a survey. UNET, London

Hudak P (1989) Conception, evolution and application of functional programming languages. ACM Computing Surveys 21(3): 359

Hudak P (1990) Tutorial on the functional programming language Haskell. Presented at the IEEE Computer Language Conference, 12 March. Available by email: hudak-paul@cs.yale.edu

Hudson M (1989) Analyst: An advisor for financial analysis of automobile dealerships. In: Schorr H, Rappoport A (eds) Innovative Applications of AI. AAAI Press, New York

Hughes J (1989) Why functional programming matters. Computer Journal 32(2): 98

Huysmans JH (1973) Operations research implementation and the practice of management. Presented at the Conference on Implementation of OR/MS models, University of Pittsburg, November

ICL (1990) A window on the future. ICL, Bracknell

Iivari J (1987) A hierarchical spiral model for the software process: Notes on Boehm's spiral model. ACM Sigsoft Software Engineering Notes 12(1): 35

Ince DC (1989) Software Engineering. Van Nostrand Reinhold, Scarborough, California

Johnson T (1984) The commercial applications of expert systems. Ovum Ltd, London

Jones A (1991) Use of new information and communication technologies: UK pressure groups and the developing world. Assignation 8(4): 15

Kanter RM (1989) When Giants Learn to Dance. Simon and Schuster, New York

Killin J, Porter D, Becker S, Vietze T (1989) Output and results 1 & 2. Task C10, ESPRIT project number 1098, The Knowledge Based Systems Centre

Knuth D (1985) Algorithmic thinking and mathematical thinking. American Mathematical Monthly, March: 170

Kress GR, Hodge RIV (1979) Language as Ideology. Routledge and Kegan Paul, London

Laessoe J, Rasmussen LB (1989) Human-centred methods – Development of computer-aided work processes. Technical University of Denmark, Lyngby

Land FF (1980) Social implications of the new technology. Presented at the ICL Seminar on Computer Based Training in Perspective, Bracknell, September

Lee S-Y (1992) Commercial research in neural networks in Korea. In: 5th European Seminar on Neural Networks and Genetic Algorithms, 12 February, IBC Technical Services Ltd

Lindsay J (1990) Teaching the environment: problems of addressing management issues in information systems design. Research Report 88-1. School of Information Systems, Kingston Polytechnic. Presented at ISTIP '90, Sunningdale

Lucas Engineering and Systems Ltd (1990) Engineering Product Design: Appraisal and Optimisation. HMSO, London

Lucas HC (1973) Behavioural factors in systems implementation. Research Paper 188, Graduate School of Business, Stanford University

Macdonald IG, Palmer I (1991) System development in a shared data environment: The D2S2 methodology. In: Olle TW, Hagelstein J, Macdonald IG, Rolland C, Sol HG, Van Assche FJM, Verrijn-Stuart AA (eds) Information Systems Methodologies: A Framework for Understanding, 2nd edn. Addison-Wesley, Wokingham

Macdonald KH (1992) Future alignment realities. Presented to MSc course in information systems, Kingston Polytechnic, March

Machine Tool Technology (1980) American Machinist 124: 105

Macro A, Buxton J (1987) The Craft of Software Engineering. Addison-Wesley, Wokingham

Makram-Ebeid S, Burel G (1992) Neural networks for industrial vision applications. In: 5th European Seminar on Neural Networks and Genetic Algorithms, 12 February, IBC Technical Services Ltd

Manley JH (1973) Implementation attitudes. Presented at the Conference on the Implementation of OR/MS models, University of Pittsburg, November

Martin J, Finkelstein C (1981) Information Engineering, Vols 1 and 2. Prentice-Hall, Englewood Cliffs, New Jersey

Martin J, Leben J (1989) Strategic Information Planning Methodologies. Prentice-Hall, Englewood Cliffs, New Jersey

Martin R (1991) personal communication

Maslin JM (1982) The importance of information in information technology. In: Hills PJ (ed) Trends in Information Transfer. Frances Pinter, London, p 16

Masters J (1990) The development of an integrated plant and circuits information system for electricity utilities. MSc project, Kingston Polytechnic

Matthews R (1989) Directors Information Systems. Metapraxis, London

Matthews R, Lowles T (1990) Executive information systems. Kingston Business School

McCullough D (1991) personal communication

McDermid JA (ed) (1991) The Software Engineer's Reference Book. Butterworth-Heinemann, London

McDonnell A (1990) Euromethod Information Notice, August. CCTA, London

McFarlan FW and McKenney JL (1983) The information archipelago – Governing the New World. Harvard Business Review, July/August

McKinsey & Co. (1968) Unlocking the computer's profit potential. McKinsey & Co., New York

Meszaros S (1988) A PC-based expert system for mold scheduling. In: ESD/SDI Expert Systems Proceedings. Engineering Society of Detroit

Milne R (1990) Amethyst: Vibration based condition monitoring. In: Keyes J, Maus R (eds) The Handbook of Expert Systems Applications in Manufacturing. McGraw-Hill, New York

Minsky M (ed) (1968) Semantic Information Processing. MIT Press, Cambridge, MA

Minsky M (1984) The problems and the promise. In: Winston PH, Prendergast KA (eds) The AI Business: Commercial Uses of Artificial Intelligence. MIT Press, Cambride, MA

Mitter S (1986) Should artificial intelligence take culture into consideration? In: Gill K (ed) Artificial Intelligence for Society. Wiley, Chichester

Moore N, Steele J (1991) Information-intensive Britain: An analysis of the policy issues. Policy Studies Institute, London, p 169

Morton MSS (ed) (1991) The Corporation of the 1990s: Information Technology and Organizational Transformation. Oxford University Press, New York

Motoda H (1990) The current status of expert system development and related technologies in Japan. IEEE Expert, Fall

Natraj N (1990) OCR integrated with imaging systems:reducing data entry costs. IMC Journal, January/February

Newell A, Simon HA (1972) Human Problem Solving. Prentice-Hall, Englewood Cliffs, New Jersey

Newell A, Simon HA (1975) Computer science as empirical inquiry: Symbols and search. Comm ACM 19: 113

Nurminen M (1988) People or Computers: Three Ways of Looking at Information Systems. Studentlitteratur, Lund

Oakley B, Owen K (1989) Alvey: Britain's Strategic Computing Initiative. MIT Press, Cambridge, MA

Oksa J (1991) Quoted in Rural Ireland: In Need of a Technology Fix? Irish Computer, August, p 23

Olle TW, Hagelstein J, Macdonald IG, Rolland C, Sol HG, Van Assche FJM, Verrijn-Stuart AA (eds) (1991) Information Systems Methodologies: A Framework for Understanding, 2nd edn. Addison-Wesley, Wokingham

Omatu S, Fukumi M, Teranisi M (1990) Neural network model for alphabetical letter recognition. In: Proceedings of International Neural Network Conference, July. Kluwer, Dordrecht

Paller A, Laska R (1990) The EIS Book: Information Systems for Top Managers. Dow Jones, Irwin, New York

Palmer C, Ottley S (1990) From potential to reality. "Hybrids": A critical force in the application of information technology in the 1990s, British Computer Society Task Group on Hybrids. BCS, London

Parsons GL (1983) Information technology – a new competitive weapon, Sloan Management Review (Fall)

Penrose R (1990) The Emperor's New Mind. Vintage, London

Peters G (1988) Evaluating your computer investment strategy. Journal of Information Technology 3(3): 178

Polanyi M (1967) The Tacit Dimension. Doubleday, New York

Polman M (1990) Foreword. In: Lane G (ed) Communications for Progress: A Guide to International Email. Catholic Institute for International Relations, London and Antenna, Nijmegen, the Netherlands, p xii

Porter ME, Millar VE (1985) How information gives you competitive advantage. Harvard Business Review, July/August

Price Waterhouse (1991) Information Technology Review 1991/92. Price Waterhouse, London

Pudar N, Harper M (1988) C-P-C stacker/destacker configuration advisor. In: ESD/SDI Expert Systems Proceedings. Engineering Society of Detroit

Quillian RM (1968) Semantic memory. In: Minsky M (ed) Semantic Information Processing. MIT Press, Cambridge, MA

Rauch-Hindin WB (1987) A Guide to Commercial Artificial Intelligence: Fundamentals and Real-World Applications. Prentice-Hall, Englewood Cliffs, New Jersey

Rauner F, Rasmussen LB, Corbett JM (1988) The social shaping of technology and work: human centred computer integrated manufacturing. AI & Society 2: 47

Reddy US (1986) On the relationship between logic and functional languages. In: DeGroot D, Lindstrom G (eds) Logic Programming Functions, Relations and Equations. Prentice-Hall, Englewood Cliffs, New Jersey

Research Software (1989) Miranda Manual and Overview, online with the Miranda System. Available from: Research Software Ltd, 23 St Augustines Road, Canterbury, Kent CT1 1XP, UK

Robinson JA (1992) Logic and logic programming. Comm ACM 35(3): 40

Rosenberg V (1974) The scientific premises of information science. Journal of the American Society for Information Science 25(4): 266

Rosenbrock HH (1974) Computer Aided Control Systems Design. UMIST, Manchester

Rosenbrock HH (1988) Engineering as an art. AI & Society 2(4)

Rosenbrock HH (ed) (1989) Designing Human Centred Technology: A Cross Disciplinary Project in Computer Aided Manufacture. Springer-Verlag, London

Rubinstein AH, Radnor M, Baker NR, Heiman DR, McColly JB (1967) Some organisational factors related to the effectiveness of management sciences groups in industry. Management Science 13(8)

Rubinyi RM (1989) Computers and community: The organisational impact. Journal of Communication 39(3): 120

Saalman W (1980) Filippo Brunelleschi. Zwimmer, Frankfurt

Senn J (1989) Analysis and Design of Information Systems, 2nd edn. McGraw-Hill, New York

Severwright J (1992) Neural networks for direct marketing. In: 5th European Seminar on Neural Networks and Genetic Algorithms, 12 February, IBC Technical Services Ltd

Shapiro E (1989) The family of concurrent logic programming languages. ACM Computing Surveys 21(3): 413

Shenton N (ed) Information Technology and the Community: Teleservices in East Manchester. Centre for Applied Social Research, University of Manchester, p 8

Sheppard J, Wang P (1992) Strategic management of information technology investment. Final report, Kingston Business School Occasional Paper, Kingston University

Silk D (1990) Managing IS benefits for the 1990s. Journal of Information Technology 5(4)

Simon HA (1969) Sciences of the Artificial. MIT Press, Cambridge, MA

Skok W and Fitz-Gerald SJ (1989) Business information technology: the way forward. Management Research News 12(8)

Skyrme DJ, Earl MJ (1990) Hybrid managers: What should you do? Computer Bulletin, May

Sommerville I (1989) Software Engineering, 3rd edn. Addison-Wesley, Wokingham

Stein J (1991) Neural networks: From the chalkboard to the trading room. Futures, May

Stewart J (1991) Can neurocomputing live up to its promise? Credit Card Management, September

Susskind R, Capper P (1988) Latent Damage Law – The Expert System. Butterworths, London

Susskind R, Tindall C (1989) VATIA: Ernst & Whinney's VAT expert system. Ernst & Whinney, London

Takahashi R (1989) "ATREX" – An automobile troubleshooting expert system. Future Generation Computing Systems 5

Tate RO (199) Deriving benefits from information technology, Kingston Business School Occasional Paper

Taylor FW (1911) The Principles of Scientific Management, Harper, New York

Taylor M (1983) Resource Centres for Community Groups. Community Development Foundation, London

Taylor RM (ed) (1989) System evolution – Principles and methods. Deliverable G9, ESPRIT project number 1098. The Knowledge Based Systems Centre

Taylor RM, Thomas M (1991) Business Driven Expert Systems. Ernst & Young, London

Thorpe S (1989) Who Wins with IT? Summary of the Findings of the CALC Project. London Voluntary Services Council, London, p 37

Tomlin R (1990) A Corporate Culture for Information Technology. A Research Report for Amdahl Executive Institute, London

Tucker AB (ed) (1991) Computing curricula 1991: Report of the ACM/IEE-CS Joint Curriculum Task Force. ACM Press, New York

Turing A (1950) Computing machinery and intelligence. Mind 59: 433 1950. Reprinted in Hofstadter D, Dennett DC (eds) (1981) The Mind's Eye. Penguin, Harmondsworth

Urquart A (1978) Intellectual and Manual Labour: A Critique of Epistemology. Macmillan, London

VerDuin W (1990) Solving manufacturing problems with neural nets. Automation, July

Wadge WW, Ashcroft EA (1985) Lucid: The Data Flow Programming Language. Academic Press, London

Ward JM (1986) An appraisal of the competitive benefits of IT. Journal of Information Technology 1(3): 28

Ward JM, Griffiths P, Whitmore P (1990) Strategic Planning for Information Systems. Wiley, Chichester

Weizenbaum J (1972) On the Impact of the Computer on Society. MIT Research Paper

Weizenbaum J (1976) Computer Power and Human Reason – From Judgement to Calculation. WH Freeman, San Francisco

Wielinga B, Breuker J (1984) Interpretation of verbal data for knowledge acquisition. In: O'Shea T (ed) Advances in Artificial Intelligence. ECAI/Elsevier, Amsterdam, p 41

Wielinga B, Schreiber G, de Greef P (1989) Synthesis report. Deliverable Y3, ESPRIT project number 1098, University of Amsterdam

Willcocks L (1991) Chairman's welcome and introduction. Presented at the Business Intelligence/Computer Weekly Managing IT Investment Conference, London

Willcocks L, Lester S (1991) Information systems investments: Evaluation at the feasibility stage of projects. Technovation, Autumn

Wills FG (1986) In: Cole JH et al. (eds) Machine Intelligence in Machine Design in Artificial Intelligence 1986 1.1

Wilmot RW (1990) Management in the '90s – Threat and opportunity. Presented at the British Computer Society Conference on Developing Hybrid Managers, September

Windsor CG, Harker HA (1990) Financial index prediction – A neural network study. In: Proceedings of International Neural Network Conference, July. Kluwer, Dordrecht

Winograd T, Flores F (1986) Understanding Computers and Cognition. Addison-Wesley, Wokingham

Subject Index

Name Index